Food Citizenship

Food Citizenship

Food System Advocates
in an Era of Distrust

RAY A. GOLDBERG

11/11/18

To Paul Shapiro,

Dear Paul,

Thanks for presenting at our 25th annual meeting of PAPSAC. Your discussion of the "Better Meat Company" will be a valuable addition to the Seminar. It will be a pleasure to have you join us —

Best Ray

OXFORD
UNIVERSITY PRESS

OXFORD
UNIVERSITY PRESS

Oxford University Press is a department of the University of Oxford. It furthers
the University's objective of excellence in research, scholarship, and education
by publishing worldwide. Oxford is a registered trade mark of Oxford University
Press in the UK and certain other countries.

Published in the United States of America by Oxford University Press
198 Madison Avenue, New York, NY 10016, United States of America.

Library of Congress Cataloging-in-Publication Data
Names: Goldberg, Ray Allan, 1926– author.
Title: Food citizenship : food system advocates in an era of distrust / Ray A. Goldberg.
Description: New York, NY, United States of America : Oxford UniversityPress, 2018. |
Includes bibliographical references and index.
Identifiers: LCCN 2017056207 (print) | LCCN 2018010243 (ebook) |
ISBN 9780190871826 (Updf) | ISBN 9780190871833 (Epub) |
ISBN 9780190871819 (pbk. : acid-free paper) |
ISBN 9780190871802 (hardcover : acid-free paper)
Subjects: LCSH: Food industry and trade. | Food supply—Economic aspects. |
Agriculture and globalization. | Food safety. | Public-private sectorcooperation.
Classification: LCC HD9000.5 (ebook) | LCC HD9000.5 .G644 2018 (print) |
DDC338.1/9—dc23
LC record available at https://lccn.loc.gov/2017056207

Hardback printed by Bridgeport National Bindery, Inc., United States of America

Cover photo credits: George Church: Wyss Institute at Harvard University;
Susan Combs: Bill Records Photography, Austin; Juan Enriquez: John Werner;
Hans Joehr: Toini Lindroos; John Johnson: David Lundquist, CHS Inc.;
Marion Nestle: Bill Hayes Photo; Gus Schumacher: Dan Rosenbaum;
Baldemar Velsquez: FLOC Archives; Danny Wegman: Kurt Brownell;
George Weston: David Hares

This book is dedicated to my wife, partner, and friend of 60 years
Thelma E. Goldberg (1934–2015)

to my children
Marc and Lorri Goldberg, Jennifer and Bill Jaques,
and Jeffrey Goldberg

and my grandchildren
Frederick and Amy, Alyssa, Meredith, Michelle, Nicole and Pablo,
and Gabrielle

Contents

Foreword

The Global Food System

The global food system is the largest segment of the world's economy. It can be viewed as the largest health system on the planet. And it is changing fast. This book takes a panoramic and in-depth look at the leaders—in government, private industry, academia, and nonprofits—who are driving a revolution, and at how they are doing it.

Perhaps no economic system is viewed with suspicion by so many people around the world as the food system. Many critics, including Marion Nestle in her excellent books *Food Politics* and *Soda Politics,* call out the food industry for its systemic problems. Abuses by firms make the headlines. Governments do not have clean hands: national and regional domestic politics can hinder trade and global cooperation on both the environment and on land and water resource management.

We must improve the food system's operations. If we don't, we will not be able to continue economic development and better manage our land and water resources, attack malnutrition and obesity, or improve the lives of people who rely on subsistence agriculture or on food and income supports to survive.

The public has an intense interest in where their food comes from, how it was grown, and who delivered it from the farm to the plate. They want to know that all the participants in the food system were treated in an ethical and fair-minded way. Few understand who the management and labor change-makers in the food system really are, or what their priority system is. This book provides some answers.

My Lifetime Study of Agribusiness

By accident of birth I grew up in Fargo, North Dakota—the only son of a father who had a farm, grain, feed, and seed business, who spent hours of time with me talking about the importance of the food system.

A farming neighbor, whose sister happened to be the president of Radcliffe College, encouraged me to apply to Harvard. I wrote my undergraduate thesis on a farmers' revolt in 1915 against the grain elevators, banks, and railroads that they felt treated them unfairly. The farmers pushed legislation to create a state-owned bank, a state-owned grain elevator, and a state-owned flour mill; to this very day North Dakota is the only state in the union with these institutions. Writing this thesis and visiting most of the original organizers gave me an understanding of the plight of those who were taken advantage of.

My PhD thesis at the University of Minnesota, on producers and processors in the nascent soybean industry, also impacted my perspective on the food system and its effect on the society it served. As I studied how a new commodity system gets developed, what impressed me was the creativity of everyone in the system, and their ability to compete and work together at the same time. I was also impressed with the role played by the university extension agents, as well as the railroads, in bringing the farmers and processors together. The farmers did not want to produce soybeans without a market, and the processors did not want to build processing plants without local soybeans to process. The railroads hosted the meetings, as they stood to benefit from the increase in transportation revenues. It turned out to be a win-win situation for all.

My work experience, and my academic experience in examining the birth of a new crop, made me want to think systematically about the food industry. I had the good fortune of meeting Wassily Leontief, who won a Nobel Prize for developing an input-output perspective on the global economy. I also met Professor Jay Forrester, the conceptualizer of the system that John Davis and I later applied to the interrelated, interdependent food system that we called "agribusiness."

When Dean Donald David and Dr. John Davis invited me to come to Harvard Business School in 1955 to help develop an agribusiness program, on the recommendation of Dr. O. B. Jessness, the head of my department at the University of Minnesota, I realized that my academic work not only influenced the way I viewed the world but also resonated with the practitioners who were the change-makers of that world.

The systems approach enables private, public, and not-for-profit leaders of the global food system to develop their own priorities by positioning their farms, firms, institutions, or government agencies within the constantly changing global system and noting their impact on the system and the system's impact on them. This approach also forces them to look at the many coordinators that hold the system together, and it helps the system adjust to change as change-makers impact the food system and the food system affects them.

I started the Senior Management Agribusiness Seminar at Harvard Business School, chaired it for most of its existence, and taught a total of over ten thousand senior managers. Many other universities worldwide now offer such programs. I have advised, taught, or helped create the agribusiness programs at universities in Costa Rica, Nicaragua, Mexico, England, Spain, the Philippines, India, and Israel.

I never planned to be an academic—I fell in love with a major economic segment of the world, one that could improve the health and well-being of plants, animals, and humans, and could also help people realize how they could work together.

PAPSAC: A Forum for the Change-Makers in Agribusiness

A quarter century ago, with the advice and help of management-labor negotiator Professor John Dunlop and Dr. Kurt Isselbacher of the Harvard Medical School, I created a forum at Harvard where the food system's decision makers could come together on neutral ground and discuss change. We called it the "Private and Public, Scientific, Academic, and Consumer Food Policy Group," abbreviated to PAPSAC. It was a seminar to broaden communication among farmers, business leaders, scientists, public policy leaders, academics, leaders of not-for-profits, and consumer activists on topics of mutual concern to participants of the global food system. I was concerned that there was no neutral territory to discuss the distrust both within and outside the food system, and felt that an academic setting would enable people to speak for themselves rather than for their organizations or constituencies.

The first meeting was a disaster, as people took positions and shouted at one another. But I was encouraged by the most thoughtful critic present, Marion Nestle, not to give up. After that meeting, participants realized that the issues we were talking about were more important than our differences, and they became eager for a second meeting. The group has met annually ever since. The questions they ask themselves are fundamental:

- How is the global food system held together?
- Who holds it together?
- What are the goals that society wants the food system to have?
- Does new technology address these goals and/or create new problems or dangers?
- Who can best assess the strengths and dangers of new technology?
- Who are the constructive gatekeepers who can provide society a better focus on the relationship of nutrition to the health of animals, plants, and humans?
- How do people and institutions help the subsistent producer and the impoverished consumer become viable participants and have a ladder to become part of the global food system and have opportunities to improve their livelihood and be successful participants in the food system?
- The cyclical nature of the food system and its many commodity and livestock systems hits hardest those least able to cope with violent swings— namely, the impoverished consumer and the subsistent farmer. What safety nets are needed for them, and who is responsible for food security in an insecure world?
- Who are the neutral evaluators who can provide safeguards against the dangers of food contamination, food fraud, nutrition misinformation, and even food terrorism?

PAPSAC attendance is by invitation only; discussions are held off the record. Some of the topics discussed include global agricultural research, food policy, nutrition, agricultural technology, food safety, and the environmental impacts of agriculture.

PAPSAC is, as far as I know, unique in the variety of sectors, constituencies, and countries represented in its membership. Some attendees fly in from distant continents and troubled home countries every year to meet for twenty-four hours with their peers, colleagues, and occasional antagonists. The discussions start at noon on a Sunday and end at noon on a Monday, but the relationships formed are so intense that attendees continue talking to each other throughout the year.

As the participants of PAPSAC began to bond and to develop a better understanding of the future of the food system and their relationship to it, I realized that I had an opportunity to demonstrate to the world that these problems require cooperation, and that people have found ways of cooperating while still maintaining their independence. I decided to interview dozens of these change-makers—most of them at the Harvard Business School as I did case studies on their work. Interviewees were also kind enough to attend the discussion of their case studies in my graduate school courses and senior management seminars. These interviews are the heart and soul of this book, and are critical to understanding the government entity, private firm, or not-for-profit institution's leadership in addressing the food system's many challenges.

Videos of the interviews are available to readers of this book, and I strongly encourage viewing them, because they capture the passion of the interviewees for their work in a way that the printed page cannot.

Overview: The Vertical Food System and How It Is Changing

This book contains the voices of change-makers of the food system—their view of the future and their role in changing it. But it is also about how the food system is converting from a commodity-driven, competitive, transactional model to a partnering, relational model that will better serve consumers and society.

Figure 1 is a simplified chart of the vertical structure of the food system, including the institutions that help the interrelated system coordinate itself and also provide shock absorbers when unforeseen climate and other changes to the system occur. It is an attempt to give the reader an overview of the participants in a food system and the types of institutions involved in holding it together.

The system shown in this figure has become more complicated as food, health, energy, and the environment have become more interrelated, and the whole system has become more consumer oriented. I call this new global food system an "agriceutical system." It is impacted by scientific discoveries and new international institutions and structures. This agriceutical system also impacts the consumer directly, with the gatekeepers of this new knowledge being the medical community. The international nature of agribusiness and the research and public policymaking in the developed and developing world make decision making even more complex. Policymakers and food leaders must consider everything from nutritional

The Agribusiness Systems Approach

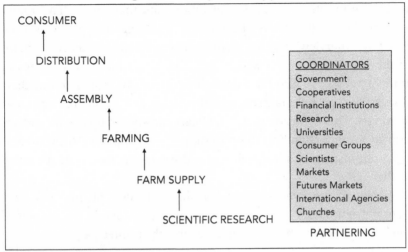

FIGURE I The agribusiness systems approach.

priorities, labor, food security, and market access to waste management and alternative energy, as well as the new coordinating arrangements that are being developed.

The food system includes all major branches of government because it involves the use of land and water resources, safety nets under both producers and consumers, creation of alternative sources of energy, development and regulation of new pharmaceuticals from plants, international trade regulation, the relationship of food to public health, and the basic fact that food security is a political issue.

Most people don't realize that the global food system is, in many ways, the biggest quasi-public utility in the world.

Figure 2 shows that the functions of participants at each stage of the vertical food system are being redefined. The farmer has become a manager of land and water resources to produce food, fiber, feed, energy, and pharmaceuticals, and has become a direct responder to the changing needs of the consumer. The input supplier has become a life science company. The commodity handler has become an ingredient supplier and a partner to the processor. The brand food and beverage company has become a wellness company. The food retailer has become a consumer advocate, food safety manager, and health, nutrition, and knowledge network supplier.

Functions Redefined

1. **Farmer**—Technology, resource, climate manager for food, fiber, feed, energy, pharmaceuticals, and land and water resources.
2. **Seed, feed, fertilizer, and machinery supplier** has become a life science company.
3. **Commodity handler and processor** has become an ingredient supplier and solutions company.
4. **Brand food and beverage supplier** has become a nutrition and taste inventor and wellness company.
5. <u>Distributor</u> = <u>Consumer advocate</u>
   <u>**FOOD SAFETY MANAGER, HEALTH, AND NUTRITION**</u>
   and knowledge network supplier

FIGURE 2 Functions redefined.

Considerations in Analyzing an Agribusiness Investment

1. Identify spreads (existing and potential) between input costs and product costs
2. Identify protections to spreads (futures markets, institutions, arrangements)
3. Identify government programs that affect spreads (price supports, Public Law 480 international commodity agreements, export subsidies and controls)
4. Identify means of convincing financial institutions to supply financing
5. Identify the importance of timing in the cycle or in the change of the market structure
6. Determine vulnerability of investment to sociopolitical pressure in agribusiness image (politics)
7. Identify extent to which cooperation is required with system participants
8. Identify special financial tools responsive to analyzing investments in agribusiness:

   - Commodity system model
   - Sensitivity analysis of factors affecting model
   - Special financial institutions catering to agribusiness investment needs
   - Leaseback arrangements
   - Special arrangements with cooperatives and financial institutions
   - Balance of product flows with vertical integration
   - Identification of special inducements to agribusiness
   - Government and joint ventures

9. Provide market access for production and coordinate production and marketing through contracts and formula pricing
10. Identify unique individuals who can provide leadership and also train others
11. Determine responsiveness of the investor to the nutritional, social, political, and economic priorities of the government or governments involved
12. Determine the long-term environmental impacts of the investment
13. Determine the creative quality and value system of the men and women needed to provide leadership for the ventures involved

---

FIGURE 3 Considerations in analyzing an agribusiness investment.

Figure 3 shows the multiplicity of constituencies—private, public, and not-for-profit—influencing any agribusiness investment made from any sector. The bottom line is only one consideration; in agribusiness it is normal to have to consider the "triple bottom line."

Constructive Criticism of the Global Food System

Critics have argued that it is impossible for food firm managers to integrate good global citizenship into earnings-oriented business practices. This book begins with an interview with Marion Nestle, the Paulette Goddard Professor of Nutrition at New York University, who is rightfully considered the toughest but fairest-minded critic of food firms' anticonsumer activities. Her most recent book is *Soda Politics: Taking on Big Soda (and Winning)*. In our interview she says that many of the corporate and cooperative managers of the food system say "the right things" but delegate many outside activities to trade associations that act more like tobacco firms once acted than food firms.

Food writers such as Mark Bittman of the *New York Times* write even more negatively of the current food system. He calls for a change in culture "to one in which eaters—that's everyone—realize that buying into the current food 'system' means exploiting animals, people, and the environment, and making ourselves sick. To change that, we have to change not only the way we behave as individuals, but the way we behave as a society."[1]

As one reads or listens to the voices of the change-makers of the future, we have to keep in mind the constructive criticism from those such as Nestle and Bittman who expect and deserve more from the food system. Some of this criticism arises from the nature of the food system and past and current mistakes and abuses within the system:

- The food system is the biggest employer in the world, and has a history of bad labor treatment in many of our major commodity systems.
- It is the biggest economic sector in the world: its sometimes sluggish and sometimes corrupt development makes people look for scapegoats.
- It is the biggest user of land and water. In many places of the world these resources are mismanaged in a manner that lessens the productivity of the soil and wastes a dwindling supply of usable water and food, making our total environment less sustainable.
- It has the biggest impact on the health of humans, animals, and plants, yet addresses health in a nonsystemic and insensitive manner.
- In many countries, overseas buyers are purchasing land as a safeguard for potential food shortages in their own countries.

Some of the criticism arises not only from the size of the food system or its history but also from the human relationship with food and reactions to changes in that relationship:

- Food is an integral part of cultures, religions, and ways of life. Any technology that changes our customs, rituals, and historical way of life is a threat to who we are and who we want to be.
- The changes from the times when nearly all people were farmers, through the Industrial Revolution and the separation of functions in the food chain, to the mechanical, chemical, genetic, bacterial, and microbial world of today, make us long for the day when we produced our own food and knew each neighbor's product and productivity. We resent consolidation and dependence on global production, even as it gives us year-round access to fruits and vegetables and a variety of unique foods from every nation in the world.

Other problems arise from the food system's complexity and its interconnectedness to other systems:

- It was much simpler to study agricultural economics, animal husbandry, and home economics as separate systems. We recognize the multidisciplinary nature of our problems, but resent their complexity and the need to understand so many different fields such as business, medicine, public health, the environment, government, molecular biology, landscaping, engineering, transportation, and life sciences to truly comprehend and affect the food system.
- In times of budget crises, governments often reduce support for those that need it most, such as food support recipients, increasing food inequity.

In spite of these and other problems and criticisms, I believe that the food industry's decision makers have the ability to create both economic value and social value—in fact, they are already doing it. More important, they are now aware that they can't have one without the other. Despite the tremendous complexity of the problems these change-makers face, this is very good news. As former Cargill chairman Warren Staley stated in one of the studies footnoted in this book, "The great challenge and joy of business is to achieve that balance." He stated further, "I believe that all aspects of good citizenship come down to a shared mindset in an organization. It is not good enough to understand what is meant by citizenship. It's not enough to believe that good citizenship is important. It only comes about by changing behavior."[2] Increasingly, Cargill's customers, and consumers everywhere, are taking a more active interest in the origins of food products and want assurances that they are produced in a responsible manner.

How This Book Is Organized

The interviews in this book are organized around the vertical food chain, starting with the consumer, showing how decision makers and critics in public, private, and not-for-profit entities at different parts of the food chain impact that consumer. The decision makers' activities and priorities demonstrate that they realize that business, public policymaking, and constructive consumer critic activities all have one thing in common: collaborating to improve the health and well-being of plants, humans, and animals and the present and future environment of the world. The interviewees' responses illuminate their value system and passion, and the variables they are juggling to fairly meet both public and private needs.

The theme of Chapters 1 and 2 is that the food system exists to promote the health and well-being of the consumers and their communities.

Chapter 3 focuses on how the food system decision maker satisfies consumers' needs by creating shared value up and down the vertical structure of the food system. Each interviewee describes how his or her firm is able to both partner and compete in the vertical food system to create a win-win relationship for all involved in the process.

Chapter 4 provides the reader an understanding of how the genetic and digital revolutions are changing the ability of the food system's leaders to respond to the health, economic development, and productivity needs of society in an environmentally sound manner.

Chapter 5 sets forth the creation of a successful resolution commission between farm workers and the firms they work with, allowing them to improve operations to their mutual benefit and that of their consumers.

Chapter 6 provides examples of large-scale farming and farm cooperative leaders taking a systems approach in relating their farming operations to a fast-changing global market.

Chapter 7 sets forth a number of leaders in private, public, and not-for-profit firms and institutions who are enabling the world's five hundred million small-scale food producers to become part of the commercial global food system.

Chapter 8 discusses the critical new role that China plays in improving the global food system, through the efforts of one of its key change-makers.

Chapter 9 provides interviews with unique change-makers who are working to create a fair and responsive global food system by creating fair trading rules, adjudicating differences, and providing equitable public policy rules and financial priorities.

Chapter 10 sets forth future trends: it describes the impact of creating shared value in a nation during a food crisis and offers an example of a systems approach to improving the taste of fruit in a way that encourages the new generation to consume more of its product: in essence, to make important foods in one's diet more enjoyable to eat.

Hope for the Future

To the best of my knowledge, no one has had the opportunity that I have had to tell the story of the global food system in the words and voices of those who are creating it. What is amazing to me is the ability these people have to recognize the changes in the food system and the extent to which they have reinvented their companies, institutions, and advocacy organizations—changes that it took guts to make. They know how to criticize one another, but also know how to develop programs, products, concepts, tools, structures, resources, and, most of all, people to tackle the developmental and the environmental challenges that face the global food system.

New types of managers know that the global food system will grow primarily in the developing world, and they must take the special needs of small-scale producers and malnourished consumers into account. They see how to adapt the developed world's technology to the developing world. They see a new kind of cooperation emerging in the developing world, leading to collaborations nobody ever thought would take place. The interviews in this book provide the reader with specific examples of what successful collaborations look like.

This book is more than just a collection of interviews; it's a testament to people who not only responded to a revolution but also have helped to create it.

Acknowledgments

SO MANY PEOPLE have been involved over the years with this book project, and with the seminar that gave birth to it, that my acknowledgments are wide-ranging.

First, this book would not have been possible without the creation of the Public and Private, Academic, Scientific, and Consumer Food Policy Group (PAPSAC) and its members, who are responsible for its success and longevity. In many ways, this is really their book. I am most grateful to each of the food system leaders in this book for being willing to be interviewed by me and giving permission for their words and video images to be used.

The late John Dunlop, Kurt Isselbacher, and I founded PAPSAC, with institutional support from Dean John McArthur of the Harvard Business School (HBS), Dean Albert Carnesale of the Harvard Kennedy School of Government (HKS), Dean Daniel C. Tosteson of the Harvard Medical School (HMS), Dean Harvey Fineberg of the Harvard Chan School of Public Health, and Harvard President Neil Rudenstine. HKS Deans Graham Allison, David Ellwood, and Joe Nye also gave support to this effort across the years, and I am immensely grateful to the current dean Douglas Elmendorf for giving PAPSAC a permanent home at the Kennedy School, and to HKS faculty member Bill Clark for agreeing to be my successor. Everyone at PAPSAC is grateful to Ayres Heller at HMS, who has managed the details of this complex international gathering with aplomb.

Agribusiness scholarship at Harvard has many friends. I am grateful to President Drew Faust for agreeing with me on the need for more multidisciplinary education at Harvard on the food system; HBS Dean Nitin Nohria for his support of agribusiness education; my HBS agribusiness faculty colleagues José Alvarez, David Bell, and Forrest Reinhardt; my colleague Jim Austin, who pioneered the HBS Social Enterprise Initiative;

and its current faculty heads Kash Rangan and Dutch Leonard. I owe great thanks to John Davis, who was the first head of the HBS Agribusiness Program and cowrote *A Concept of Agribusiness* with me, and to Hank Arthur, my predecessor in the Moffett Professorship of Agriculture & Business at HBS.

Forestry professor Michelle Holbrook and Roger Porter of HKS have both supported my activities. I am indebted to Secretary Dan Glickman, who co-taught Food Policy and Agribusiness Management with me; Robert Lawrence of HKS, who coauthored cases with me; and my former doctoral student, Dick McGinty, with whom I coauthored *Agribusiness Management for Developing Countries.*

I have known every dean of Harvard Business School except the first, but am particularly grateful to Dean Donald K. David, who was dean while I was an MBA student, and who hired me back five years later to help create an agribusiness program; Dean Stanley Teele, who rehired me later; and Dean George Baker, who granted me tenure. The fifty-seven Agribusiness Senior Management Programs I have been involved with over the years could not have happened without Agribusiness Program Manager Natalie Kindred and Senior Program Relations Director Jackie Baugher in Executive Education. And much of my work would have been impossible without the help of Theresa Sparks, who was my secretary for a quarter century.

For their excellent work in many of the cases referred to in this book, I would like to thank my doctoral students Alicia Harley and Jessica Newman, and my case writers and case researchers Kevin Allison, Ian McKowan Cornell, Noeime Delfassy, Juan Enriquez-Cabot, Lorin A. Fries, Jessica Grisanti, Kerry Herman, Allen Hirsch, Harold F. Hogan Jr., Michael Kennedy, Carin-Isabel Knoop, Kevin Liang, Katie Milligan, Meredith Niles, Andrew Otazo, Jose Miguel Porraz, Matthew Preble, Cate Reavis, Mary Shelman, Eliot Sherman, Christine Snively, Srinivas Ramdas Sunder, James Weber, Vincent N. Willis, and Jessica Droste Yagan.

I can't thank everyone in the food industry who has helped me or there would be a thousand names, but I would like to give special thanks to current Nestlé chair Paul Bulcke, former Nestlé chairs Peter Brabeck and Helmut Maucher, and former ConAgra chair Bruce Rhode for sharing their insights with me. Lisa Goldberg, assistant to Juan Enriquez, located scientific information for me a number of times. Richard Anderson of Anderson Co. has been of great support, and I am also grateful to Larry Pope of Smithfield, Paul Fribourg of Continental Grain, Wan Long of WH Group, and John Kaneb from Hood Milk for their support of PAPSAC.

Edmund O'Keefe of Pineridge Group and James Haymaker of Cargill both discussed this book with me before I started it, sharing many good ideas. My HBS colleague Mike Wheeler provided valuable advice and publishing contacts.

This book would never have been published without the sound advice, encouragement, and industrious editing from Jock Herron, my former student and now an instructor of architecture at the Harvard Graduate School of Design, and Jean Monroe or without Jacqueline Archer, document specialist in HBS Case Services, who has kept track of an ever-shifting manuscript with good humor and great professionalism. I owe a lifetime's thanks to Paula Alexander in the HBS Senior Faculty Center, who has been helping me and reading my handwriting for at least thirty years. I am also thankful for her colleagues Luz Velasquez and Jan Simmons of the Senior Faculty Center, and to Jessica Baroni, assistant director of faculty support services, for their help and patience.

I am grateful to Susan Kahn, assistant director of HBS Case Services, for approval to use my case studies, and to her department collectively for much invaluable help. Media Production Manager Tim Hogan of HBS Media Services videoed and edited the interviews, and Document Specialist Chris Jones transcribed them—large and vital tasks for which I cannot thank them enough. Thea Danato, former head of HBS Media Services, helped keep track of my interview videos over a period of years. My fellow midwesterner Alan Hutchings in HBS Operational Support Services has done reams of printing and duplicating for me, and his colleague Ramone Sharpe has done similar volumes of shipping.

IT experts Dave Dollins and Jonathan Ritter-Roderick have navigated me through the realm of system upgrades and cloud storage with calm and expertise. My friend Joan Gordon provided much support during the latter stages of this project. My agent Jim Levine of Levine Green Rostan Literary Agency sent me a very helpful submission template and shepherded this book unerringly to Oxford University Press. My kind and astute editor at Oxford University Press, Angela Chnapko, has been a joy to work with through this process, as have Alexcee Bechthold and production editor Richa Jobin.

Finally, I must acknowledge the lifelong love and support of my children and their spouses Marc and Lorri Goldberg, Jennifer and Bill Jaques, and Jeffrey Goldberg, and the love and encouragement of my grandchildren Frederick and Amy, Alyssa, Meredith, Michelle, Nicole and Pablo, and Gabrielle. I could not ask for a better family.

Food Citizenship

1

Health and Nutrition

MARION NESTLE
*Paulette Goddard Professor of Nutrition, Food Studies,
and Public Health, New York University (2014)*

Marion Nestle is one of the leading authorities and respected critics of the food system. She has a doctorate in molecular biology from the University of California, Berkeley, and is the author of numerous academic articles and of popular books for lay audiences like *Food Politics*. Her books, teaching, and lecturing have led to an increasing awareness of the shortcomings of our current food system. Thanks to her efforts, the public has responded by being more aware of the relationship between food and health and more willing to take political and economic action to change the system to make it more nutritious and health oriented. Nestle points out that the most important predisposing factor for poor health and nutrition is poverty.

RG: Dr. Marion Nestle is the Paulette Goddard Professor of Nutrition, Food Studies, and Public Health at New York University. How did you end up becoming such an unusual leader in the nutrition field? What was the motivation of your doing what you're doing today?

MN: It happened one step at a time. I got a doctorate in molecular biology, took a teaching job, and was given a nutrition class to teach as part of that job. It was like falling in love. I've never looked back. I've always loved food, and I realized right away that you could use food to teach undergraduate biology or just about any other subject for that matter. Also, the fact that my teaching could start from the science of nutrition but go immediately to its politics was very appealing. I taught nutrition to undergraduates and then to medical students for years, and then went to Washington as a nutrition policy adviser.

Soon after I moved to NYU, I was invited to a meeting at the National Cancer Institute that was run by former surgeon general C. Everett Koop. The meeting was about two behavioral causes of cancer—cigarette smoking and diet. I knew cigarettes caused cancer but had never heard anti-cigarette physicians talk about cigarette advertising in any systematic way before. They showed slide after slide of cigarette marketing in developing countries, in remote areas of the Himalayas, and in the jungles of Africa. Next, they did the same for cigarette marketing to children. I knew perfectly well that cigarette companies marketed to children. I just had never really noticed it. This felt like a revelation. I thought we nutritionists who care about childhood obesity should be doing the same thing for Coca-Cola.

So I started paying attention to food marketing, its astonishing ubiquity, and its subtle and not-so-subtle methods. I started writing articles about the effects of food marketing on food choices. Those articles turned into *Food Politics*, published in 2002, and now in a third edition. That's really when it all started, although plenty led up to it.

RG: You are considered the expert in looking at the impact of food on the health and well-being of people. You work with the private sector, the public sector, and the not-for-profit consumer activist sector. How do you see people responding to the fact that food plays such an important role in their health and well-being, and in their economic development? How do you see people understanding the importance of it, and actually wanting to do something about it in all three sectors?

MN: Food is very personal. It's something that you put inside your body, so it has deep emotional and cultural significance. I'm interested in political aspects that go beyond the personal. I want to make the personal political for people who think that what they eat is simply a matter of free will and personal choice. The way I see it, we have the choices we have because of the food system we're in. Food makes it possible to talk about political issues in a way that people can hear and respond to. Everybody can understand how the marketing environment influences what people think and do. Everyone relates to food. It's easy to talk about the politics of food; it's much harder to talk about other kinds of politics.

I'm interested in trying to get people interested in changing the food system to make it better, and in working for a healthier food environment—one that's healthier for people and healthier for the planet. It's easier to do that around food issues than trying to work on climate change or, heaven help us, changing the political system in Washington, DC.

RG: If it's much easier to do that, why do we have such an enormous problem with obesity everywhere in the world?

MN: We have an enormous problem with obesity because of enormous changes in the food system starting around 1980. That's when everything got deregulated. In the early 1980s, we had deregulated farming; farmers were paid to grow as much food as they possibly could. Farmers did a really good job of it, produced more food, increased the number of calories available in the food supply to twice as much as we all needed, and made the food system very competitive. Right after President Reagan was elected, Wall Street changed the way in which it judged corporations. The Shareholder Value Movement forced companies to provide higher immediate returns to investors and to report growth, as well as profits, to Wall Street every ninety days. For food companies, this was really difficult, because they were already selling products in a food environment with far more calories than anyone needed, so it was competition on top of competition. Food companies had to find new ways to sell food. They got a break when deregulation made it possible for all corporations, but food companies in particular, to advertise and market their foods in ways that had not been possible before.

The result: food companies made food ubiquitous and socially acceptable to eat food 24/7, and in very large portions. Large portions are a sufficient explanation for obesity. If I had one thing that I could teach the American public, it would be that larger portions have more calories! This may sound absurd, but the relationship between portion size and calories is not intuitively obvious. Large portions are a sufficient explanation for why people are gaining weight. It's not because of lack of exercise; it's because we're eating more.

RG: It sounds so simple, and yet, the problem is tremendous. Why do companies like Walmart start working with insurance companies to tackle the obesity problem from a marketing point of view, from a supermarket point of view? Do you think they can help, or do you think it's just another marketing ploy?

MN: Obesity poses a tough problem for food companies, because if people want to do something to prevent gaining weight, they have to eat less, eat better, and move more, and avoid eating too much junk food. The "don't eat too much junk food" goes under the "eat less" category. But eating less is very bad for business. The job of food companies is to sell more products and grow their returns to investors. That's their job. Healthier food is more expensive to produce and maintain, and that cuts into profits. Obesity puts food companies in a terrible position, and they know it, so they do as much window dressing as possible to get regulators off their backs. They're terrified of regulation, so they do a lot of nice things publicly. But behind the scenes, they're lobbying government not to make any rules, and doing everything that they can to fight public health measures. Even if people in these companies would like to do something about obesity—and many do—their hands are tied. They really can't take actions that might decrease returns to investors.

RG: It sounds like a terrible problem. At the same time, many of these companies—using Walmart as another example, again—they sit down with the Walmart moms, who care about their children, who care about health, who care about obesity, and they talk to them about health, and they talk to them about obesity. Do you think it's just talk, or do you think they actually have a way of working with them to help them understand to eat less and to eat better?

MN: Walmart's job is to sell more food, not less. I live in New York City; we don't have a Walmart. But I spend time upstate in Ithaca, which has a Walmart. I go to it regularly to see if what Walmart says in public is consistent with what I see in the store. I'm astounded by the discrepancy. Walmart may say it's trying to promote healthier food, but I don't see it in the store. Walmart's job is to sell food as cheaply as possible, pay its employees as cheaply as possible, and force its suppliers to provide products as cheaply as possible. That's its business model. Walmart has been astoundingly successful doing that, so expecting them to interfere with that model seems quite unrealistic. They're not going to do it because they can't.

RG: Do you think that it's just window dressing when they say they want to do it?

MN: No, I'm sure they want to do it, and I'm sure they're sincere. I've met Walmart officials. They care about promoting health, but they can only make changes that will keep sales increasing. Even though Walmart is privately held and has more flexibility with Wall Street, its hands are tied by its business model. The most effective thing Walmart could do to make America healthier is to pay its employees decent wages so they could buy better food.

RG: You really are tough on the people in the food system, and yet, when we have meetings they seem to be quite sincere about trying to improve the health of their customers, trying to find ways of getting more fruits and vegetables available to them at a more reasonable price.

MN: The Walmart in Ithaca is half a mile from a Wegmans. Wegmans is also family owned, but does all this much better, and at prices remarkably similar to those at Walmart. So I'm not impressed with what Walmart looks like on the ground. What does impress me is that a lot of Walmart's employees—I don't know the exact percentage—get food stamps. Taxpayers are subsidizing Walmart, by closing the gap between what Walmart pays its employees and what people need to live. If we want to improve the health of Walmart's employees and other low-wage workers, we have to pay them better.

RG: Forty-eight million people are on food stamps.

MN: They are indeed, and a substantial number of them work at Walmart apparently.

RG: If they were here, they would say they're trying to have low prices and be more efficient, because people are having a difficult time buying food, and what they're trying to do is actually helping them, so—

MN: Yes, but at Walmart, there's aisle after aisle of junk food at very low prices. A few little areas have fruits and vegetables, but the produce section is not well maintained, at least from what I've seen.

RG: Let's look at other parts of the system. The chairman of Nestlé, Peter Brabeck, wants to create shared value by making sure that both small-scale producers and end consumers are better off. They have health and nutrition experiments going on. The chairman was in the hospital, and the food was so miserable, he decided the whole system is at fault. Do you think they are doing anything about nutrition or not?

MN: They're changing their products in various ways, but they are still food products. If you want people to eat healthfully, you want them eating fruits and vegetables, and to increase the plant foods in their diets. That's not what Nestlé does. Nestlé makes ice cream and products you buy in packages. That's fine; they have a place in diets, just not the main place. Nestlé has the same constraints as every other food company. Profits are the number one criterion. Unless they can find a way to make healthy foods profitable, they're not going to do it. They are working hard on personalized nutrition and fortified products.

RG: At the same time, a Nestlé will go into the developing world and put a milk plant where not enough milk production is actually occurring, and wait for as much as ten years before they break even, because they want to find a way for the small-scale producer to have market access in a place for their milk. They think they're helping economic development in that process. Do you think, again, that's not really what they're trying to do, or what?

MN: They're trying to increase milk sales. I don't know whether milk is the best example. Let's talk about sodas, which I know much more about. Soda companies, like Coca-Cola and Pepsi, are going into developing areas very aggressively and setting up small businesses with carts for selling Pepsi or Coke. These people are making money off it, and it's helping raise their income level, but they're selling something the population shouldn't be drinking, or at least not drinking much [of]. So there are contradictions built into this enterprise that are complicated and not easy to sort out. That's an easier example than what Nestlé is doing.

RG: Is there any hope that in the food system itself, there are people who can actually make a difference and change?

MN: I think so, but not when the profit motive is involved. If it's a nonprofit enterprise, it has to be sustainable or it won't last. So the question is, how can you build the kinds of institutions that are sustainable in the long run?

RG: That's a good question; how can you?

MN: Well, it's not something that I'm particularly involved in, so I'm not the person who's going to do this. It's not my job to develop business models. That's your job. My job is to analyze what's going on and advocate for curbing the unbridled marketing of foods that aren't healthy for people.

RG: The people we've been discussing have looked to you for constructive criticism, but at the end of the day, you think they are unable to do what you want them to do because the system forces them to act in a way that adds to the problem rather than addresses the problem.

MN: I've been impressed that the people I've met who wanted to work from within companies to change them didn't last long. Unless their ideas were profitable, they couldn't continue, and either left in despair or found something else to do. It's asking a lot to expect companies to do this on their own. I believe in regulation. If there were regulations that restricted certain kinds of marketing activities, that would create a level playing field for food companies. It would be much easier for the companies that want to do good to actually do good if the playing field were level. Nobody wants to go first, because it puts profits at risk.

RG: Who should be the regulators and who should initiate the regulations?

MN: You could start with grassroots petitions, but we have a government that's not interested in regulation right now and wants to do away with as many as it can. This is a difficult period in American history when corporations have the rights of citizens and regulations are viewed as constraints on corporate growth. If we had a government interested in public health, there's plenty it could do. But the agencies know if they try to do the right thing, they'll be overruled by Congress. Unless we have a Congress that's more interested in public health than corporate health, nothing will change. Campaign contributions have corrupted American government. That's what has to change.

RG: You really have discouraged me in trying to find a glimmer of hope for the future.

MN: There's plenty of hope with the young people. They think the food system is hopeless and totally corrupt, and they want to change it. They know they can't change it at the national level, so they're doing everything they can at the local level. I see this in community after community, state after state. There's plenty of reason for hope.

RG: Well, that's very encouraging. Can you give me a few examples?

MN: The future is in the alternative food system. What's really exciting is what's happening in schools where we actually have some regulations that make it possible to serve healthier foods to kids. A large and increasing percentage of schools are feeding kids in a much better way. Local initiatives around farmers' markets and locally grown food are very exciting and the growth in their numbers is quantifiable. You can count the number of farmers' markets that we have now versus twenty years ago and see a huge increase. You can count the increase in community-supported agriculture programs, in the locally grown food movement, chicken-raising initiatives; people are growing a bit more of their own food. It doesn't have to be 100 percent. Just the idea that people are so interested in taking control of their own food is terrific. The movement is cutting into the market share of industrial food. It's putting enormous pressure on CAFOs [concentrated animal feeding operations] and other kinds of animal-raising operations to improve their quality, the ways they treat animals, and their environmental impact. Individuals can make a difference working in these areas. The list of movement accomplishments is really quite long. If you go into any supermarket and compare it to photographs of supermarkets twenty years ago, you can see the difference in the quality of food that is available now. The year-round availability of fruits and vegetables is a measureable change. There are vast improvements taking place, not in the conventional area of the food market, but in the alternative food market. This may only account for a tiny fraction of food sales, but the fraction is increasing.

RG: What about organics—do you think they are playing a role or not?

MN: Organics have gotten a big boost because genetically modified foods are not labeled—which I think was a political mistake from the get-go. The GMO industry is going to be paying for that mistake for a very long time. GMO companies should label GMOs and just get it over with. Labeling would solve a lot of problems. Today, if you don't want to buy genetically modified food, you have no way of knowing what is and is not GMO because it's not labeled. But if you buy organic, you know it's not GMO. That has been an enormous impetus to organic sales—the fastest-growing segment of the food system. Again, organics are only a tiny fraction of total food sales in the United States, but organics are growing. If you buy organics, you are not buying conventional foods. People can only eat so much. Buying organics is voting with your fork.

RG: If these movements are gaining strength, are the obesity problems getting less?

MN: Yes. Obesity rates have flattened out among the educated and wealthy, even among some children. Young boys seem to be a problem, and obesity is increasingly a problem of poverty. Social inequity is where we should be placing attention. Obesity is becoming a class issue and needs to be addressed as a class issue. That's why paying Walmart employees decently is so important, and why there's a national movement to get low-wage workers in farms and restaurants paid $15 an hour. Wage equity is a good place to begin.

RG: How does this relate to immigration?

MN: The wonderful thing about food is that it relates to everything. There are jobs for immigrants, but if we want people to be healthier, they have to be paid enough to buy decent food. There's all this talk about income inequality these days and its enormous effect on middle-class buying habits. If we want a flourishing, vigorous economy, people must have enough money to spend. It makes sense to me.

RG: It makes sense, I think, to many people. When you meet with different people in the food system, I think they'd all agree with what you're saying.

MN: I'm not so sure.

RG: Don't you think that they want the same results that you want?

MN: I think the individuals do, but I'm not sure about the institutions. The public face of major food corporations is, We don't want to add to the problem; we want to be part of the solution. Yet behind the scenes, the corporations are doing everything they can to defeat public health and consumer initiatives—everything they can. Look what food corporations did to defeat the GMO labeling initiative in Washington State. They put millions to fight something that I see as in their best interest. If they want the public to trust them, they have to be transparent. If food companies really cared about consumer issues, they wouldn't be fighting them the way that they're fighting them, secretly, behind the scenes, lobbying in Congress, and opposing soda taxes. I read reports about food company lobbyists, and there they are, this great big long list of issues. Every single issue I care about is on the list of what they are lobbying about, but I know they're not arguing in Congress from the same position I would be if I had the same access to Congress they do.

RG: Do you think they'll change?

MN: I hope so. If enough young people move into positions of reasonable power, the food companies will have to change. I see this in food studies. At NYU, we started food studies programs—undergraduate, master's, and doctoral—in 1996, which now seems like a century ago. When we started, we were it. There wasn't another food studies program in the country. Everyone thought we were crazy: Who would want to study about food? Now, there are five or six food studies programs in New York City alone. Every university in the country is teaching about food, because everybody has figured out that people really care about it.

RG: I know that everybody cares about it. As you talk to young men and women in food programs around the country and see a change in their interest, don't you see a change in the corporate philosophy of the companies themselves?

MN: I'm not privy to inside information about corporate philosophy. I only see the public face, and the public face is profit driven. It has to be.

RG: Historically, the food industry was considered consumer oriented. They were the face to the consumer, and consumers trusted the food system as that face. Do you think the consumer has lost faith in that system today?

MN: I can only speak for some consumers. The students I deal with, and the groups that I speak to, now see corporate food as quite similar to corporate cigarettes or corporate drugs—companies that put profits above public health and behave as those other industries have behaved. They are not mistaken. Food companies do behave the way cigarette and drug companies behave. They're using exactly the same techniques— the tobacco industry "playbook"—to win friends and influence people, discourage critics, and undermine public health initiatives. There's plenty of evidence for that. The system requires it.

RG: Why do these companies try experiments with health companies like Zoe Finch Totten's The Full Yield to reduce employee insurance premiums? Do you think they're just bumping their heads, or do you think they're making a difference?

MN: I see it the same way, because the insurance companies are largely for-profit companies. I ask myself, what industry would benefit if Americans were healthier and ate better? I am hard pressed to think of any. The one shining exception? Not-for-profit HMOs. I met with education executives at Kaiser Permanente in California and their analysis is right to the point. They spend 90 percent of their health care costs on 10 percent of their patients. If they could reduce that 10 percent by a percentage point or two, they would have vastly more money to spend on prevention, to spend on hospitals, to spend on doctors, to spend on nurses, to spend on other components of their system. But that's rare. The insurance industry is in it for profit. I belong to a for-profit medical care system, because I don't have any choice. It makes me uncomfortable. I worry that every decision in every health care interaction is profit driven. You would think that the system would change, and maybe it will if we ever get a single-payer health care system that everyone has to belong to. Then it might be obvious that we must focus on prevention to keep costs at a reasonable level. The system will change, but I don't see it changing now.

RG: I must admit, Marion, this is one of the more discouraging interviews I've ever had in my life.

MN: I'm sorry you're discouraged, Ray. I'm just trying to describe what I see.

RG: I know that, and frankly, I was always very anxious to interview you, because you've been a gadfly to the whole industry forever, and a good gadfly, I think, a proactive one, not a reactive one. If we were having this conversation ten or fifteen years from now, how will the landscape look on these issues?

MN: I have no crystal ball. I'm deeply worried about government in America right now, and the fact that the gap between rich and poor has gotten so much worse, and people on the lower end of the spectrum feel like they have no power in society. These are great threats to our democracy. People aren't voting because they feel helpless, and the political system is set up to keep as few people voting as possible. These trends are deeply undemocratic and do not bode well for the future. People concerned about America's future should be deeply concerned about the increasing threats to our democratic institutions. I've lived long enough to see how things have changed. I was lucky enough to live at a time when poor people really could get ahead. I was one of them. My single mom could not afford to send me to college, but I could go to Berkeley and get an education without ending up with hundreds of thousands of dollars in debt. I regret the disappearance of that society very much. That's what we all should be working on—ways to bring education and health to young people and not saddle them with debts it will take their whole lives to pay off. I'm trying to do it through food. I hope my students at NYU will pick up the challenge and run with it, because the future lies with them, not me.

RG: At the same time, when we started this conversation, you were quite optimistic that the younger generation gets it.

MN: I think they do.

RG: Don't you feel they're capable of making the system change?

MN: I hope so. They don't feel powerful, and how they're going to get power is a big question. The big issue in the food movement is to unite all of these diverse little organizations into one that has real political power. There are some signs that organizations can get together. I chaired a mayoral forum in New York City put together by eighty-five organizations. Twelve organizations set it up—the first time I've seen groups that usually work on different issues get together in a common cause. I wish I were more confident that they can keep that momentum going.

RG: When I ask people about consumer leadership and education, and consumer leadership and action, they all said, we've got to have Marion Nestle.

MN: That's very flattering.

RG: But also very true, and they were from all walks of life, from poor and rich, from in the food system and out of the food system, in the government and in the nonprofits. You have an enormous respect by a lot of people. Some of the people you probably don't respect, but they respect you. Do you think that an organization like PAPSAC makes any difference, or is it just a discussion group?

MN: I can't answer that question, Ray. I've never understood what your goals were. As I recall, you wanted PAPSAC to explain to food advocates why the food industry was not their enemy. That was my impression, at least. I'm not sure it's succeeded in doing that. I don't think of the food industry as my enemy, but the reality is that the goals of public health and the goals of food companies aren't the same, and they can't be as long as profit drives food company actions. Does that mean individuals won't change their minds? I cannot say. I can say it's been enormously interesting over the years to hear different points of view expressed, particularly by people who I would otherwise never get to meet. I don't spend much time with people who work for food companies, so this is a rare privilege. It's been interesting to hear the views of people at the cutting edge of issues, and useful to hear what they have to say. That's why I've enjoyed coming.

RG: Well, I've always enjoyed having you, because you've always been so forthright. Maybe, as a naïve North Dakotan, I feel somewhat more positive than you do. I worry about the same issues you worry about. I worry about the inequalities. I worry about the issues that you've raised so eloquently, but somehow, I have more faith that people in these companies realize that their long-run profitability in a poorly served society is at more risk than their quarter-by-quarter operations. A goodly number of them are looking many more years ahead, and think quite differently about the future than the generation before them. As an older person, I guess I'm more optimistic than you. You have forced people to think very differently, and have influenced people more greatly than you think.

MN: That may well be, but I'm not able to assess my impact. That's for others to do.

RG: You are rightfully impatient and upset by the slow progress that's been made. I hope you keep battling away. In closing, are there elements of hope to make the system more responsive to the real needs of society, especially those who are being more left out?

MN: The big area of hope is at the local level—getting involved in grassroots political activities. Many people get involved in food issues because they like the way food tastes. They are in it for the pleasure without realizing how political food is. If you want to change the food system, you have to get involved in the politics. I tell people to start local. Make sure your local school is serving delicious, healthy foods to your kids. Make sure that you've got farmers' markets, locally grown food, resources and people going into farming, and city councils concerned about foodshed issues. You can do that at the local level. If enough people do these things on the local level, then the issues get to the state level. And if enough states do things, the federal government has to act. I tell students: run for office.

RG: That's a wonderful way to end. Thank you so much.

SUSAN COMBS
Past Commissioner of Agriculture, State of Texas (2004)

Susan Combs, an elected commissioner of agriculture of Texas, has been a leader in collaborative efforts to provide healthier food in Texas public schools. As commissioner of agriculture in Texas, she recognized the seriousness of the obesity problem in the state, with 60 percent of the children's intake of food taking place through the school lunch program. She changed the program by getting the support of the parents and the commissioner of health, insurance, and education to get rid of all foods of minimal nutritional value. They were successful in spite of the lack of support from industry. She comes from a ranching family and has been running a cow-calf operation for nearly a quarter century. She has worked on Wall Street, has served as a state legislator, and has been a prosecutor where she handled child abuse and neglect cases.[1]

RG: You are commissioner of agriculture of Texas at a time in our country when we have so many real issues about obesity, about natural resources, about hunger, about competitiveness, about trade, about BSE, about foot and mouth disease. All of these end up at your door. How did you develop the background to be able to address these issues today?

SC: My family's been in agriculture in Texas for a very long time. We've been ranching out in the Big Ben since 1882, and I've been running my own cow-calf operation for about twenty-four years. I went east to college, then worked in New York for about six years in international advertising, Wall Street, and for the federal government. Came back, went to law school and was a prosecutor, and that was sort of a necessary predicate to part of what I'm doing now. I handled child abuse and neglect cases. Then in the early '90s I ran for office and was elected to the state legislature, where I handled natural resource issues among other things. The job I wanted was the commissioner of agriculture. It's a statewide elected job. There are fifty commissioners, secretaries, directors of agriculture in the US, and fifteen of us—I think that's the number—are elected. I ran for office in '98 and was elected, and ran for re-election, and am now in my second term as commissioner. The background I have as a prosecutor, a state legislator, and, really more importantly perhaps, a rancher has given me a background that's proved useful.

RG: Texas, because of you, is at the forefront of addressing obesity by enabling our young people to have more healthful diets. How are you doing that?

SC: Well, I tried legislatively. In the 2003 session, I tried to get legislation passed limiting foods of minimal nutritional value—and it never got out of committee in either the House or the Senate. In June of 2003 the governor's office called and asked me to take on the breakfast and lunch program. I was interested because Texas in many ways is both the best and the worst in the nation. We're the second-largest state by population, but our population is particularly prone to obesity. I was looking at what we're facing in long-range, economic terms and said to myself we had do something significant for our children. In El Paso, I've heard that 17 percent of the children in the elementary schools have signs of type 2 diabetes. If you're a policymaker, and you're looking at the consequences for your state long term, you can't afford to do nothing. When I got the power to have the breakfast and lunch program, I had the power to set policy. That means I'm able to withdraw federal reimbursement funds from schools that don't comply with my policies. I didn't believe I had a moment to waste. I got the authority to do this in July, and I started setting policy a week later for this school year we're now in.

RG: Where are you in the process?

SC: Our first salvo was to restrict all foods with minimal nutritional value. Elementary schools no longer sold hard candy, chewing gum, soft drinks, cotton candy, and some other stuff. Middle schools were restricted until lunch. I left the high schools alone because of existing contracts. We then took a broader perspective, focusing on all foods available to kids. We restricted the amount of sugar in foods. We're going to restrict the amount of fat, and ask for trans fat labeling. We're going to eliminate all food that competes with our cafeteria food service. There were reports of trolleys in elementary school halls with candy bars, and teachers selling candies in classrooms to raise funds. It was what I call food chaos. Feedback on the health side is all good; but some are unhappy because "why can't I have a cupcake?"

RG: What kind of cooperation have you had from industry?

SC: Zero. During the legislative cycle, I had absolutely none. The soft drink companies were opposed, arguing that we needed to let the kids choose. Well, there's lots of research out there that no child can make rational choices between heavily promoted items until they're eleven or twelve. I tried to work with the manufacturers as there are many good products we could put in vending machines like water. Water came out of a tap until a few years ago, and then it became intensively bottled. That's been a huge moneymaker for folks. I'm surprised no one has taken up the nutrition torch.

RG: What about the bottlers themselves? Have they been willing to cooperate?

SC: There's been a conflict between the parent company, which is generally more interested in good corporate citizenship than the bottlers. The bottlers in Texas have been very driven by cash and opposed to changing the product mix. They already view themselves as good corporate citizens. They talk about the scoreboards and scholarships.

RG: What about the school system itself? Have they been supportive?

SC: It's been interesting. During the last legislative cycle in 2003, I tried to find out how much money is received by these contracts. I made an open-records request to the 1,200 school districts in the state. We discovered that we netted about $30 million, which is chicken feed given the state's $18 billion school budget. I also discovered that if 100 percent rather than 35 to 70 percent of the kids eligible for free and reduced lunches participated rather than leaving the cafeteria line and getting a Coke and a bag of chips, the state of Texas would generate $582 million extra from the USDA. The projected health care costs—as much as $10 billion—from childhood obesity are an even bigger issue. Nutrition begins at home, but it continues at school. If the school environment is not healthy, then we're not doing our part in a publicly funded government system.

RG: When you explain this to superintendents, and when they hear these numbers, what's their reaction?

SC: The newest number, $582 million, hasn't been released yet to the general public. When they testified, they said two things. First, we need the money, and secondly, it's all about local control. The reality is that we by law make these kids go to school. These kids get 60 percent of their daily intake at school. My rebuttal to them is how dare you not do everything you can for these children? No financial argument has any merit when you look at the long-term cost. The $10 billion isn't even workforce losses. It's just health care. The superintendents, many of them, really do get it. But for some, policies imposed from outside their system make them very uneasy.

RG: What about other states? When they see what you're doing, do you get them excited about it?

SC: People are excited about it, and the USDA is too. Most every state is taking a look at its population and saying we can't keep pumping this junk into our kids and disregard the health consequences.

RG: Food doesn't kill you like tobacco, but obesity certainly adds huge health risks. Don't these firms feel they're legally vulnerable?

SC: I think so. If you're a beverage company, and if people begin to look at you as an irresponsible corporate citizen, that's a very significant risk. From a liability perspective, the schools are at risk too. It wouldn't shock me if a lawsuit was filed someplace in this country claiming that the school board trustees violated their fiduciary obligation to protect kids. I do commend Kraft for discussing a reduction in portion sizes and offering healthier products. That may be proactive as opposed to fear driven, but it's also good marketing.

RG: Every newspaper and magazine has obesity on the cover. This is not a hidden issue. If that is true, why aren't other people—you've been quoted in *The Economist*. You're speaking to the government of the United Kingdom. You're a guest in many other areas discussing this issue. I guess I'm naïve enough to not understand why industry is not really rallying to the issue.

SC: If you had spent billions of dollars building your brand, it would be awfully painful to abandon it. My response is that these drinks are fun drinks, but they're not food drinks. The minute you say you've got to have this soft drink because it's really important for your meal, you've lost the health battle. They haven't been willing to concede that ground. It's very significant that Coke says they're going to remove the large upfront payments and the liquidated damages clause. That's very positive. But to continue saying that during meal times you should drink a twenty-ounce Coke with 275 calories and sixty-five grams of sugar, well, that's not a good food message.

RG: Some of the firms, including Pepsi and Coke, are coming out with reduced-caloric drinks with reduced sugar. Do you think that's an answer, or do you think that's just a halfway street?

SC: It's a halfway step. They're talking about cute little eight-ounce cans, which are a nice marketing tool. But it's still Coke. A reduced-calorie drink is still a good step, but the sugar, of course, is the killer. Now some people are tinkering with milk, and they're adding lots of sugar. I think they're not looking at it from a health perspective.

RG: How do you see this battlefield in ten years?

SC: The companies that have transformed themselves will be hugely successful. Those that dug their heels in will be in real trouble. If it's not mandated by somebody like me, you'll see so many more hugely overweight people in ten years. I heard from the undersecretary of food and nutrition that Disney World has already had to widen its turnstiles to let people in and out.

RG: Unbelievable. Switching topics, terrorism is another concern. Many feel that the food supply is our most vulnerable area. What do you think?

SC: Parts of the food supply are certainly vulnerable. I don't see anybody going out and spraying crops. We've got enough control over aerial applicators in this country. The animal systems are especially vulnerable. A small vial in a border state worries me. We have one thousand miles of border. My ranch is in a county bordering Mexico, and I've got guys walking through it all hours of the day and night, mostly carrying drugs. We have a very poor system. Our food supply system is really good except that we're so spread out. Collaboration between the producers is key. They know better than the government who walks across their pasture or ranches. Keeping them alerted is important.

RG: It also means greater cooperation between Mexico, Canada, and the United States. How do we do?

SC: Pretty well. My scope is mostly looking at [the] US and Mexico. We do better on this than we do on drug interdiction. We do a little better moving animals. All three governments get along pretty well. We don't do well with Mexico on water. But on things like animal health, we do pretty well unless it's a regulation we wish to impose against Mexico and their producers push back, in which case the conversation becomes more heated.

RG: Codex [UN 186 = country food safety and labeling commission] seems to have done a better job in terms of labeling, in terms of other activities.

Why is Codex more successful today than OIE [World Organization for Animal Health]?

sc: Labeling is different than regulating risk. What's a parmesan cheese, and if it's not from Parma, can it be called that? Codex is more about marketing, and OIE is more about food safety. Codex has [a] higher level of support, and I think they've worked things out awfully well. People pretty much adhere to Codex and are more likely to jump ship with OIE.

rg: The reason I asked is that the WTO is pushing us to have more free trade, but the phytosanitary issues are so prevalent in all of our countries that they themselves have become trade barriers. How do we find an accommodation that's fair and equitable?

sc: If a sanitary/phytosanitary (SPS) issue is science driven, confidence goes up, but politics is still a problem. If you have a TB issue between the US and Mexico, there are good protocols for dealing with it. But if you have a government system that is responsive to its producers who say we can't be barred from this market, then it really doesn't matter to the government what the science says.

rg: There are very few people I've had the pleasure of interviewing that have had both public service and private background experience. You're the exception. You see both sides of issues. From a career point of view, how are you going to use your experience to improve things?

sc: Obesity has been interesting because it's at a confluence of policy, politics, and facts. I'm going to keep pushing that envelope. Citizens don't realize how influential they can be in making policy. I hope to be engaged on issues for a long time that demonstrate that you can get both sides—or three sides or five sides—to get down to a center point and talk about something.

rg: These problems are multidiscipline in context, and yet our schools are very turf oriented when it comes to subject expertise. Do you think we should try to find a way to get a more multidisciplinary approach to these issues?

sc: I'll give you a recent example. The four commissioners of health, education, insurance, and agriculture in Texas are all collaborating on a particular issue. We all have different facts and different perspectives, and it's making us more powerful as a group.

rg: What got you to do what you're doing? You talked at the beginning about your background, your family history and interest in agriculture.

You have taken on some of our toughest assignments in our field. What drives you?

sc: I'll divide that into two areas. On children's issues, when I was a prosecutor in Dallas, I handled child abuse cases. One of the cases was a young woman with four-year-old twins, and she thought they were nine months old, so she was starving them. My interest in children is long-standing. On the ag side, I'm lucky. Next week, I go to my ranch where I can see over distances of thirty to forty miles. I'm lucky to be in a path of thousands of years of people who roamed my part of Texas. I'm lucky to feel a linear history with people who've produced food across the globe. I feel blessed. On the other side, I guess I'm just a rabid person. A light bulb goes on, and you decide that something is really important to you. People can do powerful things. You just get the fulcrum and you find the lever.

RG: How do you enable our industry, which has lagged in professional leadership from women, to get more women involved? How would you encourage students who look to you as a role model?

sc: As women, we can clearly do anything we want. The question is, what do we want to do? I've got three children, and you have to decide what's first in your life. If you have the ability, or your children are of a certain age, then you can take on different levels of tasks. But for many women, the perception is that there's a glass ceiling. The perception may be that you won't be rewarded for your efforts. Certainly in the legislature, I didn't feel that being a woman was in any way a handicap. Women are generally perceived by the electorate as more truthful, genuine, and hardworking. The place I'm not sure women are doing as well is the corporate world, and I'm not sure why. Women generally—me notwithstanding—try to find consensus, try to find mutually successful outcomes. It's not the football game of life. It's the kitchen table of life, if that's not sounding too weird. Most successful women are better prepared. I'm not sure that CEOs understand the collective strength women bring to problem solving.

RG: When you finish up your term, what's next?

sc: I'll probably look for another elected office if there's something that's interesting, that really keeps the gray cells churning. I don't expect to be hanging up my boots—hanging up my spurs, actually, as my boots don't hang too well.

RG: I'm glad to hear that for the rest of our sakes. Thank you very much.

ICH TOTTEN

...id Founder, The Full Yield (2013)

Founder and CEO of The Full Yield, Zoe Finch Totten is a Yale-trained nurse-midwife and the daughter of a cultural anthropologist. She takes a systems approach to well-being, connecting not only food and health but also the organizations that serve them. The Full Yield's founding pilot engaged a health plan, employers, a grocery chain, food service operators, and food manufacturers and yielded both clinically significant results for participants in the program and a positive ROI for employers. She is now in negotiations with one of the country's leading health and wellness providers to pilot a more scalable version of the program as phase one of a national rollout.[2]

RG: Zoe Finch Totten is the founder and CEO of The Full Yield. Would you mind explaining what "the full yield" is?

ZT: It's an old farming term. If you start with decent seeds, take good care of your soil, get lucky with the weather and the bugs, and do what you can about watering, you'll reap a "full yield," meaning as much as those seeds can produce.

The meaning works on many levels. For individuals, your genes are your seeds. How you take care of yourself and what you eat contribute to what you're yielding every day and over a lifetime. For employers or the government paying for health care, how well we are has everything to do with yield, which can be measured in terms of productivity and/or profit and/or cost savings related to health care.

We've had plenty of evidence for a long time that we're going in the wrong direction in terms of health and productivity. My belief is that by using food quality as the pivot for the design work and for the programming around behavior change, we'll achieve the greatest results in the most efficient way in both the food and health care industries.

RG: You put this concept into practical use and involved the city of Boston, a major insurance company, and a major health company. How were you able to convince so many different kinds of people—really, for the first time—to understand the intersection was so important?

ZT: Even though it wasn't on their minds before, when folks in the grocery business and the health insurance business and people who employ people learned more about the connection between food and productivity, it made immediate sense to them. It's a pleasure talking with people about this. Having grown up off the grid in so-called third world countries and returning again and again to the States, it seemed clear that we use food to create culture. We source it together, and in the process of sourcing and sharing it, we construct meaning. There's a way to link everything back to it.

RG: Health care costs twice as much as food, and yet the connection between food and health care, which you just made, is not understood very well. How did you convince a John Hancock and the city of Boston and Harvard Pilgrim to do an experiment to show how they were interrelated?

ZT: Once they got the connection, they were willing to work collaboratively with us to improve people's health and track health metrics and then evaluate claims data to make the economic case. The work now is to scale nationally, because these connections are easier to operationalize once they're made visible to key stakeholders.

RG: You had quite a few people become part of the process. Were the results as great as you hoped they would be?

ZT: Until this is truly systems changing, I won't be satisfied, but our partners—Harvard Pilgrim, Roche Brothers, and different employers in the pilot—were immensely pleased. People really did get healthier. Focusing on food quality helped individuals improve their health and, importantly, learn greater self-efficacy, which is fundamental to health.

The claims data demonstrated that if you focus on food quality, you'll actually save on health-related productivity costs, pharmacy costs, and ultimately medical costs. Increasing demand for easier access to better-quality food creates well-identified profit opportunities for food manufacturers, retailers, and food service operators.

RG: So the claims actually went down?

ZT: Yes. Harvard Pilgrim calculated that the cost savings were almost three to one for employees who'd been in the pilot for the entire year.

RG: The largest food retailer in the world, Walmart, must be watching what you're doing—one, trying to look at their supply chain in an environmentally sound way, but also evaluating consumer purchases to see if consumers were better off not just dollar-wise but health-wise. Do you think somebody that has a 20 percent market share can have the strength to actually change that many people?

ZT: Absolutely, if they're willing to be innovative enough. The pilot is a good start, but now it's really "what's next?" Where I find myself disappointed is that there's good thinking, but the application suffers because companies are uncomfortable partnering operationally. Walmart could hook together lots of pieces inside their own operations like food and in-store clinics and in-store pharmacy.

RG: Walmart wants to standardize food quality using a "good for you" label. They've developed a common label which they hope the branded and private label companies will use. Do you think that's realistic?

ZT: Their standards are quite good. Unfortunately, that alone won't change behavior as it's lost in the cacophony of targeted noise. Shoppers need a context. They're targeted relentlessly by messages and incentives, but those don't add up to a solution, something that follows them to work and follows them home. We did that in the pilot by creating a "surround sound" effect, which recognized that people who opt for something are motivated. Their motivation created an opportunity for us to help them individually, and, collectively, it created a market demand to change all the pieces around them.

RG: Nestlé calls themselves a wellness company.

ZT: It's an excellent aspiration.

RG: And they say they want to create shared value up and down the food chain. But creating shared value among the parts of the food chain is one thing; creating shared value at the top of the food chain with the consumer is very difficult. Can they do that as a chocolate, milk, and coffee company?

ZT: They produce lots of other types of food. The one company besides Walmart that I wish would produce better-quality food is Nestlé. They make lots of frozen meals and have the capacity to partner with grocery stores to produce much better stuff that could piggyback on their other brands—weight loss brands, baby food brands, etc. I don't know why they're not doing it.

RG: What would you do if you were head of Walmart and you wanted to implement your concept?

ZT: I would focus on what most people want, which is to feel good and to have some real control over their experience. That's not how most people feel.

Starting with that and working backwards, what can I do in each Walmart store and each surrounding community to promote those feelings? An example might be when a shopper fills a script at the pharmacy for blood pressure medication, the pharmacy team can help that shopper connect to other offerings in the store in meaningful ways from food products to recipes to in-store clinics and offerings in the surrounding community. It's exhausting for people to manage all the things they have to manage these days. If they can walk into a Walmart store not only to buy products, but to get integrated support for basic healthcare in one place, they'd experience Walmart as their partners.

RG: The medical community has come into this whole program very late in the process. Why?

ZT: Lots of reasons. Reductionist modern science has done some real harm by losing track of the interconnectedness of things. For a long time, infant formula was promoted as equally good for the baby as breast milk. That turns out to have been bad science. It's much better for babies to have breast milk, and better for the mother too. We are now finally beginning to understand what's been true all along: whole foods are much better for us than refined foods. As we learn more about the microbiome, we're being forced out of the reductionist silos of scientific specialization and seeing ourselves more clearly as living systems dynamically interacting with each other and the environment.

What's happened with food is similar. For decades, we've had science supporting a message that it doesn't matter what you eat. What matters is how much. That's wrong. The most recent research demonstrates how addictive refined foods are. What we eat has everything to do with our health. By promoting largely refined foods for over three decades, we've conducted a massive, unintended experiment on ourselves the world over. The consequence has been really terrible health.

RG: What's going to make it change more rapidly?

ZT: Those who are paying for health care—employers, the government, in some cases health plans if they've got fully funded accounts—are realizing the costs are unsustainable and are putting our economy at long-term risk. There's an increased focus on human behavior and lifestyle—what we're eating, how much we're moving, how much we're sleeping, whether we're stressed—because we're all paying for poor lifestyles and higher health care costs.

RG: Can the fast food industry practice creative destruction and change who they are and what they stand for in a way that is both enjoyable and healthful for the consumer and profitable for them?

ZT: I don't think they can do it alone. Most every food company, manufacturer or retailer, has had a challenging experience offering something healthier for people and discovering that it just doesn't sell, and they lose money. Consumers will not accept healthier food options if there aren't other things going on that make them want it in the first place.

That's what we found in our pilot. We engaged people in a year-long program by asking them how good they wanted to feel. They enrolled because they did want to feel better, and part of the work was to improve the way they were eating. That was an epiphanal experience for pretty much everybody in the program. And it created a new profit center for those making and selling food.

If a fast food company—even a big one with a real impact on systems—suddenly started selling food that was better for people, they would lose a lot of customers. We've conditioned people to want a diet that's high in sugar and salt and fat. A sustained intervention is needed for us to move in a healthier direction, and the key is people knowing that they'll feel better as a result. Many pieces need to be orchestrated together. No single player is going to be able to do this in a way that's really successful.

RG: How can we make them feel better and also make them feel like they're tasting something better at the same time?

ZT: When people stop eating highly refined foods for as few as three days, they discover they like foods they thought they didn't like. I've even noticed it in myself. If I've gone off to do something celebratory for several days and eaten foods I don't normally eat, my appetite for produce diminishes, but the moment I'm back to eating lower on the food chain, I crave produce. Refined foods deaden the palate.

RG: And when we go to see our doctors, are they equipped to even give us good advice on food?

ZT: Mostly not.

RG: Why is that?

ZT: Health care is really about screening for and treating disease. It's not about teaching people how to get well and stay well. It's not their fault. The system they've come through—physicians, general practitioners—doesn't focus on being well.

RG: So the preventive part of medicine is still very weak?

ZT: Yes, historically the preventive part of health has been limited to the home and the community.

RG: Well, home economics, years ago, was a major subject. No longer. Why?

ZT: We convinced ourselves that life would be better if we handed off those skills to others who could do them more efficiently.

RG: We lost control of time too.

ZT: Part of the hoax of modern life is that we have all these things that are time-saving. But really, when I think about the people that I knew when I was a kid, nobody was frenzied in the way that everybody seems frenzied now. Yes, we've lost time.

RG: When you come to my master's class and our senior management class as well, your observations are a breath of fresh air, like somebody opened a window. Why can students and senior managers grasp what you're saying when the public per se doesn't?

ZT: People just need a bit of reorientation. I'm not telling anybody anything that isn't right there. They're just not seeing it. My seeing it, my fixation on making all this visible, is because of my upbringing, for which I thank my elders.

RG: We value certain things in this country going back to Abe Lincoln, who created the National Academy, placed extension agents in every county of every state of our country, established land grant colleges to educate people on many of the subjects you're talking about to train farmers to produce the full yield from the soil. Who's going to train humanity to produce the full yield for themselves?

ZT: That's the critical question. I suspect we'll have to experience more economic pain and more health-related pain, which will force people to look harder at where we are and what to do about it.

RG: Well, the insurance companies are getting the message, but I don't think the educational community has gotten the message. Who's going to help them do that?

ZT: I don't know that the insurance companies have really gotten the message. But there's evidence in small ways all over the country of a move to take back control and teach ourselves new competencies—how to cook, how to preserve, how to grow your own stuff in pots on your own deck. Fixing the problem won't be a single fix by a single person or a single entity. Cooperative design and orchestrating many, many levers in the market are essential.

RG: As I listen to you talk, I wonder whether the leadership is less wise than your leadership for trying to do this. I wonder if the leadership that understands this, or at least hopefully understands this, doesn't use it as a way of attacking the system rather than encouraging it to change.

ZT: I noticed as a kid how acceptable it was to simply blame others. The truth is we all got here together. Many people are surprised that I'm so pro the food industry. We need the food industry. It's already here. We all have a role to play, and if we're in agreement about what our needs are and what our goals are, we'll get there more efficiently and with more profitability as well.

RG: That's a very enlightened attitude, but I must say that there are more books written about the evils of people at the retail, processing, farming, farm supply side, blaming them for what we are and who we are, rather than looking in the mirror. Why?

ZT: There was a *New Yorker* cartoon of an adult dog telling a puppy that all dogs go to heaven because if we screw up, it's not our fault. If you look at what's not working in our culture, we can't blame any one person or system. We're all accountable in different ways.

RG: We haven't mentioned one other subject, and that's culture. Food is part of our tradition, part of our religion, part of our territory, part of our family. What makes you think that people who have grown up in this sort of environment are going to look at those traditions any differently and relate it back to what's best for them?

ZT: People tend to talk about whether a food is good or bad or how much they should or shouldn't eat. When I talk to people about food as the pivot for culture, it's a very different conversation. Culture—it's about making food visible again. Michael Pollan wrote a nice piece using Wendell Berry's line, "Eating is an agricultural act." It's a great line, but it isn't nearly strong enough, because humans have been here for six million years and agriculture started ten thousand years ago. Eating is the ultimate cultural act. We wouldn't have evolved culture, social systems, rites, and rituals if we hadn't had to figure out food together.

When people think about food that way, it becomes an invitation to take better care of yourself and to connect more fully with other people and the planet. Food becomes an exciting topic and central to systems design.

RG: If we have this conversation and I'm fortunate enough to still be alive in ten years, what do you think the world will look like on this particular subject?

ZT: Ideally, what we accomplished locally by jointly engaging food and health systems will become a national model. If not, more people will be trying to address their own discomfort and the discomfort they see in their families and communities. While that's a good thing, those efforts may conflict with as opposed to be in concert with the gigantic infrastructure we already have.

RG: Thank you, Zoe.

JASON LANGHEIER
CEO and Founder, Zipongo (2015)

Founder and CEO of Zipongo, Jason Langheier is a physician whose company is dedicated to working with corporations like Google, Microsoft, and others to promote much healthier foods. He was drawn to the field by his early experiences working with obese children at the Boston Medical Center and his own mother's struggle with weight. Langheier wanted to focus on eating well made simple by questioning consumers about their preferences and making recommendations that would both improve their health and appeal to their food choices. His program at Google with employees and their families produced effective feedback and excellent health results. The program has since been expanded to other firms in the United States and Europe.[3]

RG: Jason Langheier is the CEO and founder of Zipongo. Many people may not know what Zipongo does and may not know either your history or even why you founded it. It would be helpful to get your background and the company's background, please.

JL: Zipongo is eating well made simple. We make it easier for people to make healthier choices in their diet every single day. We work for large self-insured employers and health plans at risk for the cost of people's health care. I'm a physician by training. I went to Duke Med and then Harvard School of Public Health. I worked with great teachers like Walter Willett and became very passionate about the space when a pharmaceutical company asked me to evaluate opportunities for new drug targets, one of which was obesity. I was offered an opportunity to work for Barry Zuckerman, chairman of pediatrics at Boston Medical Center, and Carol Apovian, the head of primary care, who ran the Adult Weight Management Clinic. We developed a child obesity program called Nutritional Fitness for Life. We asked kids, What kind of food do you like? What kind of food grosses you out? And we asked their parents the same questions. We asked, Which grocery stores do you use? And what was your food budget? Many were on food stamps and had about $30 a week to spend. Asking those questions instead of starting from the medical angle and saying, Well, you have this level of insulin resistance and this level of glucose, and then just giving them a template food meal plan allowed us to build something they'd follow.

It allowed us to adjust insulin resistance as well as body mass index in the clinic dramatically. That's all well and good, but we could only see about a hundred kids. In fact, there was only reimbursement for kids who already had insulin resistance. We wanted to help kids before they become obese and prediabetic. The primary care physicians said the challenge was they don't have reimbursement to cover this and don't have enough training on food issues. They wanted an automated, digital system, like Amazon's personalized book recommendations, for families around food.

RG: Zipongo is five years old. What are the most successful experiences you've had and why?

JL: We started by focusing on helping people holistically achieve healthier lifestyles with personalized prescriptions. It became clear that what people really wanted were easy-to-follow recommendations. If we recommended a recipe, we turned it into a grocery list with a map to discounts. That's how we decided to focus on eating well made simple. We also learned that employer health plans focused on assessing risk, looking at employee biometrics and encouraging walking. Those are important, but that's where most of the funding went. Very little was spent promoting healthier eating, which is what affects 75 percent of chronic disease rates in the United States. We decided that by focusing on "eating well made simple," we could make a big impact, and in 2013 we launched a pilot program with Google. We got a very high uptake, because when people got their biometric screening results they asked for advice on what to eat. A very large percentage of people enrolled, and they kept using it because we plugged into the café and used our application as a personalized mini-menu.

RG: Thus far you've had five years' experience doing this, and how long have you been with Google?

JL: We started with Google in 2013 and are still with them today and rolling out nationally.

RG: What percentage of the workforce participates?

JL: Typically when we go through biometric screening we get 79 percent of participants to enroll. When we do a combination of digital-only and biometric screening we usually get about a third to enroll.

RG: And over the last two years have they noticed a change in their health and their body?

JL: Yes. We've seen a 1.5-inch waist size reduction over a year. We've seen a five-point drop on blood pressure. Most importantly, we've seen statistically significant drops in red meat consumption and increases in fruits, vegetables, water, fiber, calcium, fish. Zipongo is now helping companies scale nationally as well as globally down the line.

RG: Does Zipongo influence the whole family or just the workforce?

JL: The program is focused on the whole family. That's why it's both Food at Work and Food at Home. The fastest growth in health care spending is actually on family members. A lot of employee wellness programs only focus on what they control within their four walls. But an employee's food environment is dictated largely by family decisions. So with Food at Home we allow all family members to take a dietary assessment, and connect that to a meal plan. The meal plan connects to recipes. The recipes connect to a grocery list. The grocery list connects to discounts from all the grocery stores in the United States. The employer or the health plan can even fund additional rewards for buying things like fruits and vegetables. We've piloted a program where the employee can order food via the Zipongo application based on Zipongo recommendations, tied back to their biometrics and their food preferences. They could buy the food through the app, pick it up at the café, and take it home to their family. We went from 30 percent enrollment to 70 percent in three weeks when we introduced that program. And people paid full price for the food.

RG: Are the insurance companies involved in your program?

JL: Yes. We have a number of health plans. In addition to working with white-collar companies like Microsoft, we're working with people in inner-city Philadelphia. In a study that was submitted for publication by Drexel, we had a thirteen-point drop in total cholesterol and 70 percent lost weight, an average of nine pounds in six months. People took advantage of text messages recommending particular meals for dinner. People adopted Zipongo because we made their life easier.

RG: Do you have any feedback from the medical community that serves participants in the program?

JL: Yes. There's a lot of interest from the medical community going back to our original work with the Boston Medical Center. We want to enable physicians, care providers, and nutritionists to prescribe Zipongo. The reality is that as a physician myself it's not possible to spend enough time with people. We don't go into homes and help patients reset environmental cues. The system that employs us gives us only fifteen to thirty minutes with each person. The Affordable Care Act moves in the right direction by encouraging digital solutions to support the care provider community. Especially using cell phones, we can create a network of care instead of relying solely on individual care providers. Our goal is to make digital therapeutics and digital nutrition counseling an integral part of the health care system.

RG: The Mayo Clinic has been a leader in evaluating how medicine and pills interact. They've already determined that eating is more important than pills. That requires new research on the interactions between the pharmaceutical and food industries as well as the relationship between preventive medicine, food, and the health of the individual. Will the medical community be doing more research in this area?

JL: Yes. One of the teachers I most admire is Walter Willett. He and his colleagues have created large cohort studies like the Nurses Health Study, the Health Professionals Follow-Up Study, and then others before it like the Framingham Heart Study. These studies are the basis for much of what we know about nutrition today. As we aggregate anonymized versions of our data we'll be able to tie food purchases back to biometric data and we'll be able to uncover things we've never known before. Zipongo is dedicated to working with the research community.

RG: It's interesting that firms like Google and Microsoft are at the forefront in encouraging your company and using your company's facilities and results. Do you think that going forward companies will use food as a competitive tool in attracting employees to their company?

JL: They already are and Google is a pioneer. They started by simply wanting to make life easier for their employees and fuel them for the day. The productivity argument—sustainable high performance, feeling good, while you're trying to accomplish great things each day— that's a simple tenet that has been ignored by employers over the years. The phone has become their new environment. Zipongo is GPS for the food environment. It's a mini-menu that gives you all the choice in the world but it shrinks your decision set. Barry Schwartz has been a great leader in thinking about the paradox of choice. We're overwhelmed when we have too many options.

RG: What about populations that aren't in the workforce? They say that when a woman is pregnant, the future health of the child is largely determined. When people are in the last stages of their life and they leave the workforce, food becomes even more important in terms of their health. How do they get involved in what you're doing?

JL: That's really important to me on a lot of levels. Part of what inspires me is that my mom has struggled with obesity from a young age. She's in her fifties with osteoarthritis. No employer ever looked out for her and there was an enormous amount of advertising money spent marketing food to her that was not in her interest. Like so many people, she yo-yoed with her weight and struggles with it still today. The even more difficult challenge—and one I care a lot [about] from my Boston Medical Center experience—is Medicaid and inner-city populations that have even less resources than my family. When you get down into that level, we have an epidemic of malnutrition that leads to both obesity and developmental delay across so many children in America that it's extremely hard for the education system to handle. We spend so much of our GDP on the health care effects of dealing with people who are disabled, obese, developmentally delayed, because we don't make the right investments early. The people in inner-city Philadelphia that we worked with got their biometric screening and we had a chef from the community who was incredibly well received. We sent automatic text messages with recipes and we got messages back from people saying thank you, God bless you. It highlights a whole community in poverty that is looking for support wherever they can find it.

RG: How do you see Zipongo in ten years?

JL: I hope Zipongo either remains a standalone company or a standalone division of a company that is very mission driven and has really strong beliefs about what it can accomplish for the world. I would hope that we are touching people across the planet, because this is not just an American issue. We've exported the problem. There's a chance to cut off the epidemic that we've seen here over the last forty years before it fully spreads. I'm talking about obesity and the chronic diseases that flow from it. The academic in me hopes we're seeding another important cohort study that generations of scientists can use to help prevent other diseases as well: inflammatory bowel disease, Crohn's, ulcerative colitis. There's enormous evidence that cancer treatment and survivorship can be improved with the right diet. I think that Zipongo and the inevitable competitors have a chance to bring us back to our roots. Hippocrates said that food is thy medicine. We have a chance to make that true.

RG: That's a fine way to end this discussion. Thank you very much.

DANIEL WEGMAN
Chairman, Wegmans Inc. (1995)

I interviewed Daniel Wegman 23 years ago. Our conversation is included in this book because Wegmans has recognized its responsibilities to its consumers, its workforce, and its community from its very beginnings and continues to be a role model for the global food system in 2018.

The third-generation leader of Wegmans, based in Rochester, New York, Danny Wegman believes that every segment of the vertically aligned food system exists to serve the ultimate consumer. Over the course of his career, that core belief has been reinforced and other trends he has identified have come to the fore. Wegman strongly believes that Wegmans supermarkets have an obligation to improve the education, nutrition, and economic development of the communities they serve. They have done so working with the school systems, with the nutrition advice they give their consumers, and with the relationships they have with their local farm suppliers.[4]

RG: Dan Wegman is president of Wegmans of Rochester, New York, a leading food retailer in the United States. The Food Marketing Institute considers Wegmans to be a leading change maker in the food system, especially as a sensitive listener to consumers. How have you been able to achieve that?

DW: We've always had an intense focus on our customers, because either we make them happy or we're not in business. Our business has always been based on understanding our customers and giving them a unique choice that they don't have elsewhere. Sometimes it works, but you have to be ready to be wrong. We don't claim to be experts, but we sure try. There are many leaders around the world. Some of them are very small and some are much larger. We learn a lot from other folks who are doing innovative things and whose customers appreciate them. We come back and see if our customers might be interested in those kind of things. So that's partially how we try to keep up with our customers.

RG: What are some of the customer trends that you've responded to in recent times?

DW: Most of us in the food industry probably have the same list of consumer trends. Fresh food is more important, for example, than frozen or canned. There is concern about fat in products. A good-tasting, low-fat product is a home run with customers today. There's a trend toward more natural products. Fresh Fields and Whole Foods and others around the country are doing a very good job in that area. The largest consumer trend right now may be that customers don't have time to cook at the end of a day, if they're working. These seem to be the major trends.

There also seems to be a trend toward more meatless eating. There are good alternatives to eating meat—whether it's just plain pasta and vegetables—that people like. They are quick and simple to produce. Prepared foods are a response to time pressure. More people are taking foods home so they don't have to actually prepare them.

RG: What do you make available for those kinds of customers in the store, then?

DW: That's evolving. We've tried a number of different foods but aren't sure where we're going to end up. We began with Chinese food—a very significant area for us—but we sell other foods like sandwiches and Italian foods. It's an area to pursue, but we don't have all the answers.

RG: You've created a nutrition position in your company and provide nutrition information to customers in a newspaper column. How has that worked out?

DW: Mary Ellen Burris has been our director of consumer affairs for over twenty years. She's developed a reputation of trust with our customers—and that's worked out well. We try and listen to our customers, but sometimes, they don't even know what they want, so we have frank, two-way conversations with them.

RG: I imagine all it takes would be one mistake and you lose a great deal of credibility.

DW: A very high risk. When the ground beef [contamination] situation took place, it hurt the whole industry. Sometimes we're only as good as our worst member.

RG: You've been one of the few retailers that have worked very closely with your local farm producers on produce. How has that worked out?

DW: Very well. First, our customers enjoy products grown close to home. They've always liked them. It also encourages local production of fruits and vegetables. Without us, these folks really wouldn't have a business at all. We consider growers our partners, and think there's a lot more we can do with them. We're concerned about growing practices. We can work with these folks to develop integrated pest management, which enables them to grow products less expensively than they're presently doing now.

RG: You also have a reputation of producing creative private label products that are unique to your store. How do you look upon those products in the future?

DW: The customer is changing, and if we pay enough attention to our customers, we can pick up on trends maybe faster than anyone else and produce our own products—that's how we view private label for the future. Then we used to pick a national brand, match it, and sell it for less. Today, we're looking to fill a customer need and sell at a price they can afford. That's really an extension of our philosophy of selling perishable products over the years.

RG: What are the successful private label products that you've had?

DW: Spaghetti sauce, for one. There are plenty of spaghetti sauces out there, but they were clustered around the same taste profile. We introduced other tastes to our customers to go along with quick and nutritious meals. Just making the same old products didn't seem to add any customer value, but helping customers with problems they face adds a lot of value and that's where we're headed with our private label at this point.

RG: How difficult is it to get good manufacturers to provide the product to your specifications?

DW: It's very difficult because most private label manufacturers follow the old paradigm of cheap, cheap, cheap. When we said, No, we want better product—we want better-quality standards—we want you to work on your own processes of producing a better product—we've had a very difficult time in finding suppliers.

RG: Do you find that this new cooperation with brand managers—one where they understand your business better, or do they just understand the category better?

DW: If you're doing business with Wegmans, you'll understand Wegmans' business better and get better in your own category because you understand everything that's involved with distributing and getting your products to the ultimate customer. It helps brands understand where our costs are, which helps us both win.

RG: A number of companies like Tesco in England trace customer purchases by rewarding them with the equivalent of frequent flyer miles for food. Have you thought about doing that?

DW: No, but that reflects the lowering costs of technology and information. Programs like that are in their infancy. In the future, we're going to know much more about our customers.

RG: You are not only customer oriented, you are public spirit oriented in the sense of trying to make sure that the food system itself is more responsive to the priorities of the consumer. We're fortunate here at Harvard to have you as a member of [our] university-wide committee on health, nutrition, food safety, and the environment, and you've been constantly hammering this committee to be more responsive to the consumer. What should the mission of this nonpartisan and impartial group be, and what kind of focus should we have so we don't miss this opportunity to bring people with different backgrounds together to be more responsive to the changes affecting all of us?

DW: At Wegmans, every time we talk about an internal customer, we get in trouble. We've come to the conclusion we only have one customer and that's the ultimate customer. That's true for the whole food system. As a retailer, we're only a middle person serving that customer. I would love to see our group define the needs of that customer. We might have the same list, but we don't put it on the board. Without that list, you can end up with solutions that don't address the right problems. It gives us a common ground.

Without that list and without a common goal, we're all going to go in different directions and risk losing our customers' trust. Every time we lessen consumer trust, we prevent our food system from serving the customers as they should be served.

RG: You've been very community conscious in your own local community, and have worked diligently to improve education in your community. How is that working, and how can others try to achieve the same sort of success?

DW: It's working very well. We're having real success helping inner-city kids, because that's where our initial focus was. There are tremendous barriers to doing this, and the initial barrier is that most businesses don't believe it's their responsibility to be involved. We believe business is the only place that really knows what young kids need to know and can help them learn those things.

We're doing this to do something good—it does feel pretty good, by the way—but we're doing it because if we don't, these kids are going to fail, and if the kids fail, our communities are going to fail. And if we do business in these communities and the communities fail, we've got a big problem. Our own employees will have a big problem just plain living there. So, we think it's in our own self-interest as a business to get involved with communities and help them. I told my dad you were interested in his thinking about why businesses like Wegmans should help communities, and he said to tell you there's no other reason to be in business aside from helping the communities where we do business.

RG: Well, you certainly practice what you preach. The contribution you've made to both the public school system and the parochial school system in your community is a remarkable feat and an example that is cited by many people, including the president of the United States. So you have every right to be proud of that accomplishment.

How do you communicate what you've learned to other businesses in your local community, so it's not just your firm but a group of firms that try to respond to that same issue?

DW: With difficulty. We've tended—in the educational area—to put all the responsibility for good or bad education in the hands of the public school system. If the education is poor, we blame the public school system for all the wrongs in the community. I don't believe that's right. Business has a responsibility to be involved.

We tend to beat up on the public school systems. We keep pointing the finger at everyone but ourselves. I hope we look at shared responsibilities in our communities, because future success lies in shared responsibility.

RG: If you and I were having a conversation like this five or ten years from now, what will Wegmans look like?

DW: I hope we're more ethnically diverse than we are today and have more women making key decisions. We'll be selling a different range of products—far more ready for the table than today. I hope that we wouldn't be discussing how to get other businesses involved in the community—that I'd be able to say to you, Gee, Ray, we could hardly keep up with all these companies that are doing so much in our community.

RG: Well, I hope you're right on that one. One element we haven't discussed—and that is this efficient consumer response. Do you think some bulky items will be moving directly from warehouses to the consumer and bypassing the store completely?

DW: Don't know. If there's a more efficient method of distribution, that will happen. Do I think it's going to be different? Yes, it's going to be very different. As concern for time increases in the value equation, certain customers will do anything to avoid going to a store to buy certain things. What do they want delivered at home? Do they want toilet paper delivered at home? Do they want vegetables delivered at home? I don't know. We're going to continue doing a good job in our stores because customers like coming to them and will for a while.

RG: Some stores feel that they have to offer all sorts of departments—an amusement department, a dry-cleaning department, a hardware department, and so forth. How do you feel about all of those types of additional services?

DW: I'm wary of trying to be all things to all people. We're concerned about sticking to what we're good at because we think if we're not good at something, there's no reason to come to us at all.

RG: Thank you very much for a wonderful interview.

KEVIN NIELD

Director, Bishop Storehouse Warehouses of the
Church of Jesus Christ of Latter-Day Saints (2000)

In his role as director of the Bishop Storehouse Warehouse Services of the Church of Jesus Christ of Latter-Day Saints, Kevin Nield has led the church's forward-looking efforts to boost food security and preparedness at a time when global food inventories are kept very small. Nield and the Latter-Day Saints believe that the members of the church need to maintain an emergency supply of food at all times and to provide for their families' food security and for others in need. The church has built a value-added food chain in the United States to help maintain their families' food security program.[5]

RG: Kevin Nield is director of the Bishop Storehouse Warehouses Services of the Mormon Church. The church stresses self-reliance and the importance of maintaining food security for its members as well as financial security. The inventory of major grains in 2008 may be at the lowest level I think in history. Yet our population is at the highest level in history. How does the church view this situation globally, and how does that relate back to your specific program?

KN: There are more members of the church outside of the United States than within the United States, so it is a global concern. From the very beginning of the church, a goal has been to care for the poor, feed the hungry, clothe the naked, lift up the hands that hang down. Part of that always comes back to providing food. Maybe the first issue someone has to look at is employment and education, but while they're doing that some may need food so they can learn and grow and obtain the education or skills that they need. Our most recent emphasis in food security has been to refocus on family and home storage, and promote storage for a longer period against a time of greater need. Our focus is generally on personal and family preparedness. Institutionally, since the early days of the church, the welfare services program has been in place. It was formalized in the early 1930s and initially called the Church Security Program. It provided food from farms or gardens, and then from farms to processing facilities and into storehouses where bishops or congregation leaders could obtain food for those who were in need. Much of that food was provided as a service of those who have given to those who have not. In the early 1940s, a grain storage program was put into place at locations near church members, against a time of need. Those wheat inventories continue to this day. Our goal is less to take advantage of pricing opportunities than to always have grain in reserve.

RG: Do you keep these inventories turned over so they're fresh, and how do you do that?

KN: We do. We rotate the stored grain once every four years. Twenty-five percent of the product is either sold at market or we give it away for humanitarian purposes or it's used within the church organization. The wheat comes from church-operated farms and rotating it is one of our challenges.

RG: You work with agencies like the Red Cross for major catastrophes like Katrina. I understand from newspaper accounts that your institution was considered the most effective dealing with Katrina.

KN: The Gulf Coast hurricanes over the last few years have been terrible. Two things are in place that make it possible for us to respond effectively. First and foremost, there are members of the church who are organized and willing to help. In the example of New Orleans, church members throughout the South helped with cleanup efforts. Second, within a day or so, our storehouse in Slidell, just north of New Orleans, became a food distribution point serving the community of Slidell, whether they were members of the church or not. Local authorities used the facility, and we tried to help whoever was in need. We have chapels in many places and some were affected and some became convenient distribution points. We keep inventories in reserve, whether they're food or some other emergency items, so we can respond very quickly. The food is there, and the people are there to distribute it. We can be quite effective in regional or local disasters.

RG: Your members are encouraged to have a certain number of days' supply on hand of food. How many of them actually do so?

KN: Recent studies indicate that maybe 15 to 20 percent in the United States participate, which is less than areas outside the United States. The percent goes up for a global supply of food that church members use regularly. Having something on hand that can get me through a momentary crisis, whether it be personal, such as a job loss, or more widespread, affecting my community or my region, is our goal. If it's a larger scale we have some difficult challenges facing all of us.

RG: The church offers an excellent example of how managing inventories has changed in the United States. Now we have "just in time" inventory management where people try to reduce the amount of inventory on hand as much as possible. We have no more surplus storage programs in the United States, and most of the surplus supplies, if you want to call them surplus, are located outside the United States. We have an emergency oil reserve in the United States for energy and heating, but we have no emergency food relief except through conservation reserve programs, essentially land that isn't planted and lays fallow. Whose responsibility is it going to be when we now have severe shortages and people are having long-term contractual relationships with a supply chain because they're worried about having enough to even run their factories?

KN: That's a real concern. I notice lots of discussion on food safety, but very little on food security. We're all grateful for food safety, but who's responsible? It would be good if those who have taken the responsibility to feed the people in the world could figure out what to do if the supply chain breaks down in a significant way. That's very difficult because "just in time" inventories have taken over and our ability to order and deliver new goods is so constrained in an emergency. There's just this smooth line, especially in this country where food gets on our shelves seemingly without effort. I believe and the message of the church is that there's got to be some measure of individual and family preparedness. Having extra food in one's home is probably better than the large warehouse five hundred miles away in time of need. We emphasize personal and family preparedness. Responsibility goes back to individual families, and then there's the interest from the local charities, the food banks that care for those who cannot provide for themselves. It's probably the difficult question of our time: who's responsible? The land base is great and the church has a wonderful land base, but getting the food to the person in need in normal times or crisis time is a unique challenge. I don't have a great answer for you.

RG: People are becoming truly concerned about supply chains. Do we know where the inventories are? How do we measure those inventories, and do we have enough inventories on hand to make sure long-term contractual obligations can be met?

KN: Well my understanding is the world's grain supply is not quite a month's worth at the present time.

RG: For the whole world.

KN: That's my understanding. We store some grain in the church in thirty or so locations throughout the United States. Our biggest issue is to make sure those grain facilities are full. In the bigger picture, the grain we store is relatively modest, but we target a certain amount of grain to store, and when we drop below it we've bought warehouse receipts to maintain our target inventory. Recently, we've tried to find ways to improve the usefulness of warehouse receipts. My understanding is when you buy a warehouse receipt, you should know where the commodity is located, but that's becoming more difficult all the time. Back to the idea of personal and family preparedness, if there's grain in the person's pantry, the family or the person who's going to need the food knows where it is. That becomes very important in a crisis when you need to know where you can get food.

RG: The Department of Agriculture does a pretty good job tracking on-farm and off-farm storage, but we haven't a clue exactly which farms have it and we haven't a clue as to where physically it is elsewhere. Do you think we should have a food security program that actually traces where the supplies are?

KN: It's the only sure way in a time of crisis. On-farm storage isn't what it used to be. We need someone to step forward and not only put all the tools in place, but the legislation that lets us identify when grain levels drop below a target. That's quite a weakness.

RG: It's ironic that the last time people were really concerned about food supplies was in the early '70s when people had bomb shelters stored with food. Even the relief agencies today would prefer to get money to buy supplies overseas rather than have them shipped within the country to wherever food is needed. It's a monetized supply system rather than a physical supply system. We really don't know for sure whether the food is actually there. We track oil and energy inventories. Would you agree we also need a food inventory assessment?

KN: Oil and other things don't do much good if people are hungry and battling over who gets the food. The other reserves become almost useless.

RG: Do church leaders feel an obligation to discuss their program with other institutions in the hopes that that might be useful to them, or do they feel that they have enough problems doing it themselves?

KN: The church leaders are very concerned about spiritual and temporal welfare. What we're talking about here is temporal welfare. The church is pleased to participate in discussions on how these crises should be handled and what the church has done to create a food reserve. The most important message from the leaders of the Church of Jesus Christ of Latter-Day Saints would be to store resources as an individual or as a family, and look to yourself and your family or close associates first, and then to the church and the community and other institutions to help care for those in need for whatever reason.

RG: In essence, what you're saying is this is a consumer-backward program rather than a producer-forward program.

KN: That's a good way to put it. In a time of need, the consumer is the first one affected and the one that causes the most worry for everybody up and down the chain.

RG: As I think of the food chain and of supermarkets and other kinds of markets around the world that cater to the end consumer, they depend on the current global supply chain never breaking. Yet if only 10 percent of the world's annual consumption is available and most of that is probably in rolling stock moving around the world rather than stationary in any one position, it means that we're not prepared for any major challenge to the food system.

KN: That's right. In the future the warehouse is something we need to bring back. The church has established a model that is capital intensive, but it's also volunteer labor intensive and it's individual and family responsibility intensive. We use markets to make sure we have some reserves in place.

RG: The whole vertical system of farms and storehouses that you have in place has been there for some time. Do you see that system changing in the future?

KN: Not in any significant way. In the United States we've been relatively static for several decades in terms of how we keep inventories, care for the poor and needy, and promote individual and family preparedness. Some of the unique challenges we're facing internationally are in some of the big cities across the world like São Paulo or Mexico City or Buenos Aires. As far as personal and family preparedness goes, our principles are the same whether we're in Salt Lake City or in South Africa.

RG: Do you own land in those areas in order to have a vertical system or do you have to rely on others?

KN: The church owns land, but we haven't institutionalized connections between the land, the farm, the processing facilities, and the storehouses as we have in the United States. We have large agricultural holdings in Australia, Latin America, England, and a variety of places—so land is very important—but as we grow we need to consider institutionalizing some of our practices. But again personal family preparedness is not contingent upon the church or its land. It's up to the family.

RG: You are an employee of the church.

KN: I am.

RG: And a professional in your field. Are most of the operations of this vertical food chain in support of consumers' needs run by professionals or are they run by church members or a little bit of both?

KN: There's a little of both, but a lot of volunteers. The ratio of paid to volunteer is significantly weighted on the volunteer side. For example, in North America and Latin America there are 130 bishop storehouses, of which about 120 are managed by volunteers, often a couple who has finished their work and love to give their time and service to help others. The 130 storehouse operations where food is distributed are overseen by local church leadership who watch over the storehouse, provide donated labor, and then push inventory to those storehouses. We set an inventory level and when it drops below we'll ship the goods.

RG: Well you've given us a very good model. I worry about how [that] translates to the larger community, and worry even more about the risks of only having a thirty-day supply for the world's food system. But you've certainly demonstrated we have to do something. Thank you so much.

KN: Thank you.

DANIEL VASELLA

President and CEO, Novartis (2003)

President and CEO of Novartis, the first "life sciences company," Daniel Vasella has strategically structured the company to concentrate most visibly on pharmaceuticals, but with a separate division focused on nutrition, vision, and animal health. Trained as a doctor, Vasella is committed to the importance of independent scientific analysis and the constructive role corporations can play to improve people's lives. Recalling his own experience as an often-ill youth, Vasella helped build a life sciences company dedicated to improving human health and doing so in a way that does not neglect those who cannot afford their help.[6]

RG: Dr. Daniel Vasella is president and CEO of Novartis. You've been an inspiration as to how a company can plan for the future. As you look forward, how do you see your company developing over the next five or ten years?

DV: That's a multifaceted question that starts with the business portfolio and ends with how we operate within society. We're to discover, develop, and market better medicines for people, for patients. That will remain our mission, because it's impossible to eradicate all diseases, so we won't be out of work. Secondly, we need to do that better than our competition—faster with more differentiated products and better selling successes in the marketplace. We are investing now for the ten- to twenty-year period ahead. If we consider other aspects like our role in society, how well can we articulate our mission? How credible are we? How is our behavior viewed in terms of marketing and selling? How are we viewed in terms of pricing? Finally, if we look at the developing world and the moral and ethical demands on a corporation like ours, because we are in a socially important segment, we have a supplemental challenge. How do we deal with that? Our view is that we will contribute. Last year, we gave money and medicines worth about 350 million Swiss francs, about $280 million. We want to do this voluntarily and not be forced into it.

RG: We're very fortunate to have firms with that attitude. You've made an investment here in Cambridge that represents a revolutionary way of looking at a disease by working backwards from a market-oriented point of view and trying to figure out how you can look at the biochemistry and coming backwards with a solution, which is a revolution historically as to the way pharmaceutical companies work. How did you arrive at that conclusion?

DV: By ignorance. Sometimes you make better decisions when you don't know too much about history, and sometimes it's the opposite. But in this case, I think the logic says it's an approach one can and should be using. I rely heavily on really competent and engaged people. You have to trust people you don't always know well, and the trust has different levels—technical competency and decency as a human being.

RG: The people that join you are very fortunate to have a CEO with that value system. The first product of this new approach, Gleevec, really looks like a model, not just for you, but for the whole industry. How do you see it?

DV: Yes, Gleevec is a very good example, but one shouldn't believe it can be applied to each and every disease in the sense that the biologic basis, the genetic basis, of chronic myeloid leukemia (CML) was discovered in the '60s and, then, stepwise through the '80s. You can only apply these kinds of things when you have a good knowledge of the microcosm of the cell. CML isn't very prevalent, so the market was being looked at as being very small. But when we had very positive results, the size of the market can't be the criteria. If people will benefit, we have to go ahead. If the drug is good, we always make the marketing side work in the end. That's been the case with this drug too, despite the fact that we are giving it for free to indigent patients, patients who have no insurance. We make money, and the drug has taken off dramatically. Now we've discovered there are indications that it will work with other cancers too.

RG: It's a great model for everyone to follow. Getting to the environmental, social, political, societal values that you stress correctly, how do you see the brand versus private label, generic issue playing out in the future?

DV: There are limited resources for health care needs, and we know that when you get older, you get sick more often and use more health care services and drug therapies. We have to find ways to provide quality drug therapy at lower prices. Where you can substitute by generic, do it. The resources which are freed up can be redeployed for innovative new medicines.

RG: Years ago, you looked at the heart transplant area to see if there might be an alternative to the human heart, and because of my agribusiness focus I'm interested in whether the pig or hog heart will ever have a role to play in the human body.

DV: Right. Xenotransplantation is a field which for well over fifteen years has been full of promises that haven't come to clinical practice for two reasons. First, chronic rejection has not yet been mastered. Second, pig viruses are inherited from generation to generation, and even if they don't make a pig sick, they might affect humans. So I'm skeptical, but not completely negative on xenotransplantation.

RG: You were one of the first life science companies to look at health, nutrition, pharmaceuticals, and agriculture. You were also one of the first to realize that they were not necessarily mutually self-enforcing and got rid of the agricultural side.

DV: Yes.

RG: When investors look at your portfolio and when you yourself describe your company, you describe it as very focused on the pharmaceuticals side. Why bother with baby food or nutrition or all these other things [that] might take away from your mainstream?

DV: They don't. We have two divisions, one of which is mostly nonpharmaceuticals—generics and over-the-counter drugs are in there along with clinical nutrition, baby foods, CIBA Vision, and animal health. Some interact with our pharmaceuticals division; others don't. In terms of mission, I quite like it. I love a business where we promote health and nutrition and where babies would get vegetables and meat, not salty stuff, but natural food instead of French fries. Healthy food is a good mission.

RG: Getting back to the core business again, people want to trust people and businesses that have a vital stake in their health and development. In Europe, mad cow disease destroyed some of the trust people had and it shows in how they look at scientists, how they look at genetically modified foods and so on. How do academics keep their aura of impartiality so they are trusted and you, in turn, are trusted in the same way? Is there a conflict of interest for an academic to do company-sponsored research?

DV: Of course there is. In the vast majority of cases, it's irrelevant. Most people are aware of their responsibility. Our industry has worked forever with academia and with physicians, and we have all sorts of FDA regulations in place and from other authorities. We also have transparencies. If somebody is working with us, he must disclose it. You mentioned trust. The trust has been broken for big companies regardless, thanks to the Enrons. It sheds a bad light on all the big companies. At the end of the day, you have to be in sync with yourself and say, Others may be suspicions. I accept that. I just have to do what I believe is right.

RG: We have consolidation in all of our industries. You were created out of a consolidation and have an investment in Roche. How do you look at the consolidation? And where do you fit into that?

DV: There will be continued consolidation. In '88, the ten top companies in pharmaceuticals had a 25 percent market share of the world market.

Now it's 50 percent. Pfizer has over 10 percent market share. The economics favor the bigger companies. They have broader portfolios.

RG: As a consolidation occurs in all the industries, people look at size in a distrustful way and the result is we've even had countries saying they won't abide by our patent laws. How do you answer the critics in a way that makes them feel that bigness by itself is not necessarily bad?

DV: There's a spectrum of critics. Some you can talk with 24/7 and you will not persuade them. Others will accept you without any questioning. Then there's a middle spectrum who are critical but listen and are willing to interact, and we should interact with them. Sometimes they identify important weaknesses. For example, pharmaceutical companies don't do enough research and development for diseases which are primarily in the developing world, so we created the Singapore Research Center, which only focuses on those kinds of diseases. You're right: size works against trust. It's associated with anonymity, profit orientation, and lack of feelings. We have to demonstrate that people in large companies have souls and are here to serve others, not just themselves. The problem in large organizations is that the weakest link in your chain can harm you. That's a very difficult problem. I don't know what's going on throughout the corporation, but I'm accountable for it. And when you have a scandal somewhere else, it sheds a shadow over more than one company generally.

RG: Most people think we're very fortunate in this country to have a Food and Drug Administration, because they feel people trust the system because of their presence. How do we maintain that kind of quality and improve on it?

DV: Regulatory authority is essential and must be based on the impartiality of science. If you want to do other evaluations based on economics, do it, but don't mix them together. The FDA must have enough resources and qualified, adequately paid people to do a proper job.

RG: What about the precautionary principle—a concept we don't really understand very well in this country? It supports the right to control something as a precaution even without conclusive science. Do you disagree with that?

DV: I do, because these decisions are really being influenced by political thinking.

RG: What about the health system that all of us are struggling with? You mentioned that some people can't afford it. You feel an obligation to help those people. How do we develop something that makes sense? At the end of the day, if you look at food and health, it's a huge chunk of a consumer's expenditures.

DV: The thinking has become that health and access to medicine is a right. I don't believe it's a right in the sense of a human right.

RG: It's not like food.

DV: You know, in some ways both are and both are not. I believe all these things have to be deserved in one way or another. We need to work for it. There's nothing for free. Of course, everybody should have access to proper diagnosis, proper treatment, proper prevention. There are also some obligations on the prevention side. People shouldn't smoke and drink and eat like crazy. Between smoking and obesity, we would save about $280 billion a year here in the US alone. We should have a system where fundamental needs are covered. How much does society want to spend on health care? How much does the government want to spend on health care? Do you take it from the military? It has to come from somewhere. Or, do you raise taxes?

RG: Could you say a little bit about where you grew up, how you grew up, how you ended up this way. I mean, people have an interest in how a person develops and ends up in the kind of responsible position you have.

DV: I was born in 1953 Fribourg, a small city between Bern and Lausanne, Switzerland. I was the fourth child of a university history professor and was the young one. As a child, I had asthma, and then tuberculosis and meningitis, and was out of school for about a year when I was eight. I had an otherwise normal youth until thirteen when my father died after colon surgery. That was a big loss for me, but it was not the first time. My sister died when I was ten, and then my second sister died in a car accident. Disease and death have been part of my evolution, and not unimportant in my decision to go into medicine, which I did and enjoyed thoroughly. At thirty-five I felt I didn't understand anything about business or politics. I joined Sandoz and eventually became chief operating officer of Sandoz Pharmaceuticals and then CEO. When we merged with Novartis, I became CEO and then chairman and CEO. What do I want to do after I finish with this job? I would love to have a third career, something new and different.

RG: You're a young man with plenty of futures. You're a great role model. Thank you.

AUGUST SCHUMACHER
Cofounder and Executive Vice President,
Wholesome Wave (2014)

Executive vice president and cofounder of the Wholesome Wave, Gus Schumacher has been a policy innovator at multiple levels of the food system—Massachusetts commissioner of agriculture, undersecretary of agriculture in the Clinton administration, senior lender at the World Bank. Supported by government and not-for-profit funds, Wholesome Wave developed a way to double the value of food aid when purchasing fruits and vegetables from farmers' markets, thereby improving the health of both low-income families and small-scale farmers. They also persuaded the medical community to write vegetable and fruit prescriptions for their patients to supplement the payment for fruits and vegetables their patients could afford to buy. A graduate of Harvard College, Schumacher was instrumental in helping me create the PAPSAC seminar. Gus died unexpectedly just prior to the PAPSAC seminar in November 2017. He is missed by all.

RG: Gus Schumacher is the cofounder and executive vice president of Wholesome Wave. Can we start with an explanation of Wholesome Wave?

AS: We started in 2008 when my cofounder Michel Nischan and I realized that people on food stamps were not getting healthy food. Food stamps are limited to $130 per person per month, so it's difficult for a family of four to afford healthy food. New, wireless technologies were emerging, and food stamps could be credited on a mobile site, and then deducted at the store. We thought, why not try that at a farmers' market, which is what we did. We then raised money to double the value of the card, but only if you bought fruits and vegetables from a local farmer. That had two benefits. It provided fresh, local, healthy produce to lower-income food stamp families, and the money supported local farmers. A small portion of an $80 billion food stamp program could now go to small farmers and we've since expanded significantly since 2008.

RG: How big has it become?

AS: We started with four or five farmers' markets in 2008 and are now in twenty-eight states and about four hundred markets. Congress has taken that even deeper and nationally. The new farm bill provides $100 million to take the program to every state and as many farmers' markets that will accept them. The program has grown very rapidly and is an indication of how much people in America are now making the connection between diet, nutrition, and agriculture.

RG: Where does the medical community come into your program?

AS: Michel and I talked to some hospitals, and especially doctors working on diabetes and obesity. Thirty percent of our children are now obese and at risk for diabetes. We talked to doctors at the Codman Square Clinic in Dorchester, hospitals in New York, in Maine, and in Washington, and designed a program called Vegetable Prescriptions, which is a "plus up" of the nutrition incentives. If a patient is diabetic, obese, or has a high BMI, the doctor will prescribe a fruit and vegetable prescription, which provides one extra serving per week, per family member. It's an intensive diet of fruits and vegetables over twenty weeks. During the past several years we've had a 40 percent improvement in BMI.

RG: Who will be measuring the impact of this program, and how will it be measured?

AS: Doctors and researchers at the Harvard School of Public Health will be working with us to measure not just the impact on children, who have better diets when they're younger, but also on adults, and particularly on seniors. We're also in dialogue with the AARP Foundation. They are interested not just in hunger, but nutrition for seniors. They have thirty-eight million members. Probably four or five million are at some dietary risk.

RG: Will the insurance companies be working with you?

AS: Hopefully. We're working with Blue Cross Blue Shield in Minnesota, a little bit with Aetna, and did a fair bit of work with Kaiser Permanente in California. But it's a bit of a lift as they want to see evidence, which is why the research we're going to be doing with Harvard is so critical.

RG: How did you come to create the program?

AS: It was when I was working with you in 1980. My brother bought a farm in Natick and I would fly up on weekends to drive the truck to the farmers' market in Dorchester, something I enjoyed doing. One day in September I took the truck in, and when I was packing up, a pear box fell apart, and all the Bosc pears went into the gutter. I went to get a shovel to pick up the pears, and when I returned, an Irish American woman was picking the pears out of the gutter with two boys. I gave her some proper pears and asked her why she was picking pears out of the gutter in Fields Corner in Dorchester. She said her husband had left her six months earlier and she was on food stamps and couldn't afford to buy fruit for her two boys. When I was commissioner, I mentioned that to the Tufts Nutrition School, and we designed the WIC Farmers' Market Nutrition Program, which went into the Farm Bill in 1992. We then developed the Senior Farmers' Market Nutrition Program, which went into the Farm Bill in 2002, all because of that broken pear box in Dorchester. When Michel Nischan and I founded Wholesome Wave, we had a few beers and kicked that story around. Michel said there's new wireless technology that would make it easier for food stamp users to swipe their card at a farmers' market, say, in Dorchester, and then, if we could find money from foundations, we'd double it, but only if they buy fruits and vegetables with their food stamps. So the support is now at $100 million.

RG: How do you see this developing five or ten years from now?

AS: One of our colleagues, J. B. Penn, gave a brilliant talk recently in Washington about India and the need for diet prescriptions. Canadians have talked to us, and we're frequently visiting the Europeans, especially the British, because the National Health Service is very interested in exploring not just medicine, but food as medicine.

RG: It sounds like you're going global.

AS: Well, we're a small foundation, but we find it fascinating that Michel has spoken at the OECD [Organization for Economic Co-operation and Development] in Paris, and I've spoken in Italy and spent a week in the UK with doctors and had a meeting with Parliament and also the mayor's office in London. But we're going to be focusing Wholesome Wave right now on the United States. We're going to do a deeper dive with the $100 million from Congress and with the interest hospitals have in veggie prescriptions.

RG: When you were commissioner of agriculture here in Massachusetts, you not only worked with consumers, but you also worked with producers to try to enlarge the growing season of fruits and vegetables. How has that played out?

AS: My brother gave me an acre, and I worked with some of the botanists across the river to look at tomatoes. How could we extend the season with some of these new technologies? Now some of these technologies have been adopted by the USDA. They've allocated ten thousand hoop houses to extend the season for thousands of small farmers around the country. It's important that we rely less on the central valley of California, or Florida, and develop a more balanced, regional approach to our vegetable production, and to some extent small fruit.

RG: This is a bipartisan approach in Congress, which is a bit rare. How were you able to get both political parties to agree to this?

AS: It really was bipartisan. Chairman Lucas in Oklahoma chairs the House ag committee and saw our nutrition incentive program working in Tulsa at their big farmers' market. Senator Stabenow, chairwoman of the Senate ag committee, saw what our colleague Oran Hesterman was doing throughout Michigan so she put in $100 million. Chairman Lucas put in $25 million and in a bipartisan way they compromised. Proud of them both.

RG: You have people like Oran Hesterman and his not-for-profit working in the same area. Don't you think it's high time to create a coalition of groups working together both nationally and internationally rather than one particular group after another trying to do this?

AS: That's exactly what's happening. The Kresge Foundation is working with us, and the Fair Food Network and Wholesome Wave have a merged model. The AARP Foundation wants to do something nationally. A broad coalition is developing around the country driven by the health system with businesses picking up their support. Large farmer organizations like the United Fresh Food and Vegetable Association were very aggressive in supporting our program.

RG: If you and I were having this interview in ten years, how do you envision it domestically? How do you envision it globally?

AS: Domestically, there will be much more attention to diet. My mother shopped once at Stop & Shop back in the '50s and '60s. Now mothers in the suburbs and downtown are shopping twice. They're going to the supermarket for the meats and the things you need day to day; then they're taking their kids to the local farmers' market to buy fresh fruits and vegetables and participate in more of a community. As those ten-year-old children become twenty-five, they'll become the new drivers of the food system. That's going to begin to change how our supermarket system operates, and our universities too. Internationally, I see the impact on global economies. Chinese children are becoming chubbier, and the same is true in India.

RG: And how will it impact farm labor, because we're so dependent on farm labor for these crops?

AS: Exactly. That's why I'm so sad we haven't been able to get together in Congress and fix our immigration. We need to adjust our immigration policies so we can supply the diets that the hospitals, the doctors, and insurance companies are going to require, or recommend.

RG: Given your background at the World Bank, and at the Department of Agriculture, and in Massachusetts, how do you see your own professional activity for the next ten years?

AS: Ten years is hard to imagine, but new technologies and greater emphasis on food and health make for radical changes ahead. Cherries are an example. Chinese consumers are now buying cherries from farmers over the internet from Washington State. The cherries are flown to Guangzhou, and the Chinese consumers know that Harry Smith in Washington grew those cherries, which were picked fourteen days ago. They know if they're organic or IPM [Integrated Pest Management]. That's already happening. There'll be extraordinary changes in how food is grown, picked, distributed, transported, cooled, and consumed. Extraordinary changes.

RG: You're expecting a lot of knowledge by the consumer to do this. Who's going to give the consumer that knowledge?

AS: The media is changing. Seventy-four million Americans watch a food program once a week. Food is becoming more important in colleges. There were no agricultural courses at Harvard when I was an undergraduate. Now one of the most popular courses is Anthropology 105, which is food and culture. In the chemistry department, professors are teaching chemistry by bringing chefs to demonstrate the different ways foods are made. Young people are studying food as undergraduates, something I never anticipated when I was in college, and even when I was working here at Harvard.

RG: Retailers have roughly 10 percent of all the pharmacy prescriptions in the United States through their retail establishments. How will their pharmacies relate to the food in their stores and to their consumers?

AS: At Wegmans—a very sophisticated retailer—if you go to their pharmacy with a diet issue in your bio-prescription, you will get a coupon giving 50 percent off for fresh fruit and vegetables grown locally just by going next door to the produce section. Hannaford is beginning to do this, and I heard that HEB in Texas is now looking into it. If you have Humana health care coverage, when you show your Humana card at Walmart, you get a discount if you buy fruits and vegetables.

RG: Sounds like the whole economy has all of a sudden discovered that food is actually more important than pills.

AS: That's why we see doctors prescribing their veggie prescriptions, call it veggie Rx, to a farmer, who then acts as the pharmacy. It's "farmacy" with an "f" rather than a "ph."

RG: It sounds as if the genetic world is looking over your shoulder and getting feedback from the consumer and the medical community as to how to improve the fruits and vegetables in such a way that they'll be even more nutritious to the end-user.

AS: That's a key area. If you eat more fruits and vegetables, you have more fiber. You're reducing your BMI. You're improving your diabetes. But the next step is what can you build into the different kinds of fruits and vegetables? What could make them more nutritious, and how do you make them, vegetables, as prescriptions? Will there be a tomato that deals with type 2 diabetes? Can there be zucchini that has some nutrients in it that will help cancer patients recover? Companies are focused on that.

RG: You've started a revolution, and in cooperation with a lot of people around the world.

AS: The key is collaboration and networking. We have over sixty partners around the country. We're working with major agribusiness companies. We have a lot of data, which we want to make that freely available to researchers.

RG: Thank you very much, Gus.

WALTER C. WILLETT

Chairman of the Nutrition Department, Harvard T.H. Chan School of Public Health (2016)

Chairman of the Nutrition Department of the Harvard T.H. Chan School of Public Health, Walter Willett is an international leader in developing a scientifically grounded understanding about the relationship between food and health. Willett created long-term population research projects that enabled the public to better understand what foods would be useful in maintaining and improving their health. Willett also lectured in medical schools to provide nutrition training to physicians, who are becoming the "gatekeepers" in helping their patients develop and maintain appropriate diets. Willett's family had been dairy farmers in Michigan for five generations, and he grew up on a research farm near Madison, Wisconsin, where his father did research on dairy cattle.

RG: Dr. Walter Willet is chairman of the Nutrition Department of the School of Public Health at Harvard University. Would you mind talking about your background and what led you to this position?

ww: Food has been a part of my family and my life from the very beginning. The Willets have been dairy farmers in Michigan for five generations, and my father was a researcher on dairy cattle in Madison, Wisconsin, so I grew up on a research farm in Madison. I was in a 4-H vegetable garden club for many years, and won the Michigan Championship for Vegetable Grading one year. In college I studied physics and food science, but then went into medicine. All the way through I was interested in nutrition and how it relates to health and well-being. After several years in Tanzania, I got a doctorate in epidemiology, focusing on both the environment and human behavior and their effect on human health and well-being.

RG: How did you end up at Harvard?

ww: After completing medical school I came to Boston for my residency and got a master's of public health. I took some courses in the Department of Nutrition at Harvard School of Public Health, and found it really challenging to get information on what we were eating and how it affected health over time. There was a general feeling that diet was important for heart disease prevention and maybe for cancer reduction. And there were many recommendations like eat two eggs a week, and as little fat as possible. When I scratched the surface, I realized there was virtually no data to back up those recommendations. There wasn't a single study showing that people who ate more eggs had more heart attacks.

Since the late 1970s, I've been developing several large studies—now almost three hundred thousand people—that monitor what people eat over time using standardized questionnaires that are validated using biomarkers and then tracked against heart attacks and cancer. We control for physical activity, smoking, and genetic factors, so we can focus on different aspects of diet. I've been doing that for forty years.

RG: Thank goodness you've decided to get data so we could actually begin to understand how food relates to our health. But it's only been in recent years, even at the Harvard Medical School, that we've had people look at nutrition, and it's only been in very recent years that if you go to your primary care physician he even mentions nutrition.

ww: You're lucky if he or she does that, even today.

RG: But the scientific revolution has made people more aware of the fact that what you eat affects your health. How do you broaden the resources you deal with to get back to the nutrition leadership you've provided?

ww: Our studies have become platforms for bringing people together [in] all biomedical areas—geneticists, pathologists, people in every clinical area. We have very detailed information about lifestyles and unique dietary data that we've updated every four years over the decades. This is really critical because of the huge changes in the foods available over that period.

We've collected DNA from several hundred thousand people, and we've got blood for one hundred thousand or so people that create biomarkers so we can look at diet in great detail. If we had the money, we could sequence whole DNA chains. What matters most is what people put in their mouth, and monitoring the whole physiologic process including tumor characteristics that emerge decades later.

RG: You have influenced changes in the diet. Even with all your testing, they don't always listen to you as much as they do the various people who produce foods that they want to make sure are in the diet, whether it's appropriately done or not. How do you get the attention of people in an unbiased way?

WW: That's a big question beyond my area of expertise. My own mission is to have the best possible evidence, and in the long run, the best possible evidence will win. The development of evidence is a process that begins with [a] fuzzy picture, and as time goes on, we get more data, bigger numbers, more sophisticated measurements, and a sharper picture.

A major issue we've dealt with was trans fats, which wasn't about a particular food, but about how the food was processed. Partial hydrogenation was done with good intentions but caused millions of premature deaths. The American Heart Association trashed us, because they thought it distracted from saturated fat. It turns out trans fats are worse than saturated fats. The margarine manufacturers were doling out huge amounts of trans fat. Unilever, fortunately, took the science seriously and invested in ways to produce margarines free of trans fat. They became an ally, and the Heart Association eventually came along.

It started in a small town outside of San Francisco, and then Mayor Bloomberg, who is a strong health proponent, banned trans fats in restaurants, which had a ripple effect. It's a pretty unpredictable process, but it starts with having strong data.

RG: Health is more than a personal issue. It's a public issue in terms of cost of health care. Senator Harkin made it possible through Medicaid to pay doctors to talk about nutrition. My greatest concern is they're not trained to talk about it. How do you retrain a profession that wants preventive medicine rather than patients with more diseases, especially as they get older?

ww: That's a huge challenge. Our health system is seriously imbalanced in favor of drugs and procedures over prevention through nutrition, counseling, smoking cessation, and promoting more physical activity. It's not surprising. There are tens of hundreds of billions of dollars in the pharmaceutical side that influences doctors in a powerful way. Doctors are the gatekeepers for drug prescriptions, but not for eating, or for being active. Counselors can influence patients, but the reimbursements are exceedingly imbalanced. We also need better medical education. Until recently, we haven't had the information we need for educating doctors properly.

When we were getting started with our research, I was asked to teach a few courses at the Medical School, and I said I'd like to, but we just don't have solid enough information yet. Over the past decade, that's changed. We have enough information to provide good guidance.

There's starting to be interest in medical education and it's coming from students who realize it's something they're going to need. Roughly 80 percent of heart attacks and 90 percent of type 2 diabetes could be avoided by healthy diet, physical activity, not smoking, and controlling weight. Only 3 percent or so of the population we see is following a regimen of healthy diets and lifestyles.

rg: Some companies get it. Microsoft and Google compete with each other to try to provide healthy foods for their employees and their families Do you think that's going to become more important?

ww: Definitely. Many employers realize that helping their employees eat better increases productivity and helps control health care costs. Worksites are a great opportunity to promote healthy eating. We need to have every sector pushing in the right direction.

We've been tracking diet quality in the United States since 2000 using enhanced data, and we see a steady improvement in diet quality. On a score of zero to a hundred, we've gone from about forty to about fifty, so still a long way to go. Most of that improvement has been reduction in trans fat and sugar-sweetened beverages, but there are increases in fruits and whole grains and healthier fats, which is encouraging.

We've seen blood cholesterol fractions improve in the national surveys, and the last Centers for Disease Control survey recently reported that diabetes incidence has declined about 20 percent, which is very big, because it had been skyrocketing up. Most of that is due to reduction in trans fat and sugar-sweetened beverages. So we're seeing improvements. It took forty-plus years but the smoking epidemic peaked and declined, so epidemiologists are patient. We're headed in a good direction.

RG: Do you think the school lunch program has changed enough to start helping people that way as well?

WW: There have definitely been improvements in the school lunch program—not just the lunch, but sodas are out of school now. There's still [a] ways to go. Thanks to senators from Maine and Idaho, potatoes have been declared a vegetable and pizzas have been as well.

RG: Insurance companies benefit from a healthy population. Are they working with you and others?

WW: We're seeing some participation by insurance companies. It seemed logical to me several decades ago that they'd have an interest, but they were completely uninterested in promoting health and well-being back then.

One large insurance company that was equally invested in life insurance and annuities told me a revealing fact. Whether people die early or die late, it's a breakeven to them. They make money either way. But insurance companies do seem more interested in promoting the well-being of the population they're insuring.

RG: The whole food industry is beginning to change as well. They want shared value rather than an "I win, you lose" mentality. At the end of the day, the ultimate winner has to be the consumer. These companies are beginning to realize they have a responsibility not just to produce a particular product or a particular brand, but they have a responsibility for nutrition. Do you find that they come to you and begin to think in those terms? Are they becoming more health oriented, rather than just trying to sell a brand?

WW: The food industry isn't monolithic. There are some real leaders that see they can profit by providing healthy foods, which is great. Coca-Cola is panicking, because their prime product is a major cause of premature mortality and death. Unfortunately, they're taking the tobacco company script and investing billions of dollars [in] marketing Coca-Cola around the world to populations in the midst of horrible obesity epidemics. We have to find allies within the food industry.

Increasingly, though, companies are realizing that they can't ignore health. We've been working with the Culinary Institute of America, which trains people to operate major food services, and that's been a good experience.

RG: Certain populations are changing. The elder population is increasing as a percentage of the total population, and they have special problems with respect to food and health. Is anybody giving that a priority?

WW: The groups we study are aging, so we're looking more closely at elderly populations. We're giving more attention to things like cognitive function and preventing heart attacks and many forms of cancer, and we've seen life expectancy going up because of that.

When I started off in medicine, having a massive heart attack in one's midfifties was the norm. If you survived, you were lucky. Now, we have more people living into their eighties and nineties and functioning well. Diet plays an important role in maintaining good cognitive function as one ages. The good news is that diet and healthy nutrition enhances just about every function, almost every organ, even in later stages of life.

RG: Gus Schumacher and the Wholesome Wave convinced the USDA to allocate $100 million to encourage people to spend more of their money on fruits and vegetables. Supermarkets have medical divisions in their store writing prescriptions for fruits and vegetables. That's quite a change.

WW: We really need to improve the quality of what food stamps participants can buy. The diets we've analyzed of people on food stamps are recipes for diabetes, obesity, and cardiovascular disease and cancer. The nutrition gap is increasing and is similar to the income gap. In public health terms it translates directly to life expectancy and rates of heart disease, cancer, and diabetes.

RG: Our youth have rediscovered food. How can the academic community leverage that enthusiasm in terms of education and research?

WW: There's no single answer. Food can be a part of every department in the university, but we have to make the link between food and health personal for the students. We have some great people in Harvard Dining Services who are committed to providing healthier food and more food literacy as well.

RG: In the business community there are men and women who want to make a difference, but when they delegate to the trade associations the companies sometimes oppose the very things they should be supporting. How do you change that?

WW: A good question. We're supporting San Francisco in a court case to put a simple warning label on soda about the risk of diabetes, heart disease, and obesity—all well substantiated, as you know. The industry is using all its resources to stop us.

RG: What about restaurants? We keep saying we want people to know what they've ordered health-wise, but that's not really happening.

WW: Menu labeling has been an uphill struggle. Sunlight is a good cleanser. When trans fat was put on labels, manufacturers eliminated it.

RG: Another disconcerting topic is that when food firms sponsor our studies, we begin to wonder are they for real or have the studies been overly influenced by the private sector, the funding source. How do you look at that?

WW: That's a serious issue. It's pretty obvious when you look at some studies. Dr. Ludwig here at Harvard has analyzed studies on soda consumption and diabetes and found that those showing no harm were overwhelmingly supported by the beverage industries and were usually pretty crummy studies. We need to have more public funding for research. Looking down the road, there are huge uncertainties about how to sustainably feed our global population a healthy diet. We need more research.

RG: What do you want to have happen over the next several decades?

WW: I'd like to see affordable healthy food available to everybody globally and an environment that promotes activity and more social interaction. Depression is a huge problem, the primary cause of disability globally. And we need to address climate change and environmental change. Pretty much everybody's got to be involved.

RG: Thank you very much for taking on the most difficult and important task facing us, Walter.

WW: Thanks, Ray.

2

Food Safety and Food Fraud

CAROLINE SMITH DE WAAL
*Director of Food Safety, Center for Science
in the Public Interest (2013)*

A lawyer and director of food safety for the Center for Science in the Public Interest, Caroline Smith de Waal has spent a quarter century focusing on food safety and traceability. She grew up in Vermont, where her father was head of the pharmacology department at the University of Vermont Medical School. He shaped her love of laboratory science, and the family's weekend drives through the countryside shaped her love of agriculture. De Waal maintains detailed records of all food risk problems that took place in each of the major commodity food systems in the United States. She advises governments throughout the world on how best to address communication problems. She has helped author legislation that improves the testing for pathogens that identify problems in the food system, and she advises on how best to correct food risk problems.

RG: Caroline Smith de Waal is director of food safety for the Center for Science in the Public Interest. First of all, what is your background and how did you end up in your current position?

CD: I grew up in Vermont, which affects how I think about food and a lot of agriculture issues. We used to drive around the state almost every week because my parents love driving, and it's a beautiful state that probably had more cows than people. We would see farms, farmers, cows, and smell the manure. That had a really big impact on me. Second, my dad was chairman of pharmacology at the University of Vermont Medical School. He was a medical doctor, but did a lot of research on drug issues. I would go to his lab and weigh baby rats, so I saw science from a foundational level very early in my life. I'm a lawyer, which is terrific, because you're taught that you need to become an expert in lots of things, not just the law. When I started working on food issues, which I've been doing for almost twenty-five years now, I wanted to become an expert not only on the law around food issues and government systems, but I wanted to know the science.

RG: Food safety has become more important practically every year. Why has it become so important and how do you see its importance in the future?

CD: Everyone eats, so it's wonderful to work on issues that affect everybody every day. There are many things consumers want in their food, but safety is nonnegotiable. People want to be certain that when they eat a meal they're not going to end up sick. Food safety must be at the heart of food production. It has to be on the minds of people who raise the animals and grow the vegetables and process the food and transport it all over the country. Every actor needs to be aware of the part they play in ensuring safety because any gap in the chain can have serious consequences.

RG: Over the years, traceability has become more important and, with better technology, more reliable. How do you see that unfolding?

CD: The technology is advancing very quickly and consumers will benefit with higher-quality products. They'd like to use their smartphones to read bar codes to learn how and where their food was produced.

RG: Globalization has enabled the supermarkets and other distributors to have access to fruits and vegetables year round that aren't normally produced in this country. Do we have the same food safety security for overseas imports that we do for American production?

CD: Unfortunately, we don't have data today that tells us whether imports are safer or less safe than what we produce here. Of course, it's logical to think that food produced closer to where it's eaten may be safer because there's less time for the bacteria to grow and less likely that illegal pesticides have been used if the food is from the US rather than another country. But without the data, that's speculation. We do know that the way the government inspects imports isn't very rational. The USDA has an extensive system for checking the safety of meat and poultry products that it regulates. But the FDA has a take-all-comers approach. They let food come in from many different countries with very few controls. They don't have the resources to check food at the border. They're redesigning their import control system based on the Food Safety Modernization Act (FSMA), but it will probably take five years to implement. At the end of the day, we know imported foods have caused a large number of outbreaks, but we don't know whether you're more or less likely to get sick from imported or domestic food.

RG: Does consolidation in the food industry make it more likely for a mistake to be much more consequential?

CD: The outbreaks demonstrate that proposition. The spinach causing the outbreak in 2006 was probably grown in the corner of a field in the Salinas Valley. Spinach and lettuce were being washed, dried, and put into bags and shipped all over the country. Consumers learned there are dangers in their lettuce bowl they weren't aware of beforehand. It highlighted that large manufacturers can be the source of major problems. Returning to the outbreak data discussed earlier, we don't have enough information to know whether you're more likely to get sick from food produced by a large or a small processor. The industry claims they can do a better job if they consolidate by applying safety systems more broadly. The proof would be the absence of outbreaks, but we still have issues with ground beef, lettuce, spinach, and even peanut butter produced in giant factories.

RG: Identagen's been able to use DNA to identify products that normally weren't easily identifiable. What role could Identagen, for example, play in the Ireland horsemeat scandal?

CD: Identagen's new technologies could play a major role in ensuring that consumers are buying what they think they're buying. Addressing fraud provides greater assurance to both buyers and retailers.

RG: In the protein area, animals are fed antibiotics in the feed, which makes people worry that they'll get antibiotic resistance. How do you think?

CD: We're very concerned that some antibiotics critical for human medicine are being used to promote growth in animals. The use of antibiotics in food and in the animal food supply should be limited to therapeutic purposes and not just for promoting growth.

RG: Looking ahead, what are the advantages of new legislation?

CD: Our food laws were largely written in the early 1900s. Laws governing both meat and poultry are based on visually inspecting every single animal. On the one hand, we have one of the most intensive regulatory systems used in any industry with onsite government inspection checking every single animal. On the other hand, the FDA has been largely reactive, although FSMA brings the FDA forward. They can go to the country of origin rather than rely solely on border inspections.

RG: When recalls do occur, are certain companies more creative in reaching their consumer list? Companies like Wegmans and others?

CD: We're very happy that leading companies like Costco and Wegmans have customer loyalty programs and are informing their customers when they've purchased a recalled food product. Consumers often tell us they've heard from Costco or Wegmans or another retailer about a recall. It makes them closer to their customers.

RG: Can terrorists use the food system as a weapon?

CD: In 2003 Congress passed the Bioterrorism Act, which had a number of provisions dealing with imported foods. Congress has taken the concern very seriously and put a number of controls in place. After ten-plus years, the good news is we have not seen food as a target.

RG: Should companies and supermarkets have a food safety executive?

CD: Many companies recognize the critical importance of food safety and quality. FSMA strengthens the infrastructure that companies have been adopting voluntarily. Each company needs to know their product risks—not only hazards like *Salmonella* or *E. coli*, but also the risk of intentional tampering or contamination. Recalls affect every segment of the industry involved. Contaminated spinach from a field in Salinas forced spinach growers in New Jersey to plow under their fields. Consumers shift their buying behavior because they don't have the bandwidth to remember the product's brand name. Consumers simply avoid the whole category until they get an all clear from the government. Companies that avoid problems protect themselves and their customers, but also the industry as a whole.

RG: What hazards will we have to address in the future?

CD: There are a number of emerging hazards. There are *Salmonella* strains coming out of the Middle East that are multidrug resistant and chemical hazards like aflatoxin and acrylamide. It really helps to have educated consumers. I'm urging the food industry to be more transparent about potential hazards.

RG: As a consumer advocate are you called in by retailers and others for advice?

CD: Not for advice. I give a lot of speeches, but we don't really advise companies.

RG: When you want to make changes in the food safety system, do you have an advisory committee that you talk to or what?

CD: I rely on data much more than advice. At CSPI we track outbreaks. I can slice and dice data into two- and five-year segments. I can analyze whether *Salmonella* is a problem and which meat or poultry products are causing the most outbreaks.

RG: There seems to be quite a bit of fraudulent activity in the food and beverage system. A prominent soft drink company will ship syrup to a country and they'll find out that more of the finished product is produced and consumed than the syrup they sent over. How do you manage these fraudulent schemes?

CD: We're very concerned about ingredient fraud. Several years ago melamine was applied to grain and protein products incorporated in US pet foods, which caused kidney failure in many dogs and cats. We've seen the real-life consequences of intentional contamination events. It's critically important for the US to work with other governments to address these problems. The FDA should require importers to test incoming products. Some food frauds are just bad business, but some can be really harmful to the public, even deadly.

RG: Codex is one of the international agencies that seems to have some respect in terms of having a common language or common descriptions of foods. Are they very active in other ways in the food system?

CD: The Codex Alimentary Commission was formed fifty years ago by the WHO and the FAO of the United Nations. The standards and guidance that Codex produces are recognized at the WTO, so Codex standards provide a base for consumer protection when it comes to food safety, as well as standards for fair trade in food products. I've been participating in Codex for ten years now and sit on three committees. When I started I was skeptical about developing meaningful standards that truly protect the public. The Codex standards are a consensus of technical experts focused on protecting consumers rather than lawyers or trade representatives. We don't need Codex standards in the US, because our government has very qualified people who can help develop even better standards than Codex for US consumers. But Codex standards provide the foundation for food safety in developing countries.

RG: This sounds very promising. If we were having this conversation in ten years, what will be the greatest concerns?

CD: I hope we'll have strong new food safety laws in the US for FDA-regulated foods. FSMA should be fully implemented. As a consequence, we'd no longer have the outbreaks that've become so commonplace. I hope in ten years we'll be modernizing meat and poultry inspection with a system based on science rather than the individual inspection of every piece of meat. We'll still be grappling with chemical hazards and learning even more about how eating affects our health. We might be focused more on good nutrition and less on microbiological or even chemical hazards. My hope is that food safety concerns will be declining and nutrition and health will be front and center.

RG: Thank you very much.

MICHAEL TAYLOR
US Deputy Commissioner of Food and
Veterinary Medicine (2014)

US Deputy Commissioner for Foods and Veterinary Medicine in the FDA during both the Bush and Obama administrations, Michael Taylor has been a leader in improving food safety for both domestic and imported foods. Food safety became especially personal for Taylor in the 1990s, when four children died and five hundred became seriously ill from the Jack in the Box *E. coli* O157-H7 outbreak. Taylor was serving as the FDA's deputy commissioner for public policy at the time. He has worked to improve the ways in which the FDA investigates and designs safety procedures for all those involved in the vertical food chain in the United States and maintains relations with food safety officials around the world, as well as investigates plants and procedures from which we input food. He works with the EPA and USDA in improving the inspection reviews within the United States and with those government agencies that export food to the United States. As the science of detecting problems improves, Taylor utilizes the new discoveries to improve the FDA's ability to improve food safety standards. He also works with new labeling procedures designed to better educate the consumer about what is in the food.

RG: Michael Taylor is deputy commissioner for foods and veterinary medicine of the US government. You've served four different presidents: President Carter, the first President Bush, President Clinton, and President Obama. How has the FDA changed over that time period?

MT: Let's start by emphasizing what hasn't changed. We're a public health regulatory agency working within a prescribed statutory framework that Congress gave us in the Federal Food, Drug, and Cosmetic Act, and we're science based. Our mission is to protect consumers by applying law, science, and good public health policy to make decisions about everything from drugs and medical devices to food safety labeling, which is my responsibility. What's changed most is the external environment. The industries we regulate are more concentrated, the technologies are more complex, and the companies are larger and much more global. We have to be stronger scientifically and technologically more current. And we have to work in a global context.

RG: The consumer relies very heavily on the FDA for protection. It's one of the most admired divisions of our government. How have you been able to maintain that trust at a time when many agencies are under fire?

MT: Trust depends on the clarity of one's fundamental purpose and values. That's why I emphasize our public health mission. If the public believes we're committed to that mission and sees us working in an objectively scientific way, then they're more likely to trust our decisions even when they may not agree with them. We have to be fully transparent, because another environmental change for the FDA is communications and the media, including social media.

RG: Globalization has resulted in consumers relying more and more on imported foods. Are the dangers greater, less, or about the same?

MT: It's very hard to give a data-driven answer. We've had foodborne illness outbreaks from domestically produced food, as well as imported food. Our concern with imports is that we have less direct oversight of foreign producers and processors than we do with US-based producers and processors. Until the Food Safety Modernization Act (FSMA) was passed, we relied on FDA inspectors at ports of entry who could only sample on a very limited basis. In implementing FSMA we've learned that we need to be verifying that contamination is controlled at the point of production overseas. We have the advantage in this country of a very strong food safety system. We need a comparable level of oversight on imports so we can be confident we're getting the same level of protection regardless of whether the food is produced here or overseas. That's a goal of FSMA.

RG: In implementing that act, have you spent much time overseas?

MT: Yes. I travel to China regularly, and focused my personal travel on Mexico, Europe, and Canada. There's no substitute for working directly with our foreign government counterparts and for a firsthand understanding of what the practices and capabilities are in other countries. That's essential. When I started at [the] FDA in the seventies, we had no foreign offices. Over the last decade, we have established a small network of offices in China, Mexico City, Latin America, Europe, and India, and have staff permanently assigned overseas. A crucial part of our strategy is to be much more engaged with foreign governments and to educate foreign producers and processors about our requirements.

RG: What do you think are the greatest potential dangers to our food system?

MT: From a foodborne illness/public health standpoint, the major threats include *E. coli, Salmonella, Campylobacter, Listeria monocytogenes.* We're better positioned to deal preventively with these, which is what [the] FSMA empowers us to do. Over the past decade, the food industry has developed a more affirmative food safety culture that focuses more on prevention than reaction. We're on a good pathway with regard to these traditional pathogens. Unfortunately, pathogens mutate over time, supply chains and technologies change, and consumer behavior changes in ways that affect our vulnerability. Despite our successes, over 125,000 are hospitalized annually from foodborne illness and about 3,000 people die. We're also finding contaminants like inorganic arsenic, mercury, dioxin, and PCBs [polychlorinated biphenyls] in certain commodities and are also concerned about chemicals added intentionally to food. But we're making progress.

RG: Consumers are being urged to eat more fruits and vegetables for health reasons. Are they more susceptible to problems like *Listeria* or not?

MT: We want consumers to eat more fruits and vegetables, and we want them to feel very safe doing so. Unfortunately, fruits and vegetables are often packed in the field and shipped straight to consumer outlets, so there's no kill step. There's no processing to address contamination that might've come in through the environment or through the handling by harvesting and packing staff. There's more vulnerability than with food that's cooked, either by consumers or commercially.

RG: Genetically engineered foods have been in the news a great deal. Consumer advocates have been adamant about labeling GMO foods. How do you see that?

MT: I can only speak personally about GMOs, because of my history with the issue, including working at Monsanto, but I wrote about it a lot during my academic years. The starting point for me is that consumers have a right to be informed and to choose what they consume. When a new technology emerges people have concerns about it, and there has to be a way to enable them to make informed choices. I'll leave the regulatory labeling debate to others, but questions of trust and transparency have marginalized the science.

RG: Do you believe that we can regain that trust?

MT: It's an uphill battle.

RG: What's your relationship to [the] FDA, USDA, and EPA? How do you interact with one another?

MT: Operationally, we're very intertwined. For example, my program regulates the drugs used in animal food production, including limits set on the residues that could be present in the meat, milk, or eggs coming from animals that have been treated with an animal drug. Then the USDA, in its slaughter inspection program, collects samples of tissue coming through the slaughter process of pork and beef and poultry. If they find violative residues, they report that to us, and we investigate what might've happened. We share responsibility for pesticides with [the] EPA. They register chemicals, authorize their use in the field, and set tolerances for the amount of the pesticide residue that can be present in food. Our field force enforces those pesticide tolerances.

RG: Where does [the] CDC fit into your operation?

MT: [The] CDC is very important for our food safety work. They manage the surveillance systems for foodborne illness that permit us to understand what illnesses are associated with particular pathogens. We work very closely together and with the states when there's an outbreak of illness, and do the epidemiological investigation working with the states to determine what food source caused the illness. We follow up from there, taking the actions to contain the outbreak and correcting whatever problem caused it. Historically, we worked somewhat in isolation from each other, but we now work hand in glove at every step of the process. We've improved our early detection and management of illness outbreaks, and are more effective on prevention too.

RG: How do you then also work globally with the European Food Safety Authority and Codex Alimentarius?

MT: We have liaisons at the European Food Safety Authority who work with us full time. We value their risk assessments on particular substances or foods and vice versa. Codex is a crucial international mechanism for setting food safety and food quality standards. We invest a lot of energy in the Codex process, because their standards are accepted for WTO compliance purposes. We also have substantial partnerships with individual countries. The Mexican government is a particularly good example of where we have a very active partnership on produce safety. These are primary collaborative relationships that we really didn't have twenty years ago, and now they're central to our success.

RG: Some agricultural products are associated with diseases like obesity and other kinds of illnesses. Do you have a role to play, or do you leave that to the medical community? Who should think about it, and do something about it?

MT: That's a great question. I think a lot about the constituents of the diet that at a certain level are necessary for health, but at higher intake levels can be bad for you. Certain dietary fats fall into that category, and so does sodium. These are challenging problems. How do you get dietary balance? The FDA is not in the business of telling people what to eat. Our statutory role is to regulate labeling so the nutrition fact panel on all food packages provides information that consumers can use to choose a healthy diet in accordance with dietary guidelines. Right now we're updating the nutrition facts panels so consumers have better information for choosing a healthy diet. We're also working on menu labeling, an initiative mandated by Congress in the Affordable Care Act to require calorie declarations on the menus of chain restaurants. These aren't magic wands that solve obesity or any of the chronic disease concerns arising from dietary imbalances. They're part of an overall effort to give consumers better information about food choices. This can also contribute to healthier products. When New York City started requiring calorie declarations on menus, Starbucks reformulated many of their bakery items to reduce the calorie content. Diet and health is an issue that requires inclusive social effort. The FDA can't do it alone. Nutrition policy in the federal government is divided between the Department of Health and Human Services and the Department of Agriculture. We have an important role to play, but it's got to be in partnership with other elements of the government and the broader public health community.

RG: Food fraud has reared its ugly head quite a lot lately. Is that something you worry about?

MT: We're focused on it right now. Historically, the FDA has acted when overtly fraudulent practices have been present in the food supply, substituting cheap ingredients for valuable ones. We're looking now at the issue of seafood fraud. Is it farm raised, or is it wild caught? Is the fishing done on a sustainable basis or not? We're looking at ways to work with industry to manage supply chains to minimize fraud.

RG: Even though the Republican Party and the Democratic Party are at loggerheads on many issues, the one area that seems to have [a] bipartisan approach is the food industry. How do you account for that?

MT: There's something unique about the food system that makes it easier to forge [a] common purpose, particularly in food safety. It's because consumers are sovereign and have high expectations. There's a widely shared interest in doing everything that we reasonably can to make food safe.

RG: What do you think we'll be worried about ten years from now?

MT: We'll still be modernizing our approach to food safety to keep up with the changing food supply, because the food supply won't be the same as it is today. We haven't talked about developing foods with ingredients that have health benefits, so-called functional foods. Food science may permit us to understand more deeply how certain constituents of the food supply may be very beneficial from a health standpoint, not in a drug-like way, but in a nutritional way.

RG: What is there in your background that made you interested in taking on these important challenges?

MT: I graduated from law school knowing I wanted to work in government, but it was sort of happenstance that the FDA was my first job out of law school. It captured me right away as an important area, because it affects people's lives. It was incredibly challenging to incorporate law, science, public health policy, and the institutional issues given the realities of how the system works. I spent fifteen years at the FDA, and then in private law practice learning how the system really works. The galvanizing experience for me was when I was deputy commissioner for public policy at the FDA in the 1990s when the Jack in the Box outbreak happened and four kids were killed by *E. coli* O157-H7, and five hundred people became seriously ill. That's when food safety became a deeply personal issue. My experience with people directly affected is what switched everything from a fascinating professional experience to a highly motivated, very personal passion to make a difference on food safety. Along the way, I've learned a lot about [the] food system and have had amazingly rich experiences professionally. But it's the personal dimension that makes it worthwhile.

RG: We're very fortunate to have a public servant like you. Thank you so much.

RONAN LOFTUS

Cofounder of IdentiGEN and CEO of IdentiGEN's
North American Operations (2014)

As a cofounder of IdentiGEN and CEO of its North American operations, Ronan Loftus is focused on applying genomic technologies to the vertical supply chains of major commodities in the food systems. DNA tracing can authenticate olive oil as real or fake, and can also trace a foodborne illness back to its source. IdentiGEN is constantly improving the DNA techniques to identify fraud and the substitution of foreign ingredients in the food system. Food fraud is becoming more prevalent as the food system becomes more global. The substitution of horse meat for beef, and its discovery by using DNA methodology, has led to greater use of the technical knowledge of IdentiGEN. Concentration of their efforts has been in animal and fish protein. Firms such as IdentiGEN will have an important role in maintaining the integrity of the food system. Loftus holds a PhD in molecular genetics from Trinity College, Dublin.[1]

RG: Ronan Loftus is CEO of IdentiGEN's American operations and co-founder of the company. Could you give a brief summary of your firm?

RL: Our company applies emerging technologies in the DNA and life sciences area to improve quality and safety in the food industry.

RG: And the reason that you have chosen DNA technology is because it helps you in the traceability of the supply chain.

RL: Yes. A core focus of the company uses DNA to identify products. It's reading nature's bar code and that can be a very powerful tool for identifying products throughout complex supply chains. Food is sourced from many different markets and countries throughout the world. Primary production has increasingly been divorced from the consumer, and consumers want more information about where and how their food is produced. Our technology can do that in a cost-effective way without being overly disruptive to the way the industry operates.

RG: Are there particular commodities you are focusing on?

RN: We focus primarily on the protein sectors, particularly the meat sector, although we do some work in commodity crops.

RG: Thus far you've been effective in identifying problems that people didn't feel existed before.

RN: Yes. DNA unearths issues that aren't apparent to the naked eye. When you go to a meat case and buy your protein, all the steaks look the same, so there's a great degree of trust between the consumer and the grocer in terms of the provenance, safety, and integrity of the product. Our technology can underscore that bond of trust between the consumer and the grocer. It can also reassure the grocer and other stakeholders in the supply chain that the products are what they purport to be. There's enormous commercial pressure in the food system to continuously reduce price, and that creates incentives for unscrupulous individuals to cut corners, which damages the whole system. Everyone in the food system wants to make sure that a bad player doesn't undermine consumer confidence.

RG: Most of the world's leading retailers assumed that contractual relationships they had with major suppliers were well policed. Why did the horse meat scandal shock so many people?

RL: Fundamentally, there was a breach of trust that undermined the brand proposition. Some of the organizations directly implicated were very large organizations, which generated lots of media attention and reinforced a certain prejudice—wrongly in my opinion—that there is wide-ranging fraud throughout the industry. There is a certain degree of fraud in some sectors, but most folks in the industry are well intentioned and doing their best under difficult circumstances.

RG: People were shocked that some of the most prestigious firms were involved unknowingly. When a firm such as Tesco in England recognized that their suppliers were using horse meat as a mixture in their beef, there was a great concern.

RL: It did enormous damage to the company and its brand. The senior executives and the folks involved had no inkling about what was taking place. It highlighted supply chain complexity and the challenges of being increasingly divorced from primary production when you're sourcing products in multiple markets. It also underscored the damage that can be done to brand equity overnight when retailers breach trust with their customers.

RG: Has the scandal encouraged people to come to your firm for help?

RL: Yes, it highlighted vulnerabilities in the supply chain and caused firms to ask more questions about their supply base, and how products are sourced.

RG: If you go up and down the chain, who wants this test the most: the retailer, the processer, the suppler, the farmer, who?

RL: Great question. I would say the custodians of the brand. The supply chain in the protein industry has producers at various stages—there's the food processing sector and then the food distribution side. Those with brand equity see great value in some of the things we do because our technology helps convey the product story more effectively. We're getting excited about how the technology can be used to promote continuous quality improvement. In the protein industry, achieving consistent quality can be a challenge because of the fungible nature of some of these products and the variations which can occur across the production chain. Our technology helps play a role in delivering a consistent, top-quality eating experience to the consumer.

RG: An example would be Friona Industries, a leading feedlot firm that worked with Cargill and other meat processors to make sure that contractual relationships on quality continued throughout the processing phase. They then worked with the retailer Harris Teeter to make sure that the end product was consistent and reliable. The result of that cooperation resulted in a very tender quality of beef, so much so that the USDA gave a quality-of-tenderness brand to that supermarket and to that chain. Do you see that as sort of an example of what you can do?

RL: Absolutely. That's a great example of smarter vertical integration and the deepening awareness of interdependencies in the supply chain. Trading relationships based exclusively on price—don't get me wrong, price is very important—are being questioned, as producers realize consumers care about parameters other than price.

RG: The feedback mechanism that DNA gives to each partner up and down the value-added chain is critical to provide the improvement you're talking about. It's continuous improvement, not a one-shot deal. Have you been able to do what Friona's accomplished working with others?

RL: We've been told that when we've introduced the technology, there has been a radical drop in customer complaints. We have some empirical data that would demonstrate we're getting more consistent product quality. We attribute this in part to greater levels of transparency afforded by the technology. The technology is evolving, and what we're learning is evolving, but we're excited about the direction.

RG: In the protein field we've been talking primarily about beef, but does it work for pork and other products?

RL: Absolutely. We have a number of pork programs, and fish too. We're in discussions on the poultry side. The poultry industry is much more integrated and has shorter supply chains, so there may be less transformational opportunity. But with fish, sustainable sourcing is increasingly important. The origin and traceability message engages lots of different issues—sustainability, animal welfare, labor conditions of the employees.

Some retailers in Europe recently voiced concerns about sourcing shrimp from certain Asian countries because of labor practices. They wanted to verify that their production wasn't sourced from organizations with questionable work practices.

RG: There's been a lot of talk about adulteration in our food system. People talk about fish—what they think they're buying in fish is not the fish that they thought they were buying. Does DNA enable someone to protect themselves on that supply?

RL: Yes. I've spoken to a number of companies faced with the dilemma of cheating or not surviving commercially. That's shocking and not good for the consumer or the organizations involved. There's an onus on all stakeholders because ultimately the breach of trust with the consumer spreads and all stakeholders lose out. Supply chains need to be policed by those organizations directly involved, and DNA has a role to play.

RG: Do you think DNA will be used in nonprotein products?

RL: Yes, for sure—in vegetables, olive oils, honeys, things like that. If there's a strong price incentive you'll get a small number of people who engage in a degree of fraud, especially if the supply chain is complex. DNA is one of a suite of technologies that can target authenticity.

RG: Is it expensive to do this kind of work?

RL: It's surprisingly low and getting lower. In the protein sector we're talking a small number of pennies per pound.

RG: What about some luxury items? I've heard that 95 percent of the Chateau Lafitte wine sold in China—95 percent isn't Chateau Lafitte.

RL: There are a range of technological solutions depending on the type of fraud being perpetrated. DNA gets destroyed processing certain products, but isotopes have been used quite effectively [in] authenticating wine. Olive oil is another area of focus. If there's a significant price differential and the product looks visibly the same, substitution becomes quite tempting. However, people will think twice about substitution if the technology is available to expose the cheater.

RG: Where do you see your company in ten years?

RL: We're quite excited by developments on the technology side, and want to grow the business in different markets both vertically and horizontally. The challenge for a small company like ours is deciding where to focus. We want to continue growing the business and create more value by gaining broader acceptance of [the] DNA tracing concept in grocery stores and restaurants.

RG: It seems that trust in the food system in general has declined. Customers don't think it's trustworthy anymore. Is DNA one way to start recapturing that trust?

RL: Yes, and I agree that trust in the food chain has been undermined. The scientific precision of DNA and its positive perception with consumers offer reassurance in a crisis.

RG: The food system is the largest sector of the world's economy. You're a relatively small firm. How are you going to grow fast enough to cover all the parts of the food system that could use this new technology?

RL: We're both ambitious and realistic. We focus on markets where we're stronger, where we've established relationships with relevant organizations. There are a variety of markets that offer tremendous opportunities, but we need to view them strategically.

RG: Are the relationships that you develop long term in nature?

RL: Yes, they are. We're most successful when we've identified key champions who share a common vision and see both the risks and the opportunities in deploying our technology. Personal relationships are central. We probably don't spend as much time on that as we should.

RG: How do you attract and develop talented, scientifically trained employees?

RL: A great question. There's a strong technical dimension to our value proposition, so a fundamental understanding of the technology. Frequently in meetings we're asked questions—can you do this, can you do that—and in those discussions we need to respond authoritatively and give confidence to the other side that we fully understand what the technology is capable of and how it can be utilized in their organization. In recruiting and developing, we need to invest in our people and have them grow with the business and get excited and knowledgeable about our technology.

RG: Many firms involved in new technologies in the food system have developed training programs to do just that. Are you developing such a training program?

RL: We're a small organization that still needs to cultivate the right skill sets, and our HR team is evaluating ways to do that. Ultimately we're looking to recruit and retain technically capable people with a detailed knowledge of the global food industry.

RG: Historically, many universities have partnered with different parts of the food system to train and develop people useful to a particular sector in the food system. It seems to me that with new technologies like DNA there are certain schools that are educating students with those skills and interests who would love to partner with you for their students' sake.

RL: Absolutely. We already have a variety of research partnerships with universities and we'd be very excited to have conversations around how they could assist us on the training side.

RG: Going forward do you see competitors coming forth?

RL: Absolutely. If you don't have competitors, you don't have a market. We've never believed that one key piece of IP is going to protect us. We believe that complex industry knowhow balanced with a good IP portfolio will help us retain our competitive position. If we deliver real value to our customers at a price that works for them, we should do well.

RG: The food system is hungry for regaining the integrity it once had, so thank you very much for taking that leadership.

3

Creating Shared Value

JAMES HERRING
President and CEO, Friona Industries (2008)

President and CEO of feedlot operator Friona Industries, James Herring has been instrumental in developing a more collaborative approach to managing the beef supply chain in the United States. He wanted to improve the consistency and quality of meat for the consumer, but needed the cooperation of 750,000 independent cow-calf farmers, as well as feedlot operators, packing houses, and cattle breeders, along with the scientific input of Elanco. As a facilitator he made this happen, and even more importantly, he was able to get everyone to trust each other and each other's finance statements. The USDA awarded a "tenderness label" to the final product. All of this was done on a handshake up and down the vertical chain and the arrangement still exists today in 2017. Herring is a graduate of the University of Texas and the Harvard Business School.[1]

RG: James Herring is president and CEO of Friona Industries, the premier cattle-feeding and integrated cattle operation in the United States and a major leader in the global food system. The cattle industry has always been the most difficult one for people to understand—difficult in the sense of how the vertical value-added system works, difficult in the sense of trying to see how people can and will work together even though they have different objectives at every level of the system. You're the first person, to my knowledge, who's attempted to put that system into a win-win operation, rather than one of conflict. What gave you the courage to do that?

JH: We're very lucky that the McDonald's Corporation called us to a group session in the Missouri Ozarks. They had a branded franchise based on one product, beef, and they didn't know much about the product—its origin and ultimate production. We formed a five-year partnership to look at vertically aligning the beef production system with McDonald's; Excel Corporation, which is the packing arm of Cargill; and Capitol Land & Livestock in Austin. It'd never been done on a critical-size basis, so it was an opportunity to understand how much value a vertically aligned beef production system could create.

RG: The individuals who have grown up in this industry are highly independent. They're proud of their heritage and their unique role in the system, but distrust the rest of the system. They feel they're not being treated fairly. How do you get over that?

JH: We're the US facilitator between the cow-calf operator, the stocker operator, the feedlot operator, the eventual packer, and the consumer. Once you get that on paper, you see what we can do to create value for the end consumer—that's who we have to create compelling value for, the ultimate consumer. Once we started thinking consumer rather than just cattle, the whole ballgame changed. We started creating value-add for everybody in the system.

RG: The time horizon and scale for each of the players is quite different. It's fine to say you want them to be consumer oriented, but historically, their father, their grandfather, their great-grandfather have always been producer oriented: How much more gain can I get out of the animal? How much more throughput can I drive through the plant?

How do you move from that perspective to focusing on the consumer, not production, and how do you identify change-makers at each level to make it happen? How do you find charismatic leaders at each level to bring the others along?

JH: As the facilitator our job was to find the players both downstream and upstream. The upstream side, of course, was the need by Cargill Meat Solutions, the packing arm of Cargill, to differentiate their product and their value system for the retailer. They had a compelling reason to differentiate.

On the downstream side, the cow-calf operator and the stockman are basically driven by the economics. We agreed if you bring the right raw material, the right steer, the right heifer to us at the right time, there'll be an economic incentive for you, and we're in the marketplace 24/7.

We created economic incentive for both sides to create a structural partnership. It hasn't been easy, but over time it's created a compelling franchise for us as the facilitator of the whole value chain.

RG: Our industry is dramatically consolidating, domestically and globally and at every level—retailer, processor, etc. As that happens, where does meat fit in?

JH: The battlefield at the retailers and processor level is between commodity and brand. Some of the business is dedicated to the commodity side. Just create low-cost pounds, and sell pounds as best you can into an industry that's been a commodity business for years. The other path is the differentiated path that says, Rather than sell pounds, I want to sell the right kind of pounds to my customer.

Whether the industry will validate the concept of differentiated value is a real question. We think we have a differentiated system that creates a differentiated product that creates a promise for the consumer that's been validated over and over, and right now is in three thousand stores across the United States. But we're still less than 1 percent of the industry.

RG: The consumer is frustrated when it comes to meat, especially beef, because they never know whether it's going to be tender or tough. How do you address that consumer need and perception?

JH: Our differentiation is in tenderness, which we fully guarantee based on a long process, beginning with the right raw material, the right feeding process, the right pre- and postharvest technology applied to the product, and the right aging process. Each of those critical control points has been dictated not just by us as the feeder processor, but also by the retailer, so the customer sees a differentiated product. We're betting that our product is better than the commodity product and that the consumer will agree.

RG: What kind of a retailer do you want to be at the forefront of this change?

JH: The seven retail chains involved in our product are champions who believe that a differentiated meat product in the perishable section of the store wins customers who buy lots of things.

The critical piece, of course, is people. If we have a champion that understands differentiation, we've got a good chance. We've never missed selling that person. But he has to have a vision that his store will be singled out by consumers for that part of his offering. If meat is important in that sector, we're winning that battle every day in those stores. The key is having somebody willing to believe.

RG: The other parts of the meat system, like poultry—Tyson, Perdue, and others—have developed national brands. How do you get supermarkets to feel that the brand they're helping you create is also their brand?

JH: We thought we could nationally brand a meat product but were sorely mistaken. It's not possible. The stores want their own brand. What we've done is to provide differentiated raw material. Put your brand on it, and support your image in the community. We guarantee that the process and the product will fulfill that promise. That's been successful. A national brand is tough sledding.

RG: The retailer is also concerned about Walmart with their ability to compete on a global efficiency basis. How does meat fit into that?

JH: Walmart is the battlefield amongst retailers today. They're in everyone's rearview mirror. They've tried promoting a national brand, but they promote their own brands. A brand must deliver a promise, but there's no process behind branding at Walmart. We see them as a low-price commodity competitor. Our retailers are saying to the public, We have a differentiated product. Come to our store for that difference, rather than go to Walmart for price.

RG: Traceability in our food system has never been more important. Where does traceability fit into your program?

JH: We've supported a national ID system for years, but that's not happened. We've had very little buy-in from the retail sector on tracing back to the eventual animal. I'm sad about that, but we still don't see it in the United States.

RG: Can you take a leadership role there? The American people want safe food. I don't understand why an industry, no matter how independent its members are, would want their product to be in question.

JH: The impetus needs to come throughout the chain. We need retailers saying it every single day. The cow-calf producer ought to be saying, I'm very proud of my product and want to identify it. That's not happened.

RG: The industry is becoming more global. How will this affect the value-added chain going forward?

JH: American beef production is basically a premium product to the rest of the world. Our role as beef producer in the global economy is value-add. JBS, the Brazilians, market beef products on a global basis. They're going to be a very tough competitor here in the United States. It's a wakeup call for the rest of the industry to understand global marketing or risk losing out to a foreign competitor.

RG: How do you see your firm going forward? You're the change-maker in the most important industry. Beef is the most valuable food purchase a consumer makes. How can you influence both the domestic and the international scene going forward?

JH: We have to champion a better process of beef production in the United States, and we have been. The Achilles' heel for our industry is that it's very fragmented. We have 750,000 producers creating their own genetic pool and we, as the facilitator, are trying to link steps together to the eventual consumer.

We're producing half a million cattle a year, and the kill in the United States is twenty-seven million, so we're a small piece of the puzzle. But we're doing our part to change the way people throughout the industry view the cattle industry in a global environment.

RG: It's also a political industry. Many people are concerned about consolidation in our commodity systems, including beef. They want to desegregate rather than integrate the system. They don't want common ownership of feedlots and processing plants and joint ventures with cow-calf operators. They think that that's not "the American way." Why is there so much distrust of the food system by a handful of senators who feel that the farmer is losing his or her independence?

JH: If those senators understood more clearly what's happening globally in the beef industry, they'd understand that the system is actually creating bigger value. We're creating wonderful value for people downstream with 550,000 cattle a year. The same is true of 30- to 80- to 500-head cow-calf producers trying to create the right product for the right reason. We're encouraging other parts of the industry to understand they can be a part of an aligned production system creating bigger value.

In our case, we've reduced costs dramatically, we've elevated prices for our raw material suppliers, and we've created consistent business for them. We've also delivered a better product for millions of consumers in three thousand stores around the country. That's a good thing, and people need to understand that.

RG: Do they understand you're also creating a pricing system that goes beyond commodities and are giving them risk management tools that can be used over months, or even years? Do they understand you're providing long-term contractual arrangements, so that producers can plan ahead? Do they understand that instead of giving the farmer less power, you're empowering him?

JH: I'm not sure. Eliminating risk in an operation, big or small, is important. It's a value to get more for your livestock than you did last year and to have a firm that'll buy your livestock every single time without much hassle.

RG: Most people don't understand hedging. Most people don't understand that your firm and firms like Cargill and others are willing to help people help themselves. I don't understand in my academic mind why you can't convince charismatic, creative, intelligent leadership at each level to get together as you have at Friona to collaborate on problems facing the industry. Nothing we've had trouble with is due to bigness. It's our inability to work together.

JH: I have a lot of trouble with that myself. Our industry is very fragmented and is very geographic in nature. That divides us, so bringing the puzzle together hasn't been easy.

RG: Some companies, like Walmart, have been trying to get suppliers to implement an RFID program on all their products. Do you think the power of large distributors to demand traceability across their supply chain—a traceability system—will make a difference?

JH: Walmart will certainly have an impact. So will Safeway, Kroger, and McDonald's. But we need champions below as well. We need the National Cattlemen's and the processors—Cargill, IBP, JBS Swift. We need people throughout industry to understand what that can do, and to make us more competitive globally.

RG: We have the same problem at the governmental level. We have the FDA involved and the USDA, FSIS [Food Safety and Inspection Service], and the EPA. They all worry about safety, the environment, and other elements of health and nutrition. Yet we don't have a common focus. Can't a Friona take leadership and say, Look, enough is enough?

JH: Yes, we can and have, and will continue doing so. Every industry in the world does it, except for beef. We're organizing our facility so that customers know the product's value, know its direction, know its logistics to the end zone, and can deliver to the customer a consistent experience over time. We're working to create a sustainable system.

RG: Globally, it's [the] same problem: we don't have an overall focus. We now have Codex Alimentarius on labeling. OSI is trying to do the same for beef. We have global farmers, global retailers, and global processors. If we're going to have a global food system, don't we eventually have to have comprehensible global standards?

JH: Absolutely, that's a critical for international trade. The wakeup call for our industry today was JBS Swift's acquisition of National and Smithfield and a feeding operation in the United States.

We're saying to domestic producers and processors it's a global business now. We have to focus on delivery standards around the world that will make trade more efficient, straightforward, and honest.

RG: In 1955, Dean David, head of Harvard Business School, invited John Davis, who was then assistant secretary of agriculture under Eisenhower, and me to create the agribusiness program. One of our mandates was to see if [we] could get the industry to do a better job of providing nutrition, health, food security, economic development, and the society values which a food system can do.

That was fifty-three years ago. You were my student in 1974. We're talking about the same thing today. More than ever, we need to be more responsive to the needs of society. Our food system is no longer just a food system. It's a health system, an energy system, a nutrition system, and an environmental management system for water and land resources. We can't afford the luxury of looking at this on a piecemeal basis.

Politicians think from election to election, which I understand. But leaders in our industry, such as you, are thinking in ten-, twenty-, and forty-year increments, trying to plan ahead. Here's the most valuable commodity system in the world, and it's the most archaic. With your exception, nobody's taking that leadership.

JH: We're going to succeed by talking and doing and demonstrating and educating. We have the power to do that. We've been able to create an exemplary system for the beef industry. It's an effective, efficient, cost-worthy, and product-conscious delivery system. We can say, Hey, this is something for the future. I'm proud of that. However, it's a small piece of the puzzle. You're making a global case that operators in the United States and all over the world should adopt a standardized methodology for trade. Thank goodness we have champions like you.

RG: Our political candidates all say they believe in change and we have to work together. In my generation, we didn't have a Republican food policy and a Democratic food policy. We had a US food policy. This generation needs a US food policy and a global food policy.

The food system has always been a quasi-public utility. What people get paid for producing food, what people pay for consuming food, and how it affects economic development and the well-being of society make it a public issue.

Consolidation is a good thing. You can put the whole food system in one room and say, All right, we've had enough. We want the public and society to be in a better place, and we can find a way to do it together and have a win-win outcome. I'm very grateful we have a person like you who's championing that. Thank you very much.

JH: Thank you, Ray. We're going to do our part.

GREG PAGE
Chairman and CEO, Cargill (2004)

As Chairman and CEO of Cargill, Greg Page guided the largest privately held firm in the world from a transactional, price-driven commodity business to a collaborative, client-oriented partnership business without losing the company's entrepreneurial ethos. In doing so, Cargill's managers had to re-examine their strategic intent and realized that their success was not based on trading skills alone but rather on the satisfaction of the ultimate consumer of their commodities in food products. Their new mission became their desire to "nourish the world." Page grew up in North Dakota, where his father had a John Deere dealership. He graduated from the University of North Dakota with a degree in economics.[2]

RG: Greg Page is CEO of Cargill, the largest privately owned firm in the world, and one of the world's largest agribusiness firms, having sales of over $130 billion. Many people probably don't understand Cargill. How would you describe it?

GP: Essentially, Cargill takes products from places of surplus to places of deficit. We're very diverse globally. More than half our employees live outside the United States and over half our earnings are generated in about 150 other countries. We're primarily focused on food production and food processing, but we have substantial financial trading activities which grew out of our need to deal with both currency and interest rate risks. We operate as a single entity, not a conglomerate, and try to make each of our businesses valuable not only on their own but also to other Cargill businesses.

RG: Most look at Cargill as the glue that holds the food system together, from the input side to value-added products in poultry and beef to bakery products. You also have joint ventures with technology companies.

How do you see Cargill evolving from a commodity-oriented firm to one focused more on value-added-oriented businesses?

GP: Bob Shapiro, former head of Monsanto, referred to the food business as the "commercialization of photosynthesis." We're a big part of that. As the world's food system becomes more interdependent and more complicated, the knowledge a person gleans from participating in one link is valuable to other links. Our strategy is to make sure our involvement—and the associated intellectual property we create—is relevant both upstream and downstream along the chain. We evolved initially from basic agricultural marketing to simple processing. Now our customers ask us about obesity, about trans fats, about food safety.

Entry barriers are small for many of our individual activities—building an export elevator or a flour mill or a feed plant. On the other hand, operating as an integrated global system is very valuable. We emphasize the systemic value of doing business with Cargill versus doing business with companies focused on a single link. The overall system we've created has significant barriers to entry and serves the needs of our customers and shareholders well. It's a real differentiator.

RG: As you describe this system, your end-user is consolidating in every country, including our own. How will that consolidation affect you?

GP: I was in the meat business in the late '80s and early '90s in the United States when there was significant retail consolidation. Our immediate reaction was that it would be bad for Cargill, because we'd have fewer customers, and they'd have more leverage in our commercial relationship. In fact, as the retailers became larger, they had more demanding consumers and a greater need for food safety, reliable supply, and larger quantities of meat. What we thought was going to change the balance of our relationship led to greater interdependence.

Being a mere trader wasn't going to work in a world where grocery chains had few sellers and we had few buyers. Rather than see it as a negative, we asked ourselves, What's really required for a more interdependent food system to work? The word we kept coming back to was trust. A cold, bid-offer, price discovery relationship wasn't adequate. We needed to trust the large retailers, and they needed to trust us in order to serve the consumer better. There's a huge opportunity for the customer solutions model we're developing.

RG: People are worried about one company in particular in that consolidation, Walmart. They believe that a company that grows that fast and has that much buying power can dictate terms to suppliers. Do you think trust overcomes that?

GP: Not in all situations, but we've come a long way in our own relationship with Walmart. A positive about working with Walmart is their transparency and openness. They're willing to share where they're headed, what they'd like to accomplish, and why. They're not secretive.

Do they have leverage? Is purchasing power important to their business model? Certainly. Does it lead to tensions at the buy-sell level? Yes. Our relationship with Walmart is complicated. But it's based on their desire to be the best retailer in the world, and to do that, they're very willing to openly engage their suppliers.

RG: You've moved out along the chain, every link. There's a great concern that the farming community, the cooperative community, isn't responding as well to the consolidation. How does the farmer fit into your system, and how does he or she benefit from all this?

GP: It depends whether it's in livestock agriculture or crop agriculture. We've been working with a number of Midwestern pork producers and our sales office in Japan to produce meat more in line with what Japanese consumers want. We've worked with the breeding companies, changed the feeding regime and the color of the fat and age at which we market the product. We linked insights from our sales office in Tokyo with hog genetics, livestock feed, production techniques on the farm, and the farmer. The farmers feel they're producing a differentiated pork, and our challenge is to convince them that they're receiving differential value for that hog as a result of meeting a specific need. We do the same with grain crops. We still need to match supply and demand to sustain profitable prices for all participants. In a world of ever-shifting prices, our role is to find that equilibrium.

RG: Cargill also has a reputation of trying to help the farmer manage the price risks that you talked about. How has that evolved?

GP: Risk management is a big business in Cargill. It's a separate business unit that uses derivative strategies to establish floor prices on commodities, which gives lenders more confidence. The biggest challenge is the culture of primary agricultural producers. They're gamblers at heart. Giving up some topside to protect against the downside comes slowly to the prairies and the Corn Belt. Over the last eight years, our risk management business has experienced double-digit growth in this area. People realize that getting the highest price is less important than avoiding the financial duress of low prices. One of our roles in the financial system is to create new tools for commodity price discovery and risk management. Cargill customers increasingly use derivative price protection to manage cash flows over more than a single-year timeframe, which allows them to expand their business with the comfort of their banker.

RG: Your comment implies that sophistication up and down the value-added chain is also changing. You're helping your customers become more sophisticated as the system itself changes. Is that occurring?

GP: Yes, it's an educational process. I spoke only from the producer side, but the same is true for large packaged goods producers on the opposite side of the price dilemma. Their shareholders prefer consistent earnings that aren't subject to volatility in commodity prices. We're able to create products that have a smoothing effect on both costs and realized revenue.

RG: Are these types of sophisticated procedures able to be transferred overseas yet?

GP: Yes, certainly. More than a third of our volume in risk products in agriculture or food products is with foreign clients. We've had great receptivity in overseas markets.

RG: The other types of sophistication that you talked about in terms of research and development and greater utilization of every element of the value-added chain, starting with the farmer—it's sort of amazing to those outside of agriculture to see a farmer worried about not just producing food, but feed, and fuel, and even pharmaceuticals. How do you see changes in technology and genetics affecting your business?

GP: It's a huge opportunity for Cargill, because the ethanol mandate in the United States, which isn't responsive to price, creates its own form of volatility. If corn prices rise a lot, Tyson may raise fewer chickens, or Smithfield fewer hogs. But if the price of corn goes up dramatically and we have a mandate for ethanol, that is inelastic demand. When inelastic demand is introduced into a market system, you're bound to create more volatility in both directions, and volatility is something that Cargill is paid to manage.

RG: In addition to energy, pollution and environmental concerns from agricultural are a major concern. How does a Cargill address those issues?

GP: At Cargill, we have one worldwide environmental policy. Early in my career I started a poultry processing company in Thailand. We were obliged to comply with the wastewater emission standards that Cargill applied to its facilities here in North America, even though we were in Thailand. To the best of our knowledge, there were no complying food processing plants in terms of wastewater treatment. We received a visit from the king of Thailand, and were cited as a role model for other companies. So it's not simply an issue of complying with the law. In some cases, it's being a role model.

Having come from the livestock side of Cargill, I'm pleased we'll have all our major North American livestock production facilities converting their wastewater biomass to methane, so we'll have an anaerobic methane system in place. It reduces odor and makes great use of otherwise wasted biomass. We've got to meet the needs of the communities where we work. Our employees don't want to work for a company they can't be proud of from an environmental dimension.

RG: Another concern in recent years is food safety—BSE, avian flu, even terrorism or bioterrorism. How do you see us dealing with that in the future?

GP: That's a big topic. After 9/11, many companies, ours included, looked at the perimeter security of all our facilities, and how we secured in-transit products. We're members of a consortium put together by the US government that continues to look [at] ways we could use technology to control those risks. Unfortunately, we have a vast food chain, from the farm to the dinner table, so there are lots of opportunities for bioterrorism, and we need to be vigilant.

As for food safety, in terms of chemistry, food's never been safer. Some say it's too safe, and we don't build up immunities the way we used to. An old adage is that if you haven't eaten a pound of dirt by your sixth birthday, you're going to have allergies. As someone who grew up in a rural area and ate a lot of dirty carrots, I think I got my pound.

RG: Europe is addressing different issues like beef hormone and GMOs. They will allow GMOs, but as GMO "free" with less than 0.9 percent genetically modified organisms. How do you see that playing out?

GP: It's very encouraging. Whether you like the 0.9 percent or not is a different issue, but the fact that there's an acknowledgment that zero can't be the standard says we're on the right path.

RG: The standards being developed aren't just national standards. In some cases, they're global standards, with Codex and OIE and other international organizations trying to find a common standard. Do you think this is a plus, minus, or neither?

GP: It's always easier for global companies to deal with set rules uniformly applied. People's comfort level with science and with their own governments is going to vary, so we have to let people grow into this.

RG: Who do you think your competitors are? You're so unique. Are there any competitors?

GP: Yes. Our most difficult competitors are often single-industry participants in single countries or single regions. Our managerial challenge is to have a long, centipede-like footprint, and still compete with very focused entrepreneurs. I don't see any competitor being a multilegged centipede like us. But we have numerous competitors. We have competitors that only run flour mills or are only involved in animal fats or only involved in starchy products. Our challenge is to enable the leaders of our individual businesses to compete with single-minded competitors, while at the same time embracing Cargill's single global culture.

RG: The new thrust in your company affects the kind of men and women that you hire. How do you go about finding people that understand both the fork-to-table complexity of your operations, yet have the entrepreneurial focus to compete?

GP: We jokingly say we need compliant rebels. It's a contradiction in terms, but our most successful business unit leaders exemplify that. They have passion, a bias to do something, and a willingness to do so with incomplete facts. They need to fight guerrilla battles against entrenched, single-industry competitors. But they also need to be compliant enough to accommodate the needs of the whole organization. We need real entrepreneurial spirits, but also a willingness to work together on consensus-based decisions and business development. Fifteen years ago, Cargill focused disproportionately on deep analytical skills. Today it's more about emotional intelligence.

RG: Do you do much training and development inside the company?

GP: That's always been our focus. It's a great strength and weakness for Cargill, since our competitors are populated with some of our alums. In the last several years, our senior training has been done here by the Cargill leadership team. There are seven of us and we're the active instructors. It's a bit of the GE model. I was just at the senior training seminar in Shanghai, where our employees stayed in Chinese family homes and spent time with Chinese companies.

RG: What is the Cargill value system?

GP: We can't teach people to be honest, so we make no effort to do that. While Cargill generally isn't draconian, when it comes to honesty, we're very draconian. It's important to be comfortable with conflict. We're a very big company, so the failure to speak up can have the same consequences as the failure to be honest. Your job is to answer un-asked questions. There are big moments in a company's history when you make decisions that visibly define your culture. Will the company do the right thing even when it's not in its self-interest? But that does-n't happen often. Culture can't be shaped by big decision points alone. The everyday treatment of who gets honored and who gets recognized really matters. Collaborative rebels that answer the unasked questions are an important part of our value proposition.

RG: How do you think that being privately owned affects how people feel about the company?

GP: It definitely matters, but what really creates loyalty is opportunity. Young employees ask me, why am I so loyal to Cargill? I say, think of it as a business relationship. Cargill promised me opportunity and pro-vided it, and I promised to give Cargill my best effort and I did. Each party got what it wanted. I don't see myself as being emotionally loyal to Cargill. I honor and respect the things we stand for—like staying in sub-Saharan Africa, for example. It's clearly not just about money.

Employees want to work for a company they can be proud of, have a supervisor that will teach them and a company that's growing. You can have all the other things in place, but if there's no growth, how do you attract people? We call it growth oxygen. Oxygen for growth has enabled us to build a loyal cadre of long-serving employees. The seven members of the Cargill leadership team have 228 years with the com-pany. That comes from a bargain well made: Cargill portrayed them-selves accurately in the interview, gave each of us a leader we could honor and growth opportunities. That's where the loyalty comes from.

Some people say, Why is Cargill private? I always say, Because the shareholders have honored us by reinvesting their dividends in sig-nificant proportion for nearly 150 years. To the extent that a small, connected family of long-time owners continues to honor the business in that way, I think employees will always be loyal to Cargill, because that oxygen provides opportunities for thousands of people.

RG: That's a vote of confidence. How do you get young people to interact with you and your colleagues at the very highest level? How do you reach down and pluck potential leaders from the people you hire?

GP: We have formal processes, of course, with their immediate supervisors advancing them for specific kinds of training or experience. We manage expenses carefully, but it's impossible for a company like Cargill to exist without breaking bread together, so we spend money spending time together. We've been a first-name-basis company for one hundred years. Informality encourages interaction. I just got back from a trip across Romania, Ukraine, and Russia, spending time with people at their elevators and processing plants. We went bowling with some young employees and had a little vodka. They need to know you, and you need to know them, so getting out and seeing people and breaking bread together are important. In a global company, we have to make sure the best opportunities don't simply go to Americans or the Dutch.

RG: What is there about your own history that prepared you to do what you're doing right now? Where did you get your values? Where did you get your interests?

GP: Prepared is a tough word, because most days you come to work feeling unprepared. Today is going to be a chance to grow! I got my curiosity from my father, a small-town businessperson. He was a John Deere dealer for much of my youth. We had dinner together as a family, and dad had this expression—it's a sad day when you don't learn something. At dinner he would ask each of us, What did we learn today? I can assure you, "nothing" was not the right answer.

I probably got my values from my grandmother, a very strong Irish woman who spent a lot of time with me. She had eighteen grandchildren, but we all felt important, which was a good lesson that you don't need to be in a small group to be important.

I credit people at Cargill. When people ask me about my ethics, I say, I don't know yet, because I've never been asked by Cargill to do something I couldn't explain to my mother. Coming from a town of 2,500 people in North Dakota and ending up at a company like Cargill, I was touched numerous times by my immediate supervisors. I've had bosses with different styles but haven't had a single supervisor in thirty years who didn't enrich me in some way.

RG: You've seen many changes in Cargill. If we were having this conversation in ten or even twenty years, what do you think Cargill will look like?

GP: Honestly, I don't spend much time on that, because how we look will be shaped by macro events. Are GMOs accepted? Will the global food system become increasingly parochial, or will it become much more global? Will we raise food in the right place for the benefit of all mankind, or will we try to grow oranges in Minnesota? What's important for me is to create a Cargill that will prosper across all those environments, a more open global trading system or a less open global system—a system that honors science in a deep and abiding way, and where people trust the regulatory authorities.

As a company, we can't shape how that turns out. Our obligation is to deploy our skills across the great interconnected space from dirt to the dinner table.

RG: Thank you so much, Greg.

GP: My pleasure, Ray.

JOHN JOHNSON
Past President and CEO, CHS (2010)

Past president and CEO of CHS Inc., John Johnson runs the largest farm cooperative in the United States. Although a cooperative, CHS is managed as an ambitious global business that has successfully partnered with the likes of Cargill and other leading food companies to extend its reach and serve the interests of its farmer-owners. Johnson recognized that CHS was part of a global system and decided to partner with Cargill, which they traditionally considered a major competitor. They created Horizon Milling—now the leading flour firm in the United States. They have partnered with other global firms and meet with farm groups around the world. Johnson grew up in a small North Dakota farming community where he first recognized the unrealized potential of farm cooperatives.[3]

RG: John Johnson is president and CEO of CHS Inc., the largest cooperative in the United States. As a leader in the cooperative movement, how were you able to put all those pieces together, and how long has it taken?

JJ: This is my thirty-fourth year with CHS and I've been CEO for sixteen years. Our cooperative values have held the test of time, but we needed to blend our cooperative values with a more corporate culture. I took a long-term view and decided on a growth strategy to compete around the world on behalf of US farmers. In my first year as CEO I said to my board, Wouldn't it be nice if the farmers could own a Cargill or an ADM? We couldn't do that, but that was the starting point. We had to be more than just a local co-op in St. Paul, Minnesota.

RG: What was the makeup of your board—having grown out of the Farm-Labor Party—that made them willing to pick a young man in his forties with the vision to do this? Cooperatives often see the food system as an enemy, not a partner. How did they change in order to attract and identify a man like you?

JJ: When the board was selecting a CEO in 1994, some good internal choices argued, Let's keep the course. I made a high-risk proposal to compete globally, and said there'll be risks, but in ten years you're going to be proud of what we've developed.

RG: Most cooperatives find it difficult to get the financial resources to build the dream you outlined. They'd rather pay members more money for their raw material, which leaves less to build the cooperative. How were you able to change their minds?

JJ: Co-ops have no public stock for purchases and acquisitions, so we have to use cash and debt, which have limitations in volatile markets. We needed a strong balance sheet to access the debt markets.

We also need capital to expand the company to make acquisitions, build plants, and create terminals around the world. You have to balance the capital you need to grow and manage volatile markets while returning some to your owners. If you return all the capital, members will be happy in the short run, but it doesn't make them happy over a lifetime, because you won't create long-term value. I delivered that message early and they bought into it.

Our financial performance has been stellar. We've grown from $4 billion in sales in 1994 to over $25 billion. My first year as CEO, we made $50 million and our peak has been $800 million. That gives us the flexibility to pay our owners, strengthen our balance sheet, and expand the company.

It's the Pac-Man approach. We nibble away and over time we've created a big company. What's my formula? Two words—"make money." In our case, we've had a 15 percent return in cash against member equity—that's creating value for the farmer.

RG: That's wonderful value and a remarkable feat. You have a 2020 Vision program. How long have you had that, and how were you able to put that forth in an organization [that] historically, like most cooperatives, doesn't think that way?

JJ: Our 2020 Vision takes a ten-year horizon. We always focus on "what if" scenario planning. The 2020 work began the year we had all-time record earnings, and I was more nervous than I'd ever been in my career.

We engaged my senior management team and, over a period of time, had over a hundred people involved. You need buy-in throughout the organization. I'm going to be retiring at year-end, but we set five major, long-term aspirations.

RG: What are they?

JJ: As a cooperative owned by farmers, our first aspiration is to be producer focused on an integrated global basis. Our second aspiration is to support a small energy group—probably in renewable fuels. A key aspiration is expanding globally. Our fourth aspiration is continuing to build our food processing companies here and around the world. Our next aspiration involves enterprise culture. We have fourteen different business lines and have concluded we're better off operating as a business enterprise instead of a collection of independent businesses. Our fifth aspiration helps us operate as an enterprise, not as fourteen different business silos.

RG: And do you have the kind of men and women who both buy into it and can deliver?

JJ: The fundamental difference between success and failure is people. CEOs get credit for what goes right and blame for what goes wrong, but it's really the people working for you that make the difference. We have nine thousand employees around the world, and I rely on each of them to do the right thing every day.

In our 2020 Vision work, I was concerned about bench strength, so we created CHS University in partnership with the University of Minnesota business school. We've sent over three hundred of our employees through it.

RG: You mentioned earlier that production is key. At the same time, when you look at other companies like Cargill, they call themselves a solutions company for everybody up and down the chain, including the consumer. Does CHS have a consumer focus as well as a producer focus?

JJ: An excellent observation. We are so focused on the farmer that we can forget we're raising food for the consumer. If we link the farmer and consumer, we're in the middle and that's logistics, risk management, transportation, and just-in-time inventories. That's where the difference really is. We've got to make that connection.

RG: You've created a number of partnerships so that the signal from the consumer gets back to the farmer. How do you make that bridge, not just internally through logistics, but externally through partnerships?

For example, Horizon Milling. Cargill was your enemy. How did you end up partnering with them?

JJ: Early in my tenure, I knew we had to find partners. I admired Cargill, but everyone in our company hated them. Their offices were in Minnetonka; ours were in St. Paul. I called Warren Staley at Cargill and said, The world's changing; maybe we should see if there are alliances that could benefit both companies. They brought their entire senior management team over to our office, and I pulled together my entire senior team, and we sat around our boardroom talking about what the world was going to look like. One of the Cargill people who became a very good friend asked, Are you going to be my customer, my supplier, or my partner? The world says we better figure that out.

Two years later, we formed Horizon Milling. Five years after that, Warren Staley called me and said, You guys are originating 90-plus percent of the grain for the twenty-one mills and have better access to that grain and expertise than we have at Cargill. That's not taking anything away from Cargill, but we let the market decide what the Horizon Milling people needed. That partnership is absolutely phenomenal for both sides.

It gives CHS access to the consumer. We had a flour milling division but were struggling. We partnered with Cargill, because if you're supplying flour to major bakers of the United States, you better have flour mills positioned all over the United States. We couldn't build them fast enough, so we put the partnership together. We had strengths in origination and logistics. Cargill had strengths internationally as well as a national perspective on plant capacity, and additional ingredients like cocoa and sugar to supply bakers. It was a marriage made in heaven.

I've worked with partnerships all over the world. There has to be mutual reward for all parties. As businesspeople, we pride ourselves around negotiating hard, right? My test of the logic is [to] step into the shoes of my partner and see if I could live with the deal. If so, it's probably a partnership that'll last a long while.

RG: A win-win—

JJ: Has to be.

RG: On the same note, the farmers in the Midwest think of farmers in Brazil, Eastern Europe, Argentina, and China as their competitors. But you have joint ventures in all of those countries.

JJ: Yes, we do. In the global grain trade, if you don't have a global footprint, your value to the US farmer is going to diminish. Take China. They want 365 days a year. The North American market's going to supply that for six to seven months, and then South America's going to come in with their beans. I ask my board and members, Do you want me to walk away from those customers for six months? That's why we need to originate grain all over the world throughout the year. It's also essential for managing both price and geopolitical risk.

RG: Would you be willing to let farmers overseas become part of your cooperative?

JJ: We're dealing with that issue now in our 2020 Vision work. We do business with farmers all around the world, and our board is open to the idea that we would bring in farmers as members of this cooperative around the world.

RG: Some of the partners around the world are publicly owned. Are you willing to have a government as a partner?

JJ: Most of our overseas partners and customers, particularly in China, are influenced heavily by the government. We don't see undue influence, but a government policy shift could certainly interrupt a commercial customer relationship.

In 2005, after the Chinese bought a lot of overpriced soybean contracts, they defaulted on them. When prices fell, their solution was to default. Fortunately, every grain company had the same response—we're not selling unless we can tighten up these arrangements. The Chinese have been absolutely good citizens ever since. But other places in the world are not as stable, so you have to be careful. Diversifying relationships is essential.

RG: Do you have any partnerships with other cooperatives?

JJ: Yes. We partnered with Land O'Lakes in our agronomy and crop protection business many years ago and it was successful for many years. Although I'm generally known for creating joint ventures, I've also dismantled a few and that was one as it was losing its effectiveness. In my experience joint ventures with cooperatives are much more difficult than joint ventures with private and public companies.

RG: Is that because most of these other cooperatives—whether they're American, European, Asian, or Latin American—do not have the same philosophy you do?

JJ: Yes. I mean, we're both co-ops, and owned by farmers, but we operate as a commercial corporation working to be the best of the best, and a lot of cooperatives are too tied up in their political process. They spend too much time negotiating over who controls what, while I'm looking for the best execution possible.

RG: Cooperatives don't seem to trust the rest of the food system, which they see as an enemy, not a partner. Your cooperative picked you and engaged the food system not as an enemy, but as a means to satisfy consumers and society. Why haven't other cooperatives understood what you understood a long time ago?

JJ: I really don't know, but I think it's simply how you view the world. Farmers can be their own worst enemy. I love them to death. I grew up on a farm and ranch in North Dakota. Their view of the world can be very local, but in reality our farmers compete with everybody in the world. Every year I take my board—all of whom are farmers—overseas to visit customers, farmers, and government officials, so they've got a broader perspective of what we're trying to do.

Farmers are very smart, very intuitive. They like to kick tires. I can bring leading experts into that boardroom, but that's nothing compared to visiting a farm in Brazil where they're suddenly talking to a farmer managing a hundred thousand acres and he's a partner of ours. Suddenly, there's a common language.

RG: One of your predecessors and an early head of the Farmers' Union, your predecessor company, said that prices aren't made in the markets; they're made in Washington.

JJ: Farmers today are very market driven. Any larger farmer in the US will have a screen on his desk. They can check prices, trade contracts, track current prices, and make basis trades. It's all market driven.

RG: NGOs and consumer advocates are another area. They're worried about food safety, the environment, land ownership, traceability, and sustainability. How does this affect your 2020 Vision?

JJ: Given the growing population around the world, we know we've got to double food production over the next twenty years. The only way we're going to do this is through productivity. And that'll be through science.

RG: If I could ask a personal question, what influenced you growing up to become the kind of executive you are?

JJ: I think it goes back to growing up on a farm in western North Dakota. My uncles were always struggling as farmers. I watched the co-ops. Those guys were good fellows, but they weren't helping the farmer create more value.

Early in life I thought I could make a difference, but knew it had to be through corporate America. I got the opportunity and, as I look back, it's been a wonderful career.

RG: John, the American farmer is certainly better off because of you. Thank you very much.

JJ: Thank you, Ray.

BRIAN ROTHWELL

President, Bay State Milling (2007)

The fourth-generation leader of Bay State Flour Milling in Quincy, Massachusetts, Brian Rothwell has successfully positioned his family firm to compete in a commodity business by concentrating on high-value market niches. Rothwell recognized that a commodity approach to flour milling was no longer a successful approach to serving his various customers in the vertical food chain. He had to partner with the wheat grower over genetics, as well as the fast food and retail food chain he served, and had to add the expertise of a nutritionist to his family-owned firm. He also had to extend his outreach in the global economy on both the supply side and the consumer side.[4]

RG: Brian Rothwell is president of the Bay State Flour Milling Company. In our industry, many firms started as family firms. Now, we have multinational giants in the flour milling industry. The largest firms, like ConAgra and ADM, are publicly owned. Although Cargill is privately owned, it's a $75 billion firm. How does a family company like yours, that's the fourth- or fifth-largest flour milling company in our country—how do you compete in that kind of environment?

BR: Great question. Those large companies can't be all things to all people. What's kept us viable and growing is identifying niche opportunities overlooked by the large firms who don't have the scale to compete at an early stage. We spend lots of time identifying trends before they become apparent, and then going after them as aggressively as we can, and ride the wave as it grows. That's always been one of our secrets.

RG: One trend is that most people don't want to be in commodity businesses. They want to add value to their product. In a society clamoring for more value added, more nutritious, more specialized products—organic, or whatever—how do you take advantage of that trend?

BR: As value-added opportunities evolve, more and more niches are created. We've been in the organic field for seven or eight years. It's just starting to catch fire. It's a basic milling specialty, but with organic, we are partnering with early adopters in [the] supermarket field. We identify particular customers and work with them to create value.

RG: You have to work backward to the farm. How do you get identity-preserved crops and separate organic from nonorganic wheat, and then flour?

BR: It's a tremendous challenge. Supply chains have become more complicated over the past several years, so we've tried to partner with a handful of—family-owned, in many cases—elevator operators in Mexico, Canada, and the United States, so we can work backwards to secure the organic link.

It's been difficult so far, because of the unique characteristics of organic, which requires a field to be fallow for several years. It's slow to get started, and elevator operators and merchandisers have to have the same kind of commitment and foresight we do. Precious few have it.

RG: Historically, the relationship between the farmer and the miller, and the miller and the baker or the supermarket or the fast food operator has been an adversarial relationship: How much can I get: how little can I pay? Has that changed?

BR: Slowly. The more far-sighted customers are beginning to understand they need more certainty in their business. One of the largest organic users of flour was in our shop recently. They have tremendous growth opportunities but are constrained by supply. They need certainty of price and supply, so they're working with us to connect to the farms. It's a wave developing with forward-thinking companies. The survivors will have the entire supply chain covered. Our opportunity is to bring both sides together.

RG: At the same time, people want just-in-time inventory management. People keep pushing inventory management all the way back to the farmer. With six billion people now, and nine billion people projected in 2050, we have a stock management problem. When inventories are small, how do you manage a price relationship long term?

BR: No one's figured that out, and it's a challenge for us going forward. Some of the answer involves the traditional commodity merchandising system that we have in the United States, which is starting to unwind a bit. In Colorado, we're working with farms looking to get into niche businesses. They dedicate certain amounts of product for us, if we have customers with whom we have that just-in-time relationship.

RG: Do you think that consumers will pay a premium for these unique products?

BR: We want farmers to have better opportunities. Farmers need better opportunities to put more money in their pockets.

RG: Some firms are developing joint ventures; for example, Cargill will partner with a poultry company and a feed company to make sure that the ingredients for that chicken are always there. Do you see joint ventures with, say, cooperatives or others for your firm in the future?

BR: We already do. We can't be all things to all people. We have certain expertise, but not in merchandising. So in our first joint venture, we partnered with farmers to grow and store IP grain on our behalf. They're also an investor with us in one of our mills—which I daresay is a model for the future.

RG: Looking at the end consumer, many of your competitors are working with consumer-oriented companies to align future strategies. Are you doing that?

BR: We're a big small company with a thousand customers, and are busy identifying our top one hundred customers. That process involves identifying customers who are innovative, have specialty products, interesting ideas, and are willing to work with us.

We also have large customers, who can't afford the R&D that used to be taken for granted, but has been pushed back on us. That's created a much more open dialogue.

RG: Given the genetic revolution that's taking place, how do you see genetics and R&D responding to these unique demands?

BR: It's going to revolutionize our business. Wheat has been a laggard— and we're primarily a wheat miller—but will likely get the same genetic attention other commodities have had. Flour has been a traditional carrier for a lot of nutrients and vitamins and supplements over the years, so I see a genetic opportunity that will extend what's already being done.

RG: You talk about your relationship with producers in Mexico and Canada and the globalization of our industry. How do you see your firm competing in that global environment going forward?

BR: The world's getting smaller, and while we've primarily been in the States, we're selling products across North America and into the Caribbean and Central America. We're slowly but surely going abroad. I know the various players in Canada and Mexico and Europe, and a lot of them are from like-minded, private companies.

RG: Even though we have huge companies, the food business is a people business. Does being the president of a family firm get you more opportunity to work with these companies?

BR: Absolutely. It's a key differentiator. My phone calls are returned. We get the attention of the top people at firms when I go out on the road with folks to make calls. As a private company we can attract folks because of the culture we have as a company. Continuity matters.

Large public companies with milling divisions often have a revolving management door. If you have that, you lose continuity. Our customers like knowing who's at the other end of the phone.

RG: At the same time, you're competing with firms that have stock options and can provide global experiences for people. How do you compete with larger public firms in the labor market?

BR: We've been forced to confront that as our company has grown larger and become more complicated. Funnily enough, I can remember, as a young man, reading a book about salesmanship that my dad produced when he was at the Harvard Business School. In those days, the philosophy was to hire the whole man, and the expectation was, a person would work his eight or ten hours a day, and be committed to keeping the company's flag waving. In a generation, that's been turned completely upside down, and we've been forced to evolve.

We need to stay current in terms of our financial reward system, while playing to the advantages we have as a private company in terms of continuity, and having much more responsibility to create an upward curve for young employees who want to have an immediate impact on our business. That's helped us attract talented employees over the years. It's a continually evolving story. But I don't see us changing our private nature. At the end of the day, it's a tremendous advantage

RG: As a fourth-generation family firm, you have brothers and sisters and aunts and uncles and cousins and so forth. How do you manage that aspect of your firm?

BR: That's becoming more of a concern, but in a positive way. We've taken for granted that there'd be a next generation ready to step up, and, thankfully, there is. But they have to compete for jobs in an ever-changing industry. So we're developing systems to identify individuals with the appetite and ability to compete for jobs over time. It's a delicate balance, because we need to retain the continuity of a next generation with the realities of a business that needs the best minds possible to succeed going forward.

RG: One of your competitors is Cargill, which is a huge family-owned firm, uses a sort of phantom stock that's valued every year so they can reward their employees, and then, when they leave the company or retire, they can cash in their stock. Do you have anything like that?

BR: We do. In fact, it's exactly the same. It's matched up to align shareholder interests with management and, quite frankly, has been very successful in attracting candidates from among many companies, including a couple of Cargill's best and brightest.

RG: You talked about constantly renewing your people and improving their opportunities within the company. Many of your competitors have internal training programs. Do you have such a program?

BR: We're a big small company, and one of our disadvantages is we're not blessed with layers of staff to do a lot of internal training. We rely on outside programs to renew and teach our people.

RG: Another unique feature of your company is that you're in Quincy, Massachusetts. Most of the industry grew out of the wheat belt. How do you manage that?

BR: We think it's an advantage. We have the expertise needed to follow the markets, but we're not distracted by what's happening daily in the commodity markets.

We got our start in Boston, not as merchandisers but as marketers. We were brokers. Our DNA started in Boston and continues in Boston. As brokers, we identify opportunities for our customers. We're not hung up on the price of wheat every day. More important, Massachusetts has a lot of commercial and academic vigor, and offers wonderful recruiting opportunities.

RG: Historically, this industry has suffered from excess capacity, and therefore very thin margins. In some cases, if you were profitable one year, you were unprofitable the next year because everybody fought for market share. Is that changing?

BR: Somewhat. We've had a tremendous shakeout the last several years. Whether you're small or large, you have to make money to grow and prosper. We're getting a new kind of executive, even in the milling divisions of the larger companies. They're well versed in economics and business strategy.

Everyone's identifying their own strategy, deciding where to pare back and where to compete. I'm not saying we won't go back into boom-and-bust cycles, but for now, people are focused on how to differentiate themselves and how to make some money.

RG: So you're optimistic about the future?

BR: Very optimistic.

RG: Are family firms still exiting the business?

BR: Sadly, yes. A recurring theme here is my rose-colored optimism. We see that as an opportunity to grow our business, retain the culture of those that exited, and hopefully join forces and grow as they choose to exit. A lot of people haven't done the work needed to attract the next generation or they haven't differentiated their products enough to compete in the marketplace.

RG: What is it in your background, your training, and your upbringing that's affected how you view the business today and in the future?

BR: I have many answers, and they've evolved over the years. I came into the business by default, wanting to do anything but be in the family business. When I did come in, I was shocked by how interesting it was and how challenging it could be. As my interest grew, my thirst for education grew, which helped me appreciate how unique it was to be in a business as basic and as important as food.

So it was serendipitous at first. As I've grown older and understood the challenges, and what my basic makeup was, I came to realize that my background and interests positioned me naturally to get involved with management. That requires some skill sets I'd always taken for granted—being far-sighted, being interested in the sciences, being interested in people, having a well-rounded grasp of economics.

I woke up one day and said, You know, I'm in a very special place with a very special opportunity. I enjoy the business every day, and I enjoy bringing people into the business and trying to make Bay State grow and prosper, and position it so a fifth generation can be identified to sustain this wonderful opportunity.

RG: We're very fortunate to have men of your caliber and sensitivity in our industry. Thanks very much, Brian.

BR: Thank you, Ray.

GEORGE WESTON

Chairman and CEO, Associated British Foods (2010)

Chairman and CEO of his family's Associated British Foods, the largest food conglomerate in the United Kingdom, George Weston manages vertically integrated commodity operations in agriculture, textiles, food, and beverages, as well as Primark, a very successful retail clothing business. The company has extensive operations throughout the world, including China and Africa. A head office of five senior managers including Weston actively links the otherwise independent businesses together. Weston recognized that ABF's future in the food and clothing business required an understanding of the changing consumer in both industries, as well as a range of national and international governmental bodies. The consumer not only wanted quality but also fair treatment of all those involved in the vertical supply chain. When a catastrophic fire occurred in the Bangladesh factory producing some of the clothes he carried, ABF was the only firm that took care of each individual family affected. Weston's tough-mindedness in treating bribery-minded individuals in both public and private positions has set a positive example to both industries.[5]

RG: George Weston is CEO of Associated British Foods, one of the largest food companies in England and Europe and also one of the largest clothing companies. When you look at your company over the next five to ten years, what are the biggest challenges and why?

GW: We have two or three division-related opportunities and challenges to meet. In the sugar businesses, we have the challenge of developing agricultural practices in the northeast of China. In Africa, we have the challenges of operating and expanding in that continent. In our yeast business, we have a new global competitor emerging from China.

More generally, we're in a world that's changing quickly and we have to be very adaptable over the next five years. The last area is the clothing business, where there are great opportunities to expand throughout Europe.

RG: Those are four very challenging opportunities and problems. Let's take one at a time. Most people look at China as their future, because it's one-third of the world's GNP and growing more rapidly than anywhere else. It's difficult to work with small-scale agriculture that isn't prepared to use more modern farming methods. What luck have you had, if any, and how can you build on those successes?

GW: We were lucky to learn from an old manager of one of our yeast factories that a large part of the sugar industry in northeast China was bankrupt, and that the state was looking to sell it. We bought half the factories in the northeast of China over a two-month period, which immediately gave us a very big platform, and challenges commensurate with the scale we'd taken on.

Our second piece of luck was that the national government and the state government of Beijing wanted to do something with the sugar industry and with agricultural processing more generally. As a major sugar beet producer in Europe, we were welcomed into the region more openly than we would have been a few years earlier.

RG: How difficult is it to get good managers and educate the producers to change?

GW: There are good Chinese managers, but as a company we've done a poor job of hiring over the past twenty years. I don't think we realized how important it was until fairly recently.

We never established relationships with universities and HR companies, and we focused too much on English-language skills amongst Chinese nationals, so we frequently picked the wrong people for management jobs. We're getting better at all three, and now have the scale and capability to do what we should have been doing all along. We're good at taking a Chinese sugar mill or a Chinese yeast factory and improving it based on our own know-how.

The agricultural piece is much harder. One of our factories in the Northeast buys sugar from forty thousand growers, all of whom we're trying to persuade to grow sugar beets and grow differently from how they've grown them in the past. That's a big task. We went down a blind alley on this and chose the wrong scale of agricultural equipment to introduce.

We finally got onto small-scale tractors suitable for small-scale farms, but we started off with John Deeres imported from the United States that we couldn't even get down the roads and through the gates. We shouldn't have had to learn that lesson, but we did.

Our effectiveness in influencing the political environment has been mixed. In Beijing and in the provinces and, most importantly, at a regional and county level, we don't instinctually understand the politics. At the county level, we don't understand the loyalties and how things really get done.

We're getting better at it, and perhaps more trusted at the county level. But very often we've gone into a particular area, for example, in Heilongjiang, with the blessing of the governor but not the local mayor. But it's the mayor who determines whether you get your allocation of fertilizer and everything else you need to get the job done. We're learning, but if we'd had our time over again and known what we know now, we would've done a better job.

RG: Can you identify a young man or woman on the production side who could be a model for what you hope the others would be like?

GW: We're very good at doing that in Europe. We pride ourselves in taking people off the factory floor and from different parts of the operation, identifying their talent and turning them into something more than we started with. We're not good at it in China, and until we have that cadre of senior Chinese leadership, we'll remain poor at it. So the answer is no. We have another group, university graduates. We're now taking fifty graduate and postgraduate men and women annually into the business and training them. It'll take them five years to get into positions of real influence in the company. They'll form the basis of the management of the company in the future, but not just yet.

RG: That seems like a long haul.

GW: It does, and an expensive haul too. But we do have knowledge and skills that the Chinese sugar industry needs and I think we're right that China will want to produce more of its own sugar, and that sugar will come from sugar beet, not sugar cane. It'll take time.

RG: I was just going to ask you, what is the timeline you're imagining?

GW: We'll have a nicely profitable business in five years. In ten, it'll be great, and in twenty, it'll be a core of our worldwide sugar business.

RG: Comparing Africa to your Asian experience, is it farther along or farther behind?

GW: It's much more sophisticated than China. It's a sugar cane business established a number of years ago. I remember, again, being critical of a man from Booker for establishing sugar factories on a scale that was inappropriate for the agriculture in the area, but we now own that sugar factory, so I've had to change my tune a bit.

It is plantation agriculture on a huge scale. The Zambian operation is a large sugar factory surrounded by thirty thousand hectares of cane. It's very efficient. Cane yields in Zambia are significantly higher than they are in Brazil.

RG: Corruption in Africa has been a difficult problem. How do you overcome it?

GW: You don't start. You build a reputation for never taking the shortcut that corruption seems to offer. Paying a bribe is a route to nowhere. Having said that, you do need to make friends locally and at a national level. You can do both in a noncorrupt manner.

We're also very patient. We'll sit in a government office waiting for weeks and weeks if necessary to get a stamp allowing us to do something. Everyone knows there's no point asking us for a brown paper bag full of money, because we'll never pay it.

RG: What's the timeline in Africa compared to Asia?

GW: It's slow. Physical development, building a factory, can be done reasonably quickly. But setting yourself up in the first place can take a long, long time.

RG: You're very patient.

GW: Working in Africa in a commercially sustainable way takes patience. You've got to set yourself up right in the first instance. And that takes time.

RG: How did you get started in clothing?

GW: Having clothing retail paired with food retailing is less unusual than having clothing retail paired with sugar manufacturing. The general answer is we had food retail and we subsequently sold it and held onto clothing. It's evolved and it's always been supported, because it's always been successful. ABF has never believed in a single core. We support management teams and businesses that do well. And Primark was first amongst them.

RG: One of your other businesses has been flour milling. Where are you there today?

GW: We have flour mills in two countries and a share of a flour mill in a third. We mill flour in the United Kingdom, but primarily for our own bread production. We have an integrated supply chain in our bakery business, which works well. We mill flour in Australia. I got my start there. We're probably second or third there now, entirely for the domestic market.

We also have a share in a Chinese flour mill that came along with our yeast business when we bought that. It makes money, so we leave it alone.

RG: Where do you stand with your feed manufacturing business?

GW: That's been a very successful business. It began as a way of adding value to the coproduct from sugar. Sugar beet feed is a good dairy feed. We have an enzyme business in Finland where we've developed a number of molecules that are relevant to the animal feed industry. Our feed business in China combines our knowledge of how to feed pigs with our knowledge of good feed safety disciplines, both of which have relevance in China.

RG: You also have proprietary brands at the bakery level. Is that integrated with your flour milling?

GW: Yes, probably since the mid-1960s. My grandfather was a Canadian who brought North American flour to the United Kingdom to make bread. In the 1960s he bought flour mills in the UK to process EU-sourced wheat, and we've been flour millers ever since. The bakery businesses in the UK and Australia are both important to us.

RG: Twenty years from now, what will the company look like?

GW: There are two big uncertainties. One is a big series of bets, and the other one requires no sudden commitment. The big bets are around sugar in Africa and China. We're well positioned in both regions to expand our businesses substantially. If we're successful, ABF will have a much larger proportion of its whole in sugar.

The second one is back to clothing. Our expansion into Europe has been startlingly successful. It has the potential, even with the growth of sugar, to swamp the rest of the company. It would be odd if a company called Associated British Foods had 70 percent of its business in clothing. So if it succeeds, we'd likely have ABF being just food and Primark in another vehicle somewhere.

In our consumer sector, Twinings and Ovaltine are two brands with great international positions and great potential. I hope in twenty years, we'll have a very substantial hot beverages businesses established in markets we're just developing at the moment—China, Brazil, Nigeria, and other parts of the world too. A great ambition is to continue growing the Twinings brand in the United States, where it's always had more potential than sales until now.

RG: Mazola oil is another commodity you've been working on. Where does that fit into your picture?

GW: We established a retail grocery platform in the United States and Mazola is the largest part of it, though we have a number of other grocery brands—Argo corn starch, and we also have corn syrup brands and spices. It's probably subscale as a business, but it's sustainable because our branded positions are very strong, even if they're in quite small categories. We like strong category positions and would much rather have a strong category position in a small category than a weak position in a large category.

RG: Where are you in the ingredient business?

GW: We have two ingredients businesses in very different places. We're a serious player in yeast and bakery ingredients, probably second globally to Lesaffre. There's good growth potential for both yeast and also other ingredients that you sell to bakers. We've got a lot of good technology and a great route to market through the yeast distribution channels.

We've got a fair amount to prove in the enzyme business and the yeast extract business. We've invested quite heavily, firstly in Finland and building new capacity in China in the yeast extract business. We're probably the world's largest producer of medium-chain triglycerides, a business that's done well for a number of years. I don't think specialty ingredients are as significant a part of our future as we once thought they would be.

RG: Companies are highly dependent on leadership. Given your background, where do you think your strengths and weaknesses reside, and how do you see your personal leadership evolving over time?

GW: ABF is an unusual company. We look like a conglomerate, but we're really not. Leaving aside Primark, which is a special case, there's a fair degree of sophistication in our business model. In the food group we've got consumer businesses, commodity processing businesses, and specialty ingredients businesses. You look at them and ask, What's the advantage of having them all together? There is one. It's the input from the center, where there are five of us who form the management team and try to enrich thinking and the experience of our business leaders around the world.

That takes a lot of travel; it takes a lot of time. Growing up with the company, I know these businesses well and think I can contribute to management thinking in them.

The other thing that makes ABF an unusual conglomerate is that we work really hard to link the pieces together. Joint purchasing, joint HR, joint experience sharing are central to how we work. The five of us in the center are always linking up the different parts of the group.

Someone in the company said to me, ABF is unusual in that the company manages to be very entrepreneurial and yet at the same time very collaborative. If I can add something to that spirit of collaboration whilst at the same time ensuring that people think that their job is to promote the success of the part of the company they're running, that's great.

We're a family-controlled company, so I play an unusually big ambassadorial role. I travel a lot to see what our people are doing. I'm not advising them to any great extent, but am showing my face as the representative not only of the company but of the family for whom they all work.

RG: Thanks very much, George.

HUGH GRANT
Chairman and CEO, Monsanto Company (2006)

Chairman and CEO of Monsanto, Hugh Grant led Monsanto's transformation from industrial chemicals and pharmaceuticals to agriculture, biotechnology, and seeds. Monsanto's success depends on how effectively the company partners with farmers and those using what the farmers produce in their consumer products. Grant's career has involved working with small- and large-scale producers in developing and developed countries. Monsanto has partnerships with most of the world's research universities. A Scotsman, Grant worked on farms growing up and has a degree in agricultural zoology and molecular biology from the University of Glasgow.[6]

RG: Hugh Grant is chairman and CEO of the Monsanto Company, which has been transformed from a chemical company into a genetic and seed company. How did that happen? How do you create a revolution and change a whole company, culture-wise, focus-wise, technology-wise?

HG: Looking back, change always seems more gradual and planned than it really was. For Monsanto, this began between 1980 and 1985 when we stopped investing in pesticide research, so the front end was the shift in our R&D spend. Our rationale was that chemistry alone wouldn't generate the yield increases we needed. We bet the farm that genetically improved seeds would be more effective than the traditional pesticide view of the previous sixty or so years. That was the first big shift. More recently, we've moved to a business exclusively focused on agriculture and largely dependent on seed.

RG: Although it's largely dependent on seed, you consider the consumer as well as the farmer as your ultimate customer. Why do you do that?

HG: Common sense. From 1996 to 2006 our business was controlling weeds and bugs. But the next wave will be consumer driven. The macro trends include things like heart health—healthier oils and improved protein and amino acids. We also have micro trends at the consumer level. There are long R&D cycle times, say, seven years from investment to product delivery, so reading the consumer is really important. We've done a reasonable job, but there's more to do.

RG: Consumer trends have been rather dramatic. Nutrition is now at the forefront of how people look at food. Consumers want food to taste good, but they want it to be good for them. The genetic revolution indicates that the immune systems of plants, animals, and humans are quite similar, and that in order to protect the well-being of all three and the environment, you need to deeply understand genetics. How does Monsanto educate not just itself, but society and industry?

HG: That's a big question. If you take traditional plant breeding—forget biotechnology—the industry and Monsanto now have a street map for corn, soy, and a number of vegetables. Once you have that, you've got an intimate understanding of what makes that crop tick. The breeder has an algorithm based on a statistical insight into what two crosses will yield and what the offspring will look like. We're seeing more focus on nutritional targets like reduced trans fats in crops. In the future, tailoring nutrition to a specific animal species will be a commercial reality.

RG: You're going to have to revolutionize the distribution system as well.

HG: Yes, it's something we've talked about often—the relationships, the networks, and the connectivity within the chain, because it literally starts with a farmer planting a seed in the spring, and it goes all the way through to a bowl of breakfast cereal. There needs to be an economic premium.

RG: Distribution companies like Whole Foods do get a premium. They're willing to pay a premium to provide that uniqueness or that particular attribute for their customer base. You have to partner with a lot of different people. Whom do you partner with, and how does that work?

HG: We're not experts, but frankly nobody is. Creating value beyond the underlying commodity is the oil that lubricates the system. A small example is relationships with ADM, Bunge, Cargill, and Dreyfus in Latin America. They manage the interface with the grower, and often are the middleman in connecting the food companies. The first step is doing something that really adds value. When the farmer puts the seed in the ground, is there an expectation that the crop he harvests will be worth more? If the answer is yes, then relationships are easier to form.

RG: Do you deal with branded food companies and retailers more often than you ever dreamed you would?

HG: Yes. Our challenge goes back to our origin as a chemical company that sold a gallon jug of a product that kills weeds. Over the past several years, we've found ourselves in the corner offices of major food companies talking about future opportunities. They aren't simply CEO to CEO. They're technology-to-technology and fieldsman-to-fieldsman discussions. It's two different industries. Our cycle times are seven years; their cycle times are often scanner data over bar code data over one weekend. Our strength is on issues that need real technological solutions, and that's a longer-term conversation.

RG: My students have a love-hate relationship with Monsanto. They love the fact that new technology will make a difference to the well-being of the world, to the environment, to the health and nutrition of animals and human beings. But they're very fearful that your very success is primarily a one-company success. They're worried that Monsanto "controls the world." How do you answer that?

HG: I hear it—control the world and global domination—I heard it a lot more ten years ago than I hear now.

RG: Really? They think you have a monopoly on germplasm, a monopoly of knowledge in genetic technology, a monopoly on your relationships, that somehow you don't have competition. Do you have competition?

HG: Certainly. Every spring a farmer decides what bets he's going to place and runs a controlled experiment. In the developed world, if he's wrong, the bank gets angry. In the emerging economies, if he's wrong, his family goes hungry. We license the technology to about 220 mom-and-pops, and use it to leverage the brand because farmers shop. The myth is we've got an enormous germplasm share. We've got good share, but at the end of the day, the farmer selects based on the performance of individual seed. You can't force farmers to do anything they don't want to do.

RG: The farmer has a choice.

HG: Yes, absolutely. The selection of seed is very personal. The farmer decides not just what he's buying for the farm, but what he buys field by field—decisions spread across two hundred or so seed companies in the US.

RG: One of the other complaints we hear from this generation is concern about contamination and comingling. We had the Starlink case about contamination from pollen drift. How do you address that?

HG: I hear this more. Ten years ago the focus was food safety: Can I eat this? Science has prevailed on that, and ten years on it's biodiversity. There's a ton of research about [how] far pollen travels, particularly corn pollens. Does corn blow? Absolutely. Farmers grow popcorn right alongside regular corn, and the pollen blows between the two. Popcorn is worth a lot more—it puts the kids through college—so he separates them both spatially and temporally.

RG: You've always welcomed legislation that enables the consumer and producer to have a choice and to improve the knowledge about making that choice. Why is it so difficult for Europeans to embrace the genetic revolution?

HG: The straight answer is I don't know. Food is different in Europe. It's like an alternative religion, number one. Number two, there is no European regulatory standard across the whole community. Number three, ten years ago they lived through mad cow disease, and consumers lost an enormous amount of trust in government and in regulatory agencies. I'm optimistic because some of these heart-healthy oils and products offer direct and tangible consumer benefits.

RG: The new food system is a convergence of many different systems. Where does energy fit into your view of Monsanto's future?

HG: Energy is important. We've got a strong position in bioethanol, and we're looking at biodiesel. We ran the maps backwards through history and discovered varieties that aren't great for food processing but have very high sugar levels for bioethanol. Our approach has focused on genetics.

RG: Some people talk about alternative crops to corn and sugar cane, like switchgrass, that could produce some form of ethanol more effectively. How do you answer those queries?

HG: I've heard a lot about switchgrass, and I don't see it. The golden chalice in the long term is cellulosic production, which can be a real headache. The real question—long before switchgrass becomes a reality—is how corn competes with sugar cane. Sugar cane pencils down to $30 oil. Sugar cane grows very densely on an acre, and it's a perennial. You just cut it, wait for some rain and sunshine, and it grows again. Corn versus cane is a much livelier debate than corn versus switchgrass.

RG: How do you see Monsanto ten years from now?

HG: We invest on a seven-year horizon and have a board of directors that's comfortable most of the time with that horizon, and most of the time with investing exclusively in agriculture. We're spending about $1.5 million a day on agricultural research, which isn't a lot by pharmaceutical standards, but it's a whole bunch by farm standards. In five to ten years, we'll continue to be driven by the value created in the biotechnology of seed, and its performance. Farmers will buy great-performing seed. We're going to deliver more and more value to consumers, and the visibility of that value in heart health and healthier oils and improved nutrition—and ultimately, in water use—will reposition the company.

RG: Two areas that we haven't covered—fiber. Are you doing anything with fiber in terms of plastic or other kinds of fibers with respect to cotton? And finally, pharmaceuticals?

HG: Our focus in fiber has been cotton, the poor cousin behind corn and soy, probably ahead of wheat. We've started to really understand the genetics of cotton, and have been able to improve fiber length and strength. The genetic gain in many of these crops is 1.5 percent a year. We've seen that improving by three times or four times where you've got a genetic street map.

RG: What about pharmaceuticals? Is that a far reach? Will we produce pharmaceuticals in a greenhouse with plants?

HG: We exited pharmaceuticals. It's one of the first things I did. The technology is phenomenal. The science is there. The capability and capacity are there, but it's extraordinarily expensive. It will come, but we need to redefine how value is captured so the technology company shares the margin on the end product.

RG: What kind of people are you going to need in the future? Are they going to be like you? Are they going to be different, and if so, how?

HG: They're going to be different, which is the most fascinating piece of the puzzle. The molecular biologists of the next generation are now in high school. This is a very young industry. Successful leaders in the future will be comfortable with extreme ambiguity. Their effectiveness will depend as much on their scientific expertise as their ability to manage networks and build relationships with stakeholders outside their direct scientific sphere. Very often a professional scientist adores his piece of the puzzle and has no interest in anything else. That won't be acceptable in the next generation. The last piece is that the amazing benefits of these technologies can't be limited to the first world. Successful leaders in the future will be comfortable engaging with both Wall Street and NGOs to extend these technologies to Africa and India, where the economic return may not be evident, but the societal benefits are clear. That's not a business profile that exists today. Future leaders, those fifteen-year-olds, are going to be conversant with that world to an extent we can't imagine.

RG: You are the change-maker in a company that is a change-making institution. What drives you? Is it your Scottish background? Is it something from your experience at Monsanto? What is it that drives you to want to make sure that Monsanto performs in a way that benefits society?

HG: It's a strange cocktail there! It's hard for me to trace that path back, but there are a handful of experiences that shaped my thinking. I grew up on a small island. My wife's and my focus was to travel to experience other cultures and see how other people live. There are many more Scots outside Scotland than inside. From an early stage, I had a passion and curiosity about the rest of the world. I'd worked on farms as a kid and was always intrigued by them. It crystallized for me in Asia where you see farming in the raw: people living quite well on two acres, but working very hard. The epiphany was a big one, the realization that what we're doing really mattered—not in the fluffy sense of "feeding the world," but in making a real difference. I was in northern Thailand where women run the farms and make the decisions. I met a bunch of women and, through a translator, focused on weed control. Their feedback was, No, no, no, the real benefit here is we walk home in daylight and spend time with our children. We get more time with our kids and cook meals with them. Those three or four years illuminated how our Midwest company touches the world.

RG: That's a wonderful prospect and a wonderful value system. Thank you very much.

ERLING LORENTZEN
Chairman, The African Forestry Economic Development Program (2014)

Chairman of the African Forestry Economic Development Program based in Ghana, Erling Lorentzen was the founder and CEO of Aracruz Celulose, which created the largest renewable forest in the world in Brazil. Lorentzen got the global forestry industry to agree to an impartial scientific study to see if the dioxin used by the paper industry was harmful to plants, animals, or humans, and if so, to stop using it. He found a well-respected but neutral group to do the analysis. His leadership led more global industrial groups to appreciate the value of impartial assessments. After retiring from Aracruz, Lorentzen moved to Ghana, where he used his forestry expertise to boost the economy by developing biomass sources for energy. Lorentzen's forestry operations in Brazil and Ghana set examples of how reforestation can improve both the economy and the environment. He was a resistance fighter during World War II and is an alumnus of the Harvard Business School.[7]

RG: Erling Lorentzen is a leader in economic development around the world and currently chairman of the African Forestry Economic Development Program in Ghana. My first question involves dioxin in the forestry and paper industry and your work to determine whether dioxin was harmful to the environment and to people. You decided that the study needed an independent third party to review the material. Could you explain that?

EL: The forest industry as a whole on the national basis was being criticized and had no way of explaining itself. If the industry presented its own case, you might as well tear it up. We needed a totally independent study that evaluated the dioxin issue from multiple angles—industry, forest, pulp, paper, and recycling.

RG: How did you find an independent firm that had both the scientific capacity and the independence needed?

EL: That's quite interesting. I thought I'd find the people in a university, particularly a German university, as the issue at the time was particularly critical in Germany. But I was advised that universities only respond with what you want them to say.

RG: That's very sad.

EL: I gave up on universities and found a group in England, the International Institute for Environment and Development (IIED). I said I wanted a totally independent study on the whole sector, the whole question from forest to trees to paper to waste. I needed money for the study and, among others, met with the Norwegian president, Gro Brundtland. She asked, How can we guarantee that the study is independent? I told her I was going to London the next day to sign a contract with the president of [the] IIED and she said, Then you are in good hands. You have [the] support of the Norwegian government.

RG: How did you get the industry to agree to whatever the result of the study would be and to act accordingly? How did you get them to agree to do whatever the report says no matter what it said?

EL: It wasn't a question of whether the industry would like it or not. I needed the support of my own company. Although I was chairman and had started the company, I took it up with my board. One of the board members asked, How can you guarantee this study is going to go in our favor? I said, It's just as important for this board to know what is wrong and right, so the study has to be totally independent. I got the support I needed.

RG: What was the final result of the study?

EL: The study took all the positives and the negatives of the industry and one of the principal conclusions was that the world needs to plant more trees.

RG: But the conclusion also said that dioxin was harmful.

EL: We, Aracruz, invested $100 million in the problem and after a while came to the conclusion that there was no problem.

RG: Turning to the future, how did you get interested in trying to do for Africa what you did for Latin America? And why?

EL: I resigned the chairmanship of my own company—I didn't own it but had created it—in 2004 after forty years. I'd gathered experience that could be of value in other places, especially Africa. Finding countries where I could utilize my experience took me a little while, because corruption was a problem in some of the countries I visited. I'd started my business life in Brazil by saying that if corruption is necessary, forget me. Corruption was very, very much part of the first two countries I visited in Africa. Then some friends introduced me to Ghana where I ended up working. I've worked there now for over seven years and there hasn't been one question of corruption. I'm happy to do something of value for a country, in this case, Ghana. It's a basic philosophy.

RG: What progress have you been able to achieve thus far?

EL: I'm working on two projects. My original idea was to create a correct legal basis for others to work out further. I've gone further with another project, because I felt that electric energy is the basis for development. People need electricity for most everything. You can see statistically how electricity generates growth. Some electricity, for instance, in Ghana, is created with fossil fuels, and that's expensive. So with my friends, I worked through the complications and the bureaucracy and started on a biomass-powered, electric plant. I'm very happy with the progress. I'm not 100 percent happy but we're very close to being able to start a power plant project. In the meantime, we're developing a eucalyptus plantation. We've completed testing for the right type of eucalyptus for energy and the right spacing of the trees and are carefully looking for the right way to plant. I worked with Aracruz to develop eucalyptus for cellulose, but eucalyptus trees for energy are different. We're now ready with four thousand hectares.

RG: What will the eventual size of this forest operation be?

EL: We've already planted four thousand hectares and are building five to six per year over a five-year period. When some people hear we're going to burn the annual crop, they react, but I have no problem with environmental ashes burnt. The crop regrows all the time, and we power a sixty-megawatt plant. The net CO_2 of the project becomes neutral, and we have a substitute for fossil fuel.

RG: Does the Ghanaian government approve of what you're doing?

EL: They're very anxious to see this happen, and give us a lot of support. There are other parts of government that we have to go through a process. I have to be sure I'll get paid when we sell our power. Who should guarantee that is now being analyzed, because the electricity company itself isn't adequate from a financial point of view. The payment guarantee from the government has to be higher up.

RG: I assume there's a shortage of power in·the country.

EL: Yes, there's a tremendous shortage and a large part of the energy consumption is based on fossil fuel. Practically every house has an extra generator. There are blackouts all the time.

RG: Do you have people opposing your program?

EL: I can't think of anybody. I've met with Kofi Annan, who is Ghanaian as you know, and he's very much in favor. So is the president of Ghana. The first time I saw him, he said, I wish I had four Erling Lorentzens.

RG: That's quite a compliment. At the end of the day, do you feel that this will be a model that others will follow?

EL: Exactly. We want to demonstrate that this is a way to solve problems. One of the most important aspects is that we'll be needing four thousand to five thousand employees for the first phase. That's very satisfying.

RG: You're improving the environment, you're improving employment, you're improving energy, and you're improving economic development.

EL: This is an economic development model, which can be replicated in many African countries. They all need energy.

RG: You've changed another part of the world, made it more environmentally sound and economically prosperous. What would you like to see this look like in ten years?

EL: Ten years from now? You know, I'm not a spring chicken. But I want to see that the world becomes more realistic in its attempt to solve our environmental, economic, and social problems. I don't think it will ever happen, but we can make a lot of improvements over the next ten years.

RG: You've given us a wonderful model and, as per usual, provided leadership the world desperately needs. I can't thank you enough, Erling.

EL: Thank you, Ray.

SHELDON LAVIN
CEO, OSI Group (2015)

As CEO of OSI Inc., Sheldon Lavin operates one of the largest suppliers of beef, poultry, pork, and fish in the world. OSI began supplying hamburger meat to McDonald's in 1955 and they remain their largest supplier. The relationship to this day relies on a handshake rather than a contract and the ongoing commitment to product improvement by both parties. Lavin is a lawyer by training, who is committed to preserving the decision-making benefits of keeping OSI private well into the future.

RG: Sheldon Lavin chairs the board of the OSI Group. Could we start by having you explain what OSI does?

SL: OSI Group is a vertically integrated company focused primarily on proteins. We have approximately sixty business units around the world with facilities in sixteen countries serving over forty countries. We're in the protein business—basically beef, pork, and chicken, with a little fish in a couple of countries and also a dough-based company, a company that sells prepared meals, and we do a lot of beans, salsa, and produce.

RG: McDonald's has a method of relating to long-term suppliers, domestically and globally. You're one of their biggest suppliers.

SL: Yes, probably their biggest in protein. It's been sixty years now. We supplied the hamburger patties for their very first store in Des Planes, Illinois, in 1955. That tells you how long we've been there.

RG: It's my understanding you have no written contract.

SL: No, we don't. Everything is by handshake and has been for over sixty years.

RG: Given your long-term relationship, do you sit down with senior executives at McDonald's and develop strategies together?

SL: We work very closely together—not so much on their long-term strategy of the company, although I've been involved in strategic discussions over the years. I've known every CEO and been pretty good friends with all of them. We focus on innovation. In areas like food safety, we meet often.

RG: Do you have joint R&D activities, and do you develop specialty products for them?

SL: Yes. For example, in 1983 or so, we developed the McRib in conjunction with Iowa State University, which made a special plate for us. We've developed a lot of things over the years.

RG: Nutritionists are concerned about meat consumption. How does that affect McDonald's and how does that affect you?

SL: Years ago I was part owner of some local banks in Chicago and we had a very famous woman doctor, a pediatrician, on one of our boards. We were talking about what to eat and what not to eat and she said anything that tastes good is bad for you, but anything you eat in moderation is okay. I never forgot that statement. We're seeing requests for different flavors mostly from millennials, who seem to have different tastes. I see that even among my grandchildren. They're very different today than we were.

RG: In what way are they different?

SL: They're more conscious about what they're eating. They eat meat, but they're very picky. I have a grandson in California who makes his own food, because he wants dinner made a certain way. They don't eat a lot of sweets and are much more conscious of organic foods and foods that don't have an overabundance of salt or sugar. They draw their own conclusions.

RG: Does this group affect your business or not?

SL: They impact the fast food business. Everybody including McDonald's is trying to develop products that appeal to millennials. There's clearly an impact on the food industry right now—not sales so much as the necessity to develop products which appeal to them. That's a big group from eighteen to thirty-five.

RG: Years ago McDonald's tried veggie burgers and was unsuccessful.

SL: Interestingly, country clubs generally have a veggie burger on at lunch.

RG: When you look at your company, do you vertically integrate back to the grower or just contract with them?

SL: We do both. In the United States we have poultry companies in South Carolina and Maryland where we grow larger poultry. In Europe, we have five beef abattoirs. Farmers bring the animals to the slaughtering site. In China we're growing and slaughtering about 80 million chickens a year. We'll be boosting that to about 180 million. In China we own the farms too. In the US we supervise and contract the farms, but don't own them.

RG: Is it difficult to get managers of farms in a country like China?

SL: We've been blessed with some very good people, including a lot of original staff from when we started twenty-four years ago. We haven't had too many problems with people.

RG: As I recall, you had to teach Chinese farmers to grow lettuce and tomatoes, because you didn't have a supply of them.

SL: Yes. We got into the produce business quite a few years ago, and now grow our own vegetables in China or contract for them.

RG: Success in the fast food industry, especially for a company like McDonald's, seems highly dependent on long-term relationships.

SL: Fred Turner—Ray Kroc's first grill man in the first store—was the second in command at McDonald's and really grew the company when Ray stepped back. Fred coined the phrase "three-legged stool," meaning the corporation, the franchisees, and the suppliers all have to be functioning properly to succeed. That's been the go-to phrase ever since.

RG: Are you publicly traded?

SL: We're not publicly traded, Ray. You go public for two basic reasons— first, to liquify your assets, or second, you need money. I don't have to liquify my assets right now, and we're fortunate to have a syndicate of banks that finance us at very comfortable rates.

RG: The continuity of family firms is important for long-range planning and relationships. How do you keep the management and the family together at OSI?

SL: We have great loyalty among our people. More importantly, preparing for the future, almost thirty years ago I began a college intern program in the summer. In the first class there was a fellow who caught my eye. He was a top graduate in animal science at Iowa State. Each intern has a project and has to critique the company. In that first class, he was the only one that criticized us, so I hired him as my understudy. Today, at fifty, he's president and COO of OSI and running the business. This summer we had fifteen interns, two or three of whom were sent to Mainland China. The intern program has been a wonderful success.

RG: You've always taken a systems approach when you look at the food system, and were always consumer oriented. How do you think about the future and the changes that are going on?

SL: Change is always good, but you have to be ready for it. OSI is an old company, but we're young too. Take me out of the equation and our average employee age is probably under fifty. We have a well-equipped culinary center with talented chefs where we entertain lots of customers. We have one in China, and are opening one in Augsburg, Germany. We have a separate plant, an R&D center, maybe two miles from corporate headquarters in Aurora. We have small models of our production equipment there, so we can experiment with small batches of new products. I'd like to say we're on top of this millennial change right now, because I know some of the products we're working on.

RG: Are those new products both protein and nonprotein?

SL: Yes, both.

RG: And when you look at the food system and the changing attitudes of the millennials you're talking about, does OSI have to change a great deal?

SL: No. At OSI, we've been adapting to change all along. We see a lot through our diversified customer base and benefit from their research and development as well as our own.

RG: You have an excellent record in social enterprise and respect for the consumer and respect for the environment.

SL: Food safety too.

RG: How long have you been able to keep that leadership role, and when did you start?

SL: We intend to hold on to it forever, and we committed to those values right from the beginning.

RG: If we were having this conversation in thirty years, what will OSI look like?

SL: First of all, I won't be around, but we have very capable people in place and continue to train more. Assuming the company isn't sold, we'll be quite a bit larger. We can't slow down. I have to step back and let the younger people, as we say, "have their head."

RG: There's been a movement among the protein companies to recognize the new consumer, the younger consumer. They look at organic foods. Hormel recently purchased Applegate. As you look to the future, will you acquire companies in that space or build internally?

SL: We're starting with antibiotic-free chickens, because of customer demand. I want to accelerate our program so we can be ahead of everybody.

RG: When Cargill changed from being a trading company to a solutions company that looked forward from the consumer and backward from the producer, they changed the very nature of Cargill. OSI seems to have had that attitude right from the beginning.

SL: Right from the beginning.

RG: So all the changes we see in the food industry and how these companies are changing were part of your idea from the beginning?

SL: No question.

RG: Why were you so far ahead of your time?

SL: I'm not sure we're so far ahead. It's very different being a privately held company. We're not talking to analysts every quarter and don't have shareholders looking over our shoulders. We can do a lot of things as a private company that are more difficult as a public company.

RG: Jim Perdue talked about being antibiotic-free and also about being privately held and what that means. Do you think that private firms like yourself and Perdue will be able to stay private for the long term?

SL: At OSI, we'll move heaven and earth to stay private. If something should happen to me, and of course it will, my older son, who is vice chairman, will vote the shares. He's very close with Dave McDonald, the president. They'll run the business together with Steve as chairman and Dave as CEO. I think we're ready.

RG: In addition to being head of your company, you're on the board of Rabobank. Is that correct?

SL: The North American advisory board of Rabobank.

RG: It's a Dutch bank that came to the United States when we were having trouble. Every other bank ran away and they came and embraced American agriculture. What kind of leadership do they provide?

SL: Rabobank is a very unusual bank. They focus primarily on agriculture and don't panic when there are big commodity swings. Four years ago, the bottom fell out of the poultry industry. They came and spoke to the other banks and syndicates. The American banks are getting used to it, but they tend to panic when there's something like that.

RG: Do you think people are finally beginning to understand the food system rather than simply finding fault with it? Reading the editorial pages of many newspapers, people feel that the food system has let them down: You don't care about nutrition or the consumer. You sell sugary drinks. You advertise to children. You'd think the food system isn't a good citizen.

SL: The NGOs representing small groups make a lot of noise and the media blows it up out of proportion.

RG: So how do you counteract that so the average consumer doesn't lose faith in the food system?

SL: Some of the big companies like McDonald's are going antibiotic-free on chicken. That sounds good for the consumer, but probably only to consumers really interested in food.

RG: If the consumer wants veggie burgers or to eat less meat, you're more than willing to provide an appropriate product.

SL: There's nothing we can do. It's the consumer's choice. It's the same thing with children and obesity. If parents let kids eat anything they want, they're going to get fat. You have a choice.

RG: I can't thank you enough.

SL: Thank you, Ray.

HANS JÖHR
Corporate Director of Agriculture, Nestlé Company (2017)

As corporate director of agriculture for Nestlé, Hans Jöhr helped create the multi-stakeholder Dairy Farm Institute to address serious quality management issues in the Chinese milk industry. Jöhr heads up their "farmer connect" program, which involves 375,000 farmers who supply Nestlé with milk, coffee, and cacao products. Nestlé was asked to create the Dairy Farm Institute in China to help fix a broken dairy system. The stakeholder groups include universities in Wisconsin and China, twenty-four business firms, and two farmer cooperatives all dedicated to improving the milk system of China. The firms and the government have created a model for other commodity systems around the world. Jöhr grew up on a family farm in Switzerland, studied agriculture in school, and was a farmer in Brazil before joining Nestlé.[8]

RG: Dr. Hans Jöhr is head of agriculture for the Nestlé Company. Would you tell us about your personal background before we start so people will know a little bit about you?

HJ: I was born on a family farm in Switzerland, and studied agricultural economics in school. I wanted to become a farmer, but couldn't do that in Switzerland, because we mainly [do] gardening rather than farming. I tried to go to Canada but I didn't have enough money, so I went further south and spent twenty years in Latin America before joining Nestlé, back in Switzerland.

My big passion was always farming and being meaningfully involved in the world food system. At Nestlé, we started many activities, mainly focused on sustainability. We started the Sustainable Agriculture Initiative, which fifteen years later inspired the idea for the Dairy Farming Institute in China.

RG: Few understand the unique significance of the Dairy Farm Institute— the amount of collaboration between different parts of industry, academics in this country and China, the US government in this country and China. No one has ever tried to put so many different people in the private, public, and not-for-profit sectors together to improve a major commodity system. What do you believe the Dairy Farm Institute will accomplish? And how many people are involved in putting it together?

HJ: Nestlé has existed for about 150 years and has always been directly linked to farmers, something we now call Farmer Connect. It's in our corporate DNA. We strongly believe that linking farmers to consumers will be a competitive advantage in the future, because we know the source of the raw materials we use in the products we serve our consumers. By doing so, we earn the trust and the credibility of consumers. Very simply, we think in a totally different way when we go with food transparency and the traceability of all our raw materials.

We were pushed in China by the government to help transform the entire milk sector. Putting it in perspective, ten years ago we had thirty-six thousand smallholder milk farmers in the Chinese supply chains. We now have fewer than five hundred, and we're producing more milk. The transformation at the farm level has been monumental—the biggest farm is operating with twenty-eight thousand milking cows, and the smallest has five hundred cows. That's a totally different structure in only ten years.

Operating the business is totally different too. Our people need different skills, which is why we came up with this approach. We invested in both people and new technologies. Our people weren't fully prepared to use the new technologies, which is why we had to partner. We invited all the relevant stakeholders to work with us.

RG: In order to appreciate the enormity of the collaboration, who are some of the partners involved?

HJ: In genetics, we have the Alta-Agricorp group. For feeding, Land O'Lakes. On the buildings and farm equipment, there's a local company called East Rock. For dairy cow health technologies, we have a company called SCR. Our total solutions provider for dairy farming and milking equipment is GEA. And for dairy nutrition and health we have companies like Alltech.

Then there are the animal health and welfare companies—Elanco, Boehringer Ingelheim, Zoetis—and the academic partners like the University of Wisconsin at Madison University and the Northeast Agricultural University in China. [The] International Farm Comparison

Network from Germany helped us put all those things together. But that's just the tip of the iceberg.

RG: I've never seen companies so enthusiastic about working together. Why is there such enthusiasm for collaborating in this particular project?

HJ: Many of them are excited about this big, huge Chinese market. By partnering, you can learn more quickly and lower some risks. Partnering with highly professional people gives you a safe haven for sharing experiences. In the UK, there is the Chatham House rule, which a lot of people like, because you share information freely you normally don't get in the business world.

RG: Many people believe that the Dairy Farm Institute could be a model used all over the world. Do you agree?

HJ: It's a useful general recipe, but the ingredients are extremely local. It has to be adapted, not cloned. Over the past two years, we've taken the same approach in Latin America, beginning in Mexico without the big infrastructure of the Dairy Farming Institute, but doing it in a similar way, and it works. It also works in Brazil, but in a way that's totally different from Europe.

In Europe, we're still in silos, and don't cooperate as much as other parts of the world. The adapted model works in milk sourcing. But we believe we can also use it to source coffee and cocoa.

Coffee and cocoa are two crops produced mainly by smallholder farmers. On the African continent, over 90 percent of these crops are produced by smallholder farmers.

We organize using the DFI concept of taking the beans to cooperatives and then from cooperatives to the grinders and then from the grinders either using it locally for the next step of processing or shipping the beans to European grinders and then finally to the chocolate industry. Slowly but steadily we've extended what we learned from the value chain of milk to the value chain of chocolate beverages and other chocolate products. The key has been linking smallholder farmers in a decent way with full transparency and traceability to the market and finally to the consumer.

RG: Were the universities—Northeast in China and Wisconsin in the United States—able to develop a curriculum that effectively served all these types of people?

HJ: In general, yes, but we've adapted our model so that our business partners also send in their professionals to teach. We have a mix of good academic knowledge blended with technical training from partners that are practitioners. We take students directly to a farm to teach them outside the classroom as well. We have a unique mix of practitioners working with academics to teach the students. We're in the third year, and have put more than 2,500 students through the Dairy Farming Institute.

RG: When we have major breakthroughs in bringing people together, people often wonder whether we can evaluate the success not only commercially, but from a social, educational, and environmental point of view as well? Is anybody from the outside evaluating this?

HJ: That's a very relevant question. In measuring success, the first thing to ask is whether students are interested in what you have to offer. I'm happy to report that during [the] first three years we had 2,500 students attend and we've established a personnel base for running more professional and highly technological milk farms in China.

More importantly, we're running the farms in a very competitive environment. That means we understand our production costs and are better able to make environmental improvements, because we have to comply with local regulations. Until recently, animal health and welfare wasn't a concern in China, but that's changed. Chinese consumers—as in the United States—want to know, Do you take care of the animals? Do you feed them well? Do you follow decent standards? That's absolutely new in China, and taught for the very first time through our DFI courses. This is restoring consumer confidence in locally produced milk, which goes hand in hand with government policy.

As you know, there are many different stakeholders with many different performance indicators to evaluate. We'll analyze DFI performance using the scorecard approach with different stakeholders mapping out the indicators. This is still in the making, because it's more complex than using an accounting statement. We're evaluating this, and will definitely need external help to put the key PIs together to really measure ourselves.

RG: People are concerned that men and women may not look at agriculture as an opportunity. Do you think DFI will appeal to the younger generation?

HJ: That's a crucial question. Some years ago, Nestlé created a training program call Agripreneurship specifically designed to engage talented young people and make sure they had good reasons to stay in rural areas. Talented and educated people need to have at least the same lifestyle as in urban centers. That goes for smallholders as well as more commercial farmers. Using more technology, earning more, and having a better lifestyle are critical success factors for the DFI.

RG: The governments in China and the United States want to make sure the food system improves nutrition and environmental quality.

HJ: Governments are focused increasingly on the nexus of agriculture, nutrition, and health. The relationship between environmental and human health is increasingly acknowledged. That helps us as a company, because we're on track to affordable, nutritionally rich food that has a positive impact on health.

RG: Your new CEO comes from the nutrition area. Does he see the importance of DFI for his mission as the new president?

HJ: He likes our end-to-end approach of interacting with farmers, taking care of natural resources, and making sure that consumers are getting not only the nutritional benefits but also lots of other benefits from the world food system.

RG: Is DFI also reinforcing creating shared value, which you lead the world in?

HJ: Yes. If there's no clear value proposition for the students—if they can't lower production costs or increase the productivity of the cows or their fertility, if there's no added value—then the whole system collapses. Having access to consistently high-quality, fresh milk for our factories adds value that goes through the value chain into finished products and benefits our consumers. If you're doing the right thing the right way, shared value is an outcome.

RG: Does Nestlé believe you can put these commodity systems together on a win-win basis at every level?

HJ: Yes, it's the journey we've embarked on. We're also in a very competitive system, so in addition to what I've described here, at the end of the day we also need a clear, compelling financial advantage. But we're absolutely convinced we can achieve this. We see it on our own two farms when we benchmark them against other farms of the same size. We have a working model that is economically attractive and environmentally sound, and good for farm workers too. It's also the right thing to do. I think we've developed a compelling role model for other farmers to copy as we work towards a more sustainable dairy industry throughout the world.

RG: I can't thank you enough for discussing the Dairy Farm Institute. The kind of food system you're creating is a win-win for all. Thank you very much, Hans.

HJ: It was absolutely my pleasure. Thank you very much for helping us go in the right direction.

4

Technology—Coding Life

JUAN ENRIQUEZ

President and CEO, Biotechonomy (2014)

Managing director at Excel Venture Management and president of Biotechonomy, Juan Enriquez is an author, investor, cabinet member in the Salinas Mexican government, two-time research assistant of mine, and founding director of the Life Sciences Project at the Harvard Business School. His careers in the private, public, and academic world have given him an unusually broad perspective on the food system. He recognizes the deep importance of science in every aspect of the global food system, and the need for putting a much higher priority on education at all levels for both the United States and the world.[1]

RG: Juan Enriquez is a managing director at Excel Venture Management and the president and CEO of Biotechonomy. He's contributed enormously to the agribusiness program at the Harvard Business School, as the founder of the HBS Life Sciences Project and coauthor of a major article in the *Harvard Business Review* on life science. You've argued that the genetic revolution is the most important change-maker in all of our history. Why is that?

JE: The difference between ourselves and animals is that we've learned how to pass on knowledge across time. So even though there's a very small difference in DNA between ourselves and monkeys, we teach our kids to do music and science, how to read the weather and grow crops. We get more and more skilled at learning and teaching.

We once taught using pictographs, then with Kanji, and eventually with ABCs. Recently all languages have collapsed into two digits. The digital revolution lets us use cellphones to bring together all types of music and images, all words written and spoken in any language. Today 99 percent of all data transmitted in the world is in this digital alphabet. Now we're learning the language of life. Between 1970 and 2000 we transitioned into the digital era. Between 2010 and 2050 we're transitioning into the era of coding life.

RG: Coding life is critical to plants, animals, and human beings. How do they interact with one another, especially in their immune system?

JE: First, there's an enormous overlap in the gene instructions between ourselves and a whole series of different species. The difference between ourselves and mice is about 5 percent, between ourselves and monkeys is about 1.27 percent. There are even significant overlaps in gene code between ourselves and plants and even bacteria. The instruction sets that allow us to produce, synthesize, and modify organics in plants may also be applicable to bacteria, and vice versa. We're starting to see plants producing vaccines and bacteria growing organic plastics, and vice versa. A cholera vaccine can now be programmed into tobacco, or a potato, or a banana or a bacterium.

RG: If life code is programmed into plants or the milk of animals, what does that do to the cost structure in industries like agriculture, petrochemicals, and pharmaceuticals?

JE: Coding life can have an enormous impact on the cost structure of various industries. For one, it brings together agriculture and energy—not efficiently or subsidy-free yet, but more and more petrochemical processes and ethanol production will depend on living factories. We'll rely less on million-year-old plants that under pressure have become oil, and short circuit the entire system by programming corn to produce biodegradable plastics. Life sciences will push down prices of commodity products. Walmart already offers disposable salad containers made from biodegradable plastics grown in either bacteria or in corn.

RG: Which also improves the environment in the process. Many farmers throughout the world look at the genetic revolution as a threat. Is it a threat or a savior?

JE: It's a big problem for the uneducated farmer in the same way that open markets were a big problem for the uneducated farmer who didn't know how to use futures markets, international options, credit markets, and the latest yield technologies. If you keep doing what grandpa did, and the system changes, you can get into big trouble. On the other hand, if your animals are producing a medicine, let's say a goat or a cow that's producing a compound to fight cancer, it isn't worth the price of the steaks; it's worth about $1 million. The economics, the value added per animal, is much better if the animal has been bred to produce a life-saving medicine rather than hamburger.

RG: In other words, the farmer is becoming a pharmaceutical and an energy producer, as well as a food, fiber, and feed operator.

JE: Exactly. You're changing how you use a square meter of farmland. You can use it to plant crops, preserve the environment, grow chickens, or whatever. The biotech revolution is allowing farmers to code life or move from farming to pharming, or store information in living things or produce plastics. A few already produce broccoli that helps fight cancer, but that's the exception. Right now we have a system where "all-natural corn" might sell for $2, and "genetically modified corn" only $1.50, because consumers tend toward all-natural. But someday the sign won't read "genetically modified corn"; it'll say corn that helps you fight cancer or process certain fats and the modified corn will sell for $4. Eventually the value added to plants and animals will have more consumer pull. Today, most of the input traits increase yield. As consumer-friendly output traits come to market, not only will the price structure change; farmers will have a chance to get real branding and potentially build a far stronger sales story than through the current commodity system.

RG: What type of education should that farmer have in order to be able to make use of these emerging technologies?

JE: Farmers who don't understand the digital world and international markets will be at a huge disadvantage. There are very few farmers who don't understand what's happening to prices globally and how to navigate subsidy structures. Big and little soybean farmers look at the weather in Brazil as well as their own, because it has an impact on prices and availability. The farmer will also need to be genetically literate to understand the value of various modifications, as well as the risks.

RG: Will the life science input companies change dramatically as well?

JE: Yes. Several decades ago, the digital revolution upended some of the most powerful companies in the world. Silicon Valley in 1960 was basically an agricultural backwater, and Seattle, Washington, wasn't exactly the center of the technology world. A few individuals and a few companies can make a huge difference in terms of regional wealth and vitality. Attracting these people makes a difference in real estate values, schools, restaurants, museums, and music. It can make communities viable and vibrant, or not. Areas like Flint, Michigan, that depend on once-leading technologies but didn't substitute and grow are in big trouble. Areas that developed new technologies have become very powerful.

RG: Many look at Monsanto as a threat rather than people that [are] trying to help change the system. Will Monsanto benefit from this revolution or will they also be threatened by it?

JE: In 1935, if you were one of the five hundred largest companies in the world, your corporate life expectancy might be ninety-odd years. Today, a company that becomes a Fortune 500 company might expect to be there for fourteen years. New technologies put enormous pressure on companies. Maybe Monsanto will be a very powerful company in twenty years, or maybe they'll be challenged by competitors who aren't in the agribusiness chain today—companies in pharmaceuticals or information technology or even insurance. The value will shift from molecules coming out of the ground towards molecules as information systems. Farming may become a genetic code business as opposed to a labor business. These transitions tend to quickly upend companies that don't understand where they're playing.

RG: So the competitive environment is up for grabs?

JE: Very much so. One prediction I feel comfortable making is that some of the largest companies in the world will be life-science driven. A second prediction is that you will find some very unexpected mergers and competitors. A merger that surprised me was General Electric— a manufacturing company that became a finance company and is now a health care company—buying Amersham Pharmaceuticals. Who's going to be buying into agribusiness? We've already had the seed companies acquired by chemical companies. Pharmaceutical companies may become consumer products or cosmetics companies. There are so many opportunities for little seeds to reproduce various life codes. Perhaps, now that the seed companies have merged, people will start making stuff using bacteria instead of seeds.

RG: Can you recreate the germ plasms that exist in seeds in bacteria?

JE: We can't yet write very large chunks of the genetic code accurately. We can insert single genes or a couple of genes. During the past fifty years we've been discovering how life is coded, figuring out how instructions are transmitted using the basic four-letter ATCG code of DNA into proteins that execute the code. Recently we've seen a few maps of whole systems, entire operating cassettes for viruses, and a few bacteria. Eventually we'll modify the source code for maize, drosophila, and even humans.

When we're able to rewrite very large stretches of gene code and execute specific life instructions, we'll be getting closer to the software scenario where ever more complex programs drive a huge change in computing and in industry structures.

RG: As we move up the value-added chain into assembly and processing and then ultimately distribution, how will each of these stages be affected by the genetic revolution? Do you think we'll have more identity preserved? Will we have more segmentation, or will we have something else?

JE: Every single aspect of the agribusiness chain will change. You'll be able to trace the origin of every living thing, learn how it evolved and when. Identity preservation becomes almost trivial. Programming what you want a living thing to do becomes a really interesting question, because we don't recombine at random. Your own DNA is not a random recombination of half your mom, half your dad; it's a code transmitted in big chunks of DNA, what they call haplotypes, that you take either from your mom or your dad. As we understand more about these haplotypes, we'll get better at predicting how groups of people differentially react to cholesterol, or why they metabolize medicine in different ways, or have different sleep patterns and get sick from different things. The first broad effects of these new discoveries will be in agribusiness and they'll affect production, distribution, marketing and alter almost every aspect of the agribusiness chain.

RG: It's very much consumer driven, because people now look upon food as nutrition, as health, as safeguarding an immune system. As people think of food that way, as well as enjoying it, how will that shape the production and distribution system and the kind of firms that will be in it?

JE: Firms across the agribusiness chain will be driven by information as opposed to physical structure. You'll see a transition similar to what we had in computers where the big iron, hardware companies were dominant, but now it's the software companies that generate the most value and create the most wealth. Agribusiness will move in the same direction as information and knowledge drive more and more of the wealth within the system.

RG: An issue the agribusiness system faces is bioterrorism. Will science make traceability more effective in dealing with bioterrorism?

JE: We know that every new technology has been misused to hurt people, by accident or on purpose. It'd be very hard to have World War I or World War II without steel, without electricity. But as a great historian once wrote, "I'd rather live in a world that's not just lit by fire." Abusing genetic code for ill is a concern. We need much stronger bioterrorism and bioweapons conventions and rules. We also need to learn how to defend ourselves by making vaccines more effectively and getting them to market more efficiently. Most every new technology has been misused at some point. But I'm an optimist. Despite the tragedies of the twentieth century, we added forty years to the average person's life expectancy and lifted huge chunks of humanity out of dire poverty and starvation. Kids born today will likely live healthy lifestyles past one hundred.

RG: People are the driving force in addition to the science. This country historically has been at the cutting edge of change, and of information, and of technology, yet when you pick up a newspaper today you see people are concerned that we're falling behind, that other nations are doing a better job of educating their people, doing a better job of identifying quality scientists and helping them change. What do you see developing here?

JE: The US has to start taking education in math and science as seriously as it takes football. We often treat education as a remedial program. Only rarely do we focus on the really talented kids before they get to college or graduate school. After decades of treating scholastics just as we treat varsity sports, other countries are building out national teams. We need higher standards, or we're not going to be competitive. There's no testing gap between minorities in our military schools and on military bases, because the expectations are, I'm going to promote you if you achieve a certain standard, not because of the way you look.

RG: The agribusiness and agriceutical systems benefited enormously from the land grant college system that Abraham Lincoln established. He also developed the National Academy of Sciences. He enabled people to apply their education to the most important industry of its time, which was agriculture. Today the money invested in research at the land grant colleges on biotechnology, genetics, and genomics is less than what the private sector invests. Should that be changed?

JE: The curve of government investment in scientific research in terms of absolute dollars still goes up. But as a percentage of the economy, it's been coming down for decades, and that's just wrong because research is the gasoline that fuels our future economic growth. Technology generates most of the new wealth in the world. And yet as a percentage of the economy, we're being careless about funding talented people to do smart research.

RG: When you also look at the education system and the amount of multidisciplinary relationships necessary to do the kinds of work you just described, you have to be an agronomist, a geneticist, a businessperson, and an economic development person. You need all those skills. How do we change our educational system to cross-pollinate departments and learning?

JE: You now have to go to school for life, because often the technologies that you learned ten years ago are completely different today. If you don't keep upgrading you become obsolete. Executive education becomes a driving force. The military is out ahead of civil society in understanding this. When you get promoted from major to colonel you better have a master's, and from colonel to general you often have to have a PhD equivalent. A lot of the military curriculum is based on hard sciences like physics and math, because those subjects truly matter if you're making decisions in a technology-driven world.

RG: Consolidation in every part of our industry continues. Is there new pressure on the survivors to play a bigger role beyond the corporate role in response to society's needs?

JE: It's really worrisome how we demonize others today. It's all the government's fault, or the president's fault, or all the greedy businessmen driving the world to perdition. There are evil people in every profession, but by and large, people want to do things right. They have kids and a community and pride. We have to be careful about our incentive mechanisms and simplify things like tax codes, regulations, and laws. We have to make it harder to tweak the system in favor of an already privileged few. We need a more transparent system grounded in common sense. We'll all do better except the lobbyists and those few favored by the status quo. That's equally true in business and government.

RG: Given your multinational background and the evolution of your own interests over the years, what's been important to you in the past, and how do you see yourself five or ten years from now?

JE: I've had a very good life. I've been very lucky in my personal life, and been very lucky in finding mentors like you to teach me different ways of seeing the world. It's been a great adventure, because I've been able to move from government into academia, into business and writing. Each place has a different structure and it teaches you. It's like a jigsaw puzzle, putting little pieces together to try and make this part better and that part better and this part better. Usually, it's just really fun to get up in the morning, particularly if you're working in an area like life sciences and technology, because it's like Christmas. It's a lot of creative people doing a lot of interesting stuff in a lot of different places in the world. My grandmother once told me, Never travel without a purpose. Exploring science and technology, building stuff that matters always gives you purpose, keeps you on your toes, and surprises you. It allows you to learn from and work with interesting people. That's really a huge part of life.

RG: As your former professor I'm very proud of what you've accomplished and what you will accomplish, but more importantly I'm proud of your value system. Thank you very much, Juan.

JE: Thank you, Ray.

GEORGE M. CHURCH
Professor of Genetics, Harvard Medical School (2016)

George Church is one of the world's leading geneticists. Professor of genetics, Harvard Medical School, he has been at the forefront of applying the gene editing technique known as CRISPR to a wide range of fields including medicine, agriculture, and the resurrection of the wooly mammoth. Stepson of a doctor and first introduced to computers as a ten-year-old at the 1964 World's Fair, Church grew up in Florida fascinated by links between plants, animals, computers, and medicine. His CRISPR-related discoveries will create gene drives that will profoundly affect humans, plants, and animals. He is also a thought leader in the prospective use and misuse of powerful new genetic technologies.

RG: Dr. George Church is professor of genetics at Harvard Medical School, Harvard University. You've changed the world more than any other scientist I know. In the process, you're going to change plants, and animals, and human beings, and crops more than any other person will in the future. How did you get interested in this?

GC: I got interested in science very young. Nobody in my family was interested in science. My mother was a bit of a math phobe, but she got a vicarious pleasure from me doing it. I was really interested in the plants and animals that were in my backyard. I lived on the water with mud flats. My third father was a physician, and I was fascinated by the inventions that were in his medical bag. He used to do house calls back then. I also got entranced by computers when I went to the New York World's Fair when I was ten. I returned to Florida where I found no such thing. I started trying to make connections between these things—the backyard plants and animals, medicine and computers. In college, I majored in chemistry and zoology and finally found a good connection, which was crystallography. I spent most of my time in the lab and graduated in two years, because I didn't want to spend my parents' money. I was working in college to help pay my way. I became a graduate school student where they pay you, but I worked so hard at the research, I flunked out—that was at Duke University. I worked as a technician, and then came to Harvard as a graduate student with Wally Gilbert. Business interested me too, not just science, which was quite rare at the time. I consulted for a company called Bio-Rad in graduate school, and then Wally did something very unusual at the time, which was start a biotech company, one of the first. The company was Biogen, and I became one of the first employees as I finished up my PhD. I got hooked on the whole technology aspect working on crystallography and then sequencing technology. I eventually worked on stem cells as a postdoc in San Francisco with Gail Martin. I then set up my lab, and have continued ever since developing technologies for biology and medicine.

RG: There's remarkable range to your work. You created an amino acid that never existed before, and you're working on plants whose drifting pollen won't affect the crop next to it. How soon will these things be available? People are really worried about the science—the risks—but also the impact on the world to which they're accustomed.

GC: We do a fair amount of what I would categorize as "safety engineering for biology." There's safety engineering for almost every field of engineering, whether it's civil engineering, bridges or automobiles, jet liners—everything has some safety component to it. But there was relatively little for molecular biology, which is why we developed a strain of industrial microorganism that was dependent on an amino acid that didn't exist in the wild and would have the lowest possible escape rate.

Back in the '70s when there was a recombinant DNA moratorium, the NIH mandated an escape rate of one in a hundred million—one in ten to the eighth—that's never actually been achieved, in my opinion—maybe one in a million. We worked it out to where it's probably now one in ten to the fourteenth. So it's one in a hundred trillion rather than the previous record, which was around one in a million. Most of what you develop in the laboratory would not survive in the wild. But every now and then, you'll develop, say, herbicide resistance. Even if escape probability is very low, it could creep into the weeds. You get herbicide resistance because you're applying lots of herbicide—same goes for pesticides, and antibiotics. We're developing alternatives to these things.

RG: Are you getting close to that?

GC: Your question was, How long do these things take? Some things happen much more quickly than expected. We helped bring down the price of genome sequencing by about three-million-fold so far. That took less than a decade. Some said it would never happen, and the optimists said it would take six decades. It was more like seven or eight years. There's been a similar revolution in changing the genomes, which has become increasingly precise and safer. The most recent example is CRISPR, a method for changing one base pair so it's no longer transgenic—moving a gene from one organism to another. By that definition, it's not a GMO [genetically modified organism], because it's no more genetically modified than a random mutation. We've done this since the dawn of agriculture ten thousand years ago. So we now can do with precision what we've been doing randomly without moving genes from one organism to another, which has caused great concern. Many people worried about taking a jelly fish gene and putting it into a plant, or putting human genes into plants and so on. All those have been assessed as generally safe, but we're entering a new era with high promise and new risks. It involves engineering the wild, so if you take an herbicide-resistant weed, you can restore it to herbicide sensitivity. But to do that, you're engineering the wild, because the weed is a wild plant. It's not even an agricultural species. You can do that with CRISPR gene drives. But you need to really know what you're doing. You can engineer mosquitoes and other disease vectors, like an invasive species, with the same CRISPR gene drives. But these are all wild animals, and you need to make sure that there's no other animal that depends on them, including plants for pollination. You need to make sure that what you're spreading doesn't spread to other organisms. You have to do all this in a process that's somewhere between a laboratory test and a field trial. You can't do it in a field trial if it's going to spread, so it has to be on the scale of a field trial, but in physically contained space like a laboratory.

RG: What about the problem we have with mosquitos now and the diseases they carry? Is it possible to do something with a mosquito to reduce a level of that disease?

GC: Many diseases, especially in developing nations, are associated with agriculture and related to irrigation and large pools of stagnant water. Mosquitoes spread serious diseases like malaria, dengue, yellow fever, and so on. You can either aim antibiotics at the disease itself, which is not the mosquito typically but a parasite or a virus or a bacteria, or you can aim a pesticide at the mosquito or you can make vaccines against the disease. Each of these eventually develops resistance. So a new strategy is to develop malaria resistance in the mosquito or other disease vectors. Generation after generation, that spreads exponentially. You can simultaneously decrease the mosquito population and the malaria inside the mosquito if you need to do both at once. To get a new vaccine or a new drug approved is likely a much harder process than getting the mosquito to be resistant.

RG: There was a herd of goats here in Massachusetts that produced a drug cheaper than you could produce using other devices. I'm not sure whether it still exists today, but do you think using milk, and a particular special herd of goats or something like that, to produce a pharmaceutical is practical or not practical?

GC: Plant and animal proteins are among the least expensive sources in the world, and they're commoditized. Many pharmaceuticals are nothing more than a protein. Now, the major milk proteins and seed proteins are hard to completely replace, but you can manufacture things in large fermenters at the multimillion-liter scale. Depending on the drug, you can produce up to tens of grams per liter. All these flowers are blooming right now, whether made in animals, plants, or—mostly—cultured in cells. One new thing you can do with animals that's very hard to do with plants or microorganisms is to produce organs for human beings. Essentially all the organs that a human needs can be harvested from a single pig. That's now feasible using new genome editing tools that we and others have developed. We may be a year or two away from primate-human testing.

RG: If that really works, then instead of people waiting years to get an organ when someone dies in a car crash, they'll be able [to] get a mass-produced organ on demand, perhaps from a pig.

GC: Right. Some people think the problem is getting a match, but there's simply not enough donors even if everybody matched. It's hard to assure physiological health due to the time delay of many hours, but also whether there's an undetected viral infection. We've shown you can get rid of pig viruses genetically.

RG: That's a huge breakthrough. When you look at crops, some people talk about producing vaccines in tobacco and other plants. Is that possible?

GC: Yes—a vaccine is a protein. There are protein pharmaceuticals that are not vaccines, and these can be made in any microorganism, animal, or plant. But there's been a concern about transgenics, moving one from one species to another, especially if those transgenics are out in the wild. If they're in some factory in a stainless steel, million-liter fermentation facility, that's more acceptable than if they're growing in a banana plant on a big plantation in the middle of nowhere.

RG: If we were having this conversation ten or twenty years from now, many of the things we're talking about will be reality.

GC: Yes, there'll be new things we haven't even thought of yet. All we can do is encourage innovation and, especially, encourage the safety test. We need both innovation and safety in testing to make sure we don't get setbacks that can push back the timeline.

RG: Do you think the public will understand the CRISPR revolution enough to realize that it doesn't create GMOs?

GC: That's still up in the air. It's certainly not a transgenic. You can use CRISPR to make transgenics, but the most common use is genome editing—a single-point mutation which is indistinguishable from random mutation and selection. I suspect CRISPR will be accepted as being benign—possibly, more benign than random. If I were to eat or inject something into my body, I would far prefer that it be precise rather than random. I might be concerned about the transgenics. In the end, the line probably shouldn't be drawn by the method, but by effectiveness and by safety for humans and the environment.

RG: Europe has been the most leery of genetically modified anything, primarily because of Hitler and his Nazi-era experiments. How do you get that kind of mindset changed?

GC: I think it's more complicated than that, and the complication actually gives us hope. The Germans practiced a form of eugenics, which had begun in America and other countries in [the] 1920s and went well beyond World War II to the 1970s. People don't realize just how widespread eugenics was. Even if the science had been good, which it wasn't, it would have been unacceptable in modern terms to tell people how to reproduce. Fast forward to the present: you've got GMO issues that had little to do with Germany and eugenics. England and [the] Netherlands had no particular stake in eugenics or in Hitler's Germany. I think what happened was that a large monopolist from another country, Monsanto, didn't play well with others. Europeans basically said, What's the advantage to us of surrendering our agribusiness to an American monopoly? And they looked at the cost benefit and there was no obvious benefit. It also became a bit of a class war. That's what I mean by "it's complicated." Many of those most opposed to GMOs were either opposed to an American monopoly in Europe or they were wealthy and didn't care about the nickel-and-dime difference between a genetically modified soybean and the organically farmed version. I think if a new technology develops that isn't a monopoly, or is a European technology that provides more than pennies-on-the-dollar benefits to farmers and consumers, then they might accept it. Golden rice is a good example. It could have annually saved a million people with a vitamin A deficiency. It's been ready for approval since 2002, but there's been serious resistance to it. It's been an interesting battlefield to watch.

RG: When you talk to nonscientific groups, do they still bring up monopolies when they discuss the issue with you? Or don't you talk to nonscientific groups?

GC: I talk to nonscientific groups quite a bit. Monopoly is rarely brought up in public discussion. You'll see it occasionally in socially and tech-savvy journals and books when analysts try to sort out what's really behind the resistance. Part of it was NGOs like Green Peace, who were having trouble raising money in Europe around the time Monsanto came in. When they saw Monsanto, they concluded, Here's an issue we can exploit. Nonprofits are businesses just like everybody else. Their donations grew when they positioned themselves as fighting a monopoly that was not interacting well with the community. Monsanto assumed they could win based on merit, or based on value to the farmer, or even value to their stockholders, which really wasn't the correct algorithm for winning the hearts and minds of people around the world.

RG: The National Academy is doing one more study this year on the safety of GMOs. Do their pronouncements mean anything to the public?

GC: Yes, they have an impact. When the National Academy of Science reports on controversial topics—whether it's global warming or industrial pollution or agriculture—the world is desperate for a source that can engage opposing views, hear many voices, and document it all in a very thick book. The reports serve a purpose, but they're pretty high level, occasionally esoteric, and are government oriented rather than oriented towards the people.

RG: If the scientific world is going to change the food system and a great deal of the health system, it's also going to affect climate. What are we doing for forests and things like that?

GC: Forests have historically been part of the collateral damage of our growing population. We're now, easily, twice the holding capacity of the planet pre–green revolutions. We probably can go higher, but at some cost. The goal for technology is to make our currently arable land more productive per hectare. One approach is to examine how much carbon and protein we create and use producing food. Some animals require a great deal more hydrocarbon and solar input per gram of protein than makes it to the table. Getting rid of animals is not a panacea, but it's part of the solution. So is focusing the crops that are the most efficient at utilizing water and sunlight. This involves cultural preferences, so we need to focus on broader recipes, not just technology.

RG: It also has to do with nutrition. People want you to have more fruits and vegetables. They want your diet to improve health. Even your moods are related to what you eat. In a way, what you're doing is giving the world an opportunity to look at the end product and relate it back to the technology. Who does that well? You do it, but do other people look at that?

GC: No one person can span that great an interdisciplinary range. In building interdisciplinary teams, each person has to be as interdisciplinary as possible but also have real depth too. You also need international sensitivity, because interdisciplinary initiatives can maximize your local environment but impact another one. We're all becoming geo-engineers, which is to say we're affecting the climate worldwide. There are going to be winners and losers, because—for example— making the world warmer might benefit northern climates preferentially while turning a lot of currently productive equatorial regions into deserts. We need to be careful about the global impact of local initiatives benefiting a particular group. It's not just about nutrition or fresh fruits. There are lots of ways to pack nutrition into things that are inexpensive—like golden rice with vitamin A for people who can only afford rice, which is one of the cheapest foods on the planet. We're increasingly understanding, microorganisms are kind of like vitamins. If you have too much of one kind, it's unhealthy, and if you have too little of another, you may be depressed or susceptible to obesity. Some people simply need a lot more food to attain the same level of health depending on the microorganisms in their gut.

RG: Is the scientific community working with the medical community on these issues?

GC: There's some overlap between agriculture, pure science, and medicine. I don't think it's nearly enough. There are lots of silos, where people become highly specialized and hoard their data rather than sharing it. This is especially true in medicine where the stakes are very high, or in newly arising, information-rich fields.

RG: How do we get someone with your background to take a leadership role in putting these pieces together and, more importantly, putting the people together to look at it and cooperate, so that the world will have the leadership it richly needs?

GC: Scientific leadership is quite different from political leadership. Scientific leadership can move mountains and nations with a powerful idea, and a willingness to share the idea and collaborate with others. Working with companies and nonprofits and debugging ideas doesn't appeal to that many academic scientists. More could cross over and cover the range between basic science and debugging societal systems.

RG: Why doesn't it appeal to the scientists?

GC: Everybody has their own idiosyncrasies. When I was a student and a postdoctoral fellow, we looked askance at any business involved in biology. Technology and business were both considered less worthy than basic science. When I was a student, the more esoteric your science, the better. That's mostly been corrected, but there's still a lingering feeling. Specialization may even be more important. You can become an expert in your field, and when your field shrinks, you become a very deep expert on something that is very small. You not only avoid social issues in business and ethics, but you avoid adjacent fields. In business, you can be a generalist or a specialist, but in science specialization is complicated, because there's a great tendency to specialize.

It's very hard to do something well with deep knowledge, and also bridge more than one field.

RG: We're fortunate to have a George Church who does just that, so thank you very much. You're giving us a lot of things to be excited about in the future, but you're telling all of us that the barriers remain tough as well.

GC: Yes, don't underestimate the difficulty of planning very complicated global systems with high levels of safety and security.

RG: We're fortunate in this world to have you. Thank you very much, George.

Farm Labor

BALDEMAR VELASQUEZ

President, Farm Labor Organizing
Committee (FLOC) (2014)

President of the Farm Labor Organizing Committee, Baldemar Velazquez worked with former US secretary of labor John Dunlop, then of Harvard University, and George McGovern of Campbell Soup to create a mutually beneficial, multistakeholder forum known as the Dunlop Commission to give voice and protection to farm laborers who were explicitly excluded from the National Labor Relations Act. The commission was effective, and now under Velazquez's leadership efforts are underway to extend their work to other commodity systems. Velazquez was raised in a poor family of migrant workers treated poorly by their employers. His spiritual faith helped him approach life "as a process of reconciliation rather than a struggle to get even." He was awarded a MacArthur "genius" grant in 1989.[1]

RG: Baldemar Velasquez is president of the Farm Labor Organizing Committee (FLOC), which represents farm labor groups in the United States. He's successfully developed working relationships with the total food system, and won a MacArthur "genius" award when he worked with John Dunlop to develop an informal labor relations board for both farm labor and the companies employing them. You created working relationships that have stood the test of time. How do you account for that?

BV: There were a couple of cornerstone pieces set in motion in the 1980s when Campbell Soup asked Dr. Dunlop to create a blue ribbon commission to address workers suffering in the tomato industry in northern Ohio. The manufacturer didn't intend to create a labor relations unit, but Dr. Dunlop and I agreed there should be a mechanism for workers to address issues directly on their own. Agricultural workers were outside the National Labor Relations Act so they had no right to collective bargaining, so we pressed the companies to create an independent commission to act as a labor board by private contract. That was the key to setting guidelines for representation with the companies in their supply chain. After the Campbell Soup campaign, which also included Vlasic Pickle, Heinz, and others, we demanded that they recognize the commission as opposed to just recognizing the union. More than anything, that helped us sustain the systemic representation created by the Dunlop commission. Working without the commission framework would make our efforts on the bottom of the supply chain worthless. Our current campaign against big tobacco— Phillip Morris, Altria, Reynolds, and the leaf brokers—is contingent on their recognizing the commission. So yes, it's stood the test of time.

RG: Have you been happy with the results?

BV: I can't be sad, because workers have improved their lives. It's allowed them to be recognized as human beings and speak about the troubles in their lives. When they go out in the fields in rain or in sun, in the dirt and dealing with hazards like nicotine and pesticides, they need the opportunity to speak about safety conditions and minimizing workplace hazards. No matter what government regulations are in place, the test is what happens on a day-to-day basis. They're migrant workers in strange communities. When they have an organization, they can advocate for themselves.

RG: Now that the organization has more than just recognition, can you talk to managers of these various companies and plan for the future by figuring out how to work collectively to respond to new trends, new issues, and new products?

BV: That's one of the key lessons I learned working with Dr. Dunlop. He helped all sides better understand the needs of the manufacturers, growers, and farmers, and our needs as well. It's a two-way street. For example, in northern Ohio the manufacturers wanted grade number one cucumbers for pickling. They put them in jars, so the cucumbers must be less than one and one-sixteenth inch in diameter. When companies pay by weight, grade number one gets a premium price. We learned that the larger sizes can be harvested mechanically, because they're cut up as relish or slices, so bruising the skin is okay. When whole cucumbers are jarred for pickles, you've got to handle them delicately and harvest by hand. When we learned about the distinction, we trained workers to use a picking rotation that keeps cucumbers small. Using that rotation, we increased the percentage of number ones harvested to 40 percent from an industry average of 18 percent. The manufacturers and farmers got more of what they wanted, and the workers made more money. It was a win/win situation, because we understood the need and trained accordingly. There's nothing genius about it. It's just being practical and understanding one another.

RG: Do you think what you've accomplished with cucumbers can extend to other commodities?

BV: Yes. The agreement that we signed with the Mt. Olive Pickle Company and the North Carolina Growers Association is an organizer's dream, because the workforce is involved in the main crop running through North Carolina, which is tobacco. These same workers harvest thirty or so other crops—everything from sweet potatoes to cucumbers to strawberries to wine grapes, even Christmas trees. We are just beginning to unravel the production needs in those commodities, but they look to be similar to what we found in Ohio.

RG: Do you think the company leaders in these commodity systems understand what you've been able to accomplish with Campbell Soup and others in the pickle and tomato industry? Do they understand how much of a win/win relationship was achieved through collaborative learning?

BV: I don't think so.

RG: How are you going to change that mindset? Wouldn't the business leaders in these other commodities want to sit down with the business leaders of the new commodities and encourage them to work with you?

BV: The impediment is sharing power and the threat to profits. You have a very marginalized workforce in agriculture across the entire United States. The manufacturers and retailers are businessmen focused on pleasing their shareholders. When you talk to them about a long-range plan to transform the industry so there's equity across the supply chain, it's very difficult for them to grasp, because that's not what they're paid to do. They're paid to operate systems that make quick profits. Not all of them are that way, but most industries operate like that. It takes a while to get their attention about the inequities, because the people at the top designing the supply chains are so far away from the people on the bottom. It's not their job to think about them. They have other players in their companies who work with the lower levels of the supply chain. The decision makers at the top are very hard. Over the years we've campaigned publicly to get their attention and mobilized church networks and now the labor movement to address these issues. When we make enough noise, they get concerned about their image and their brand and we get their attention. We try to be clear that we'd like their business to prosper, because we also make our living in it. We don't want to take over the business. We're the workers, the people that do the stoop labor in the fields. But we want to live and work with a status that isn't as close to slavery as it is.

RG: I'm very disappointed to hear you have to struggle so much given the success you've already had. Some companies live quarter by quarter and worry about short-term profits rather than long-term profits, but I thought the culture in our country was shifting. I thought people were beginning to develop long-term relationships throughout the supply chain. Why hasn't this moved more quickly?

BV: The partisan political environment hasn't helped. Politicians have used immigration to get votes. The anti-immigrant rhetoric over the last decade has made it difficult for politicians to work with open-minded employers in their districts. People rail against undocumented workers, yet they utilize them every day. We keep bringing it to their attention until they get to where, Okay, we'll finally recognize you as human beings and negotiate with you about your families and your needs as a worker in our supply chain. That's how it is for agricultural workers in this country.

RG: How do we provide a vehicle for labor and management leaders to understand how important it is to have fair-minded labor relations with a fair-minded path to citizenship as opposed to lives as second-class participants in the food chain? How do we do that?

BV: Part of it is our educational institutions. I gave a graduation speech at a northwest Ohio university some years back and reread it a couple of weeks ago. It addresses your question. We need new leaders with the courage to say, Look, we have to find systems that are equitable and give everyone a fair chance. Anyone doing hard, physical labor ought to be able to feed, educate, and clothe their own families, and not rely on public subsidies for it. Businesses need to design their supply chains humanely. We need to move beyond the selfish polarization of wealth that's driven our country in the past. Henry Ford created a more equitable supply chain when he started making the Model T. He said, If I want the guys making these cars to buy one, I've got to pay them enough to afford one. If more people thought that way, you could legalize the twelve million undocumented people in this country and create a whole new consumer market. There's a big win/win opportunity if we had a corporate or political leader who thought in that fashion.

RG: John Dunlop did a wonderful service to our food system by creating your organization and finding you. Where are the next Baldemars?

BV: We have a core of young leaders we're developing. I take them under my wing and spend a lot of time with them trying to teaching the good principles I've learned from others. Dr. Dunlop showed me how to practically apply things that most people just think about philosophically. My grandfather-in-law worked with Gandhi in India and I sat at his feet listening to stories of his conversations with Gandhi about the objective of nonviolence and winning the opposition over by exposing injustices and offering solutions.

RG: Dr. Dunlop together with other faculty members here at Harvard created a trade union program for labor leaders and managers. I don't think that exists anymore. How can we develop the academic leadership to do more of what you're talking about, getting people like you together with company heads to think more positively and practically about the future?

BV: Some of those classes need to be away from the classroom and out in the fields. We've run a camp for the last couple of years that brings church leaders, labor leaders, and community leaders out to the tobacco fields and into the labor camps to talk to the workers, witness the squalor they live in, and hear the human side of their story. When you make it human, your philosophical thinking comes to life. I have great faith in consumers and the American people. They have a good conscience, but they live in cloistered communities and can't connect with the suffering of others. When they do, they have a heart for others.

RG: I noticed you didn't say business leaders. I wonder how many of them have ever walked in your shoes.

BV: I've invited them, and only two executives from Reynolds Tobacco came out and walked with us into some of those labor camps. They're caught in a vice because they're managers within a frozen institution. There are a lot of corporate leaders who are good people, but they're stuck in institutions that thrive on inequality.

RG: My classmate, Gordon McGovern, was head of Campbell Soup when you were involved and he understood that finally. I really think the CEOs in all of the major crop systems have to begin to walk in your shoes. They have to understand that at the very top, not just at the bottom. Years ago there was a famous interviewer by the name of Edward R. Murrow. He used to broadcast from Europe during World War II. When he came back to this country he produced an important film. It was shown on CBS and the chairman of Coca-Cola saw what was happening to the orange grove workers and appeared before Congress to publicly apologize for what was going on and changed many things in that company. We could use a few more Edward R. Murrows.

BV: I agree.

RG: Most decisions made by organizations are made by unique individuals. What was there in your background that enabled you to create a win/win relationship with the rest of their industry? What was in your historical background? You mentioned your grandfather. You mentioned Gandhi. What's enabled you to do what you've done?

BV: A couple of things. I was raised in a poor migrant worker family watching my mom and dad, with nine mouths to feed, get cheated on wages and my mother get mistreated by field men and supervisors. That made me angry and fueled me to do something. But the other thing was a spiritual conversion through which life became a process of true reconciliation rather than a struggle to get even. I opened the Scriptures and the words of Jesus crystallized for me what needed to happen. A supply chain is like a big family trying to accomplish something. When there's inequity, it's like a dysfunctional family. What does a good pastor do with a dysfunctional family? Sometimes you have to separate the feuding parties, counsel them separately, and then bring them together. That's what John Dunlop did. He got the feuding parties together, got them to understand one another, and reconciled the differences so we could move forward together. I've read all the community organizing manuals, but the best are the Scriptures. When Jesus said, Love your neighbor as yourself, he didn't say love your neighbor if he looks like you or is in the same political party. I grew up mad at God and would tell my mom, who was a charismatic Catholic, if there's a god it must be a pretty lousy god to keep us in this situation. When I became a believer, I imagined hearing, Well now, Baldemar, I know you've gone through all these nasty things growing up, but if you hadn't gone through those things I wouldn't have a spokesperson to address them.

RG: Thank you for a wonderful interview.

Large-Scale Farming

JACK HUNT
Past President and CEO, King Ranch (2006)

Past President and CEO of the King Ranch, Jack Hunt manages one of the world's largest farming, ranch, and mineral operations. He has worked extensively with farmers' co-ops and partnered with migrant workers. He opposes mandated markets, such as ethanol, in part because they create more price volatility in the system. Jack is a self-described "Navy brat" who worked as a cowboy/tractor driver on his uncle's ranch. He graduated from Williams College and Harvard Business School.

RG: Jack Hunt is president and CEO of King Ranch, one of the largest farming operations in the United States. Most people don't understand King Ranch. Could you give a rough idea of the number of acres you manage, what kind of activities you engage in, and the type of ownership that exists in the company?

JH: King Ranch is a privately owned company whose stockholders are all direct descendants of Captain Richard King, who founded the company in 1853. We own over one million acres in Texas and Florida and farm approximately 110,000 acres of that with a variety of crops. The balance of the land in Texas is devoted to livestock, cattle operations, and wildlife recreation activities. We've established a sod business in Texas and have purchased Young Pecan, which buys, processes, and distributes pecans to retailers and food processors. We have a retail business in catalogs, a saddle shop, and brand licensing, like the King Ranch Ford pickups, and a gun line we have with Beretta. We also manage about 1.2 million acres of minerals.

RG: What about your own personal and professional background prepared you for your current position?

JH: I was a Navy brat so I never really lived anywhere, but my uncle owned ranches and farms in Texas and New Mexico. As a kid, I worked for him as a cowboy/tractor driver and did whatever else they needed. He was a well-known leader in agriculture and a role model for me. He's probably why I went into the cattle business once I finished my schooling and military service.

RG: You went beyond college and got an MBA here at Harvard Business School. Do you think the men and women who manage production agriculture in the future will have to go beyond an undergraduate education?

JH: The ideal employee today has an undergraduate degree in some aspect of agriculture, has gone out and really worked in the field, and then studied for an MBA or some related degree. They may have an MBA, but they love agriculture and are out driving around in the orchards or in the feedlot getting dirty like everybody else. Those are the kind of people we need in agriculture today.

RG: Some consider agriculture a quasi-public utility, because political as well as economic factors determine what producers get paid and what consumers pay. Will the government always be part of production agriculture?

JH: Yes. Anything involving lots of land like agriculture is going to have heavy government involvement at the local, county, state, or federal level. There are other issues too, like crop programs where the history is long, deep, and at times confusing. Being in agriculture requires an ability to work with government agencies at all levels.

RG: Managing the land and water resources of a country is critical to the country's economic and environmental development. From a social point of view, we have safety nets under other parts of our economy, and since the Depression of the '30s there's been somewhat of a safety net for farmers. Do you feel that should be the case?

JH: You have to have something. The government can make life very difficult for farmers, or they can make it better. The global farm economy is always government to government, so the government's going to have a role.

RG: People generally want government to be market oriented when it's influencing what's produced and how. At the same time, we need rules and regulations. You've served on a number of government committees focused on water management, trade, and immigration. How do you see those issues from a producer's point of view?

JH: That's a big question. The government's always been heavily involved in water, particularly in the West. From a producer's standpoint, there's a long history shaping the evolution of the water system and a lot of that's been capitalized in the land. So changing the way farmers are charged or the way water's allocated can make life very difficult for farmers. On trade, we have to make sure our government does a good negotiating job and protects our producers. It's a very complex process between governments.

RG: Historically both the Republicans and the Democrats have tried to treat agriculture on a bipartisan basis. Do you think that that's still the case?

JH: Yes. There'll be differences depending on where a particular chairman is from and what's grown in his area. But overall it's been fairly bipartisan. One problem is people making decisions at the executive level who don't understand agriculture. Congress has to play a stronger, more bipartisan role, because they know their producers and have to worry about getting re-elected every two or six years.

RG: An important issue in agriculture and the food chain is food safety. We've had a couple of cases of mad cow disease now in the United States. We just had an *E. coli* scare in spinach, for example. How good a job are we doing on traceability?

JH: You have to look at the various commodities. On spinach, they found the source relatively quickly, which may reflect the way that industry's changed. The livestock producers have a real problem, because the industry is very fragmented with small cattle producers the dominant source of cattle. I'm as worried about the animal health side as the food safety side, because the part of the cattle industry that's closest to the consumer is very concentrated, and I worry about diseases like hoof and mouth disease, which we'd have a very hard time tracing.

RG: There's been some discussion about using DNA as a way to trace pork and the hog economy. We've considered RFID [radio frequency identification technology] tags. Can we become more sophisticated even at the small herd level?

JH: It's possible, but difficult politically. I worked with a group of producers on the long-range plan for the National Cattle and Beef Association. A really smart guy from Missouri described how difficult it would be to get part-time cattle producers to participate in any program at all even though they represent the bulk of the mother cow herd. The average animal changes hands four or five times, so building the tracing system is organizationally very complex even though we have good technologies.

RG: Volatility is also a concern. We've experimented with crop insurance and other kinds of producer insurance. Will that be more important in the future?

JH: Crop or revenue insurance requires some government support because private insurance would be too high at the outset. It's a better way to go than the government constantly forking over disaster relief on an ad hoc basis.

RG: In Europe, they're developing a program that makes the farmer responsible for land and water resources, essentially paying him to maintain and nurture those resources. How do you feel about that?

JH: I'm not that knowledgeable about Europe, but they seem more protective of the rural environment. We have some of that here. People say the ethanol deal might bring ten million acres out of CRP [Conservation Reserve Program]. That's upset the hunters and enviros, because they'd rather have pheasants than corn. It depends on the habitat. There's an experiment with rainfall insurance that pays growers if there's no rain, rather than paying based on cattle or crop losses. That's moving more in the direction you're describing. Again, it's different regionally and by crop and not a general movement as you probably have in Europe.

RG: When you mentioned ethanol, you raised the issue of energy. Farmers aren't just producing feed and fiber and food; they're also producing energy and to some extent pharmaceuticals as well at the farm level. Starting with energy, you've got ethanol, you've got plant sources for ethanol, and you've got wind and solar power at the farm level. How do you see this kind of activity?

JH: At King Ranch, a 51-cent-per-gallon subsidy on ethanol adds over $1 a bushel to the price of corn, which lowers the value of our calves by about $2 million a year, and for the industry that's about $6 billion. My problem is that subsidies affect other commodities involved, and in the case of wind the assets involved. Environmentalists love to talk about not accounting for externalities. In the case of ethanol, there's a lively discussion about whether corn ethanol is even energy. Wind is another issue as wind machines aren't necessarily compatible with urban landscapes, yet heavy subsidies make the economics attractive. Urban areas seem to be in a reflexive guilt trip over global warming.

If it's renewable or green it's good, and we should subsidize it extravagantly without fully understanding the impact those subsidies have on other commodities, the landscape, or individuals. As you can tell, I'm frustrated by the nonthinking approach to renewables.

RG: A technology company just received the opportunity to plant a farm or implant a pharmaceutical into a rice crop in Kansas. What do you think of that?

JH: It's probably a good thing, if they can manage it. What's worrisome is that we don't have a good record of controlling experiments like that. They don't grow a lot of rice in Kansas, so it's a pretty good place to experiment. But there have to be extremely rigorous controls and the government needs to be involved to ensure there's no cross-contamination. Excitement about new technologies can result in mindless behavior.

RG: Another issue in agriculture is immigration and farm labor, which unfortunately has become a political issue as well. How do you see that being resolved?

JH: I have to compliment President Bush on wanting to do the right thing on this problem at the outset. He comes from an area where he understands the problem, and I think I do too. Most of the people that want to come into the US legally or illegally want to come here for opportunity, not to blow us up. We need to let those people come here and work via a guest worker agricultural jobs program that identifies workers and lets them go back and forth. That's what most of them want to do. Border patrol, particularly along the southern border, would be much easier if they didn't have to spend all their time chasing the 97 percent of the people that want to work and pick oranges and pick lettuce and do the things that we can't find American workers to do anymore. They're being paid minimum wage and benefits, at least by our company. It's an enormous problem. Florida had the smallest orange crop it's had in fifteen years. Several million boxes simply weren't picked last year. Growers across the US are being hurt by lack of labor. We're trying to grow our sod business in Texas, and we're having a terrible time finding labor to work in the fields and stack the sod, because of the documentation requirements. Anyone living in the southern tier of the States knows those economies would come to a crunching halt without access to these workers. I've been around them. They're good people, people with a lot of charm and grace, strong values, most of them, and it's just a shame that the immigration thing has deteriorated the way it did prior to the last election. I'm hopeful we'll get a comprehensive approach to this problem and that ag will be able to get a decent ag jobs program. But it's an enormous problem with huge personal costs. We find bodies on our ranches in South Texas almost every week—people simply hoping to work. There aren't many Americans who want their children to pick oranges and work in the lettuce and sod fields. We need these workers.

RG: Looking ahead, how do you see American agriculture, say, ten years from now?

JH: We're going to see continuing growth in the larger operations, more diversity within the larger operations across a mix of product lines, more integration in both directions among the larger operations, and a continuing increase in the number of smaller, part-time lifestyle-related operations in farming. Overall, farming is getting so complex that you have to be big enough to afford the talent needed to operate in that environment. Size will continue to be an important factor, which isn't what people like to hear. The guys in the middle are going to have a tougher and tougher time. That's not a new observation, but it's one I continue to have.

RG: You've been very gracious. Thank you.

JH: Yes sir, thank you.

RON OFFUTT
Chairman and CEO, RDO Company (2008)

Chairman and founder of the privately held RD Offutt Company, Ron Offutt used central pivot irrigation, access to light, sandy soil in Minnesota and North Dakota, and well-aligned strategies with customers to build his company into the largest potato grower in the world. RD Offutt is also the largest John Deere dealership in the world, in part by offering dealers an opportunity to sell their franchises and retire. Offutt graduated from Concordia College with a degree in economics.

RG: Ron Offutt is chairman and CEO of the Offutt Company, a major producer of agricultural products throughout the world. You grew up in agriculture. Your dad was a farmer. You've been and are a farmer. How do you explain the enormous transition that's occurred from the time when your father farmed in Minnesota and North Dakota to today?

RO: When I was growing up and working with my father, it was all about making a living and paying the bills for normal living expenses as a family. Today, our operation looks at production agriculture as a return on investment. We measure ourselves by what we can do with capital, just like any other business.

RG: You're the largest potato producer in the world. How did that happen?

RO: It's the old story of finding a need and rapidly expanding to fill it. In my life, the best example was when center pivot irrigation arrived in the early '70s. We had an opportunity to buy cheap land, but it was quite sandy and needed additional water. The new irrigation system solved that. Potato production was growing to meet the needs of French fryers. We aggressively pursued that niche market, and one thing led to another.

RG: But you did much more than simply satisfy a market. You developed a well-aligned strategic plan with Frito-Lay and Lamb Weston. How did you get top management's attention and become a partner in the process, not just a supplier?

RO: When we started out, we filled a present need. In doing that, our organization became more professional, both agronomically and operationally. We were a major supplier, so Frito-Lay wanted to get our opinions. Our size enabled us to leverage those relationships to other geographic areas where we could fill their need for raw potatoes and logistically save them lots of freight dollars. We moved production closer to where they process the potatoes.

RG: Did you begin to think in terms of global production as well?

RO: Yes. About fifteen years ago, McDonald's went into Russia with their very first restaurant.

RG: Their most successful one.

RO: Yes. They wanted Russian potatoes if they could get them. So Lamb Weston and we tried raising potatoes good enough for their French fries. The program was only moderately successful for all kinds of reasons. But it opened up other opportunities for us, and we got to know the country and the agricultural area. We were much more successful in the Russian John Deere equipment business than we were producing Russian potatoes.

RG: Talking about John Deere, in addition to staying on the agricultural front from a production point of view, you became the number one dealer of farm machinery and construction machinery in the world. You were a farmer. Why would you want to take on a dealership?

RO: When I graduated from college, my father and I became partners. We raised potatoes and marketed 'em pretty much the way we had during his lifetime. I did that for about three years and saw we were making a living, and that was about it. I borrowed some money to buy a John Deere store, but quickly realized I wasn't very good at running it. I hired a manager and went back to farming. I learned it's a lot easier for me to manage a manager than it is to manage a store. I went back to potato production, but because I was in the equipment business I learned about the center pivot system to irrigate land. That sprung us into potato production in the sand lands of central Minnesota, which led to our rapid growth in potato production.

RG: But you grew the John Deere dealership in such a way that it was successful, and it became more than just a store. It helped you understand the current and future needs of your fellow farmers.

RO: I could aggressively grow the John Deere business, because I didn't have day-to-day responsibility for operating our stores. Being an aggressive entrepreneur, I saw people wanting to exit the equipment business as an opportunity to buy their store. We provided an exit strategy for people wanting to retire. By having John Deere stores in about four geographic areas and construction in about three, we got geographic as well as business diversity and a lot more stability than if we'd stayed in one geographic area.

RG: In addition to investing in potatoes, you've looked at other parts of agriculture. Don't you have a dairy operation? How'd you end up doing that?

RO: We bought a large farm in Oregon, which had 29,000 acres of irrigated land on 130,000 deeded acres. The sheer size of the farm lent itself to a large animal enterprise, because from the center of the farm we were more than ten miles from any neighbors who might resist a large animal enterprise. I bought the farm to raise potatoes, but you can raise potatoes only once every three years on the same ground. Commodity prices were cheap, so there was no way to make money growing corn or wheat. I thought, Let's put a large animal enterprise in and feed 'em whatever the farm produces. But let's also sell the production preprice so we don't have to fight the market.

Long story short, a local cheese manufacturing plant in Oregon wanted to expand. We agreed to supply up to 65 percent of their milk at a fixed price, if they built their cheese plant adjacent to our farm. That's exactly what happened. All we had to concentrate on was producing milk. So at fifty-eight years old, I went into the dairy business for the first time in my life. I'd never milked a cow before.

RG: The principle of starting with the market and moving backwards has been part of your success in both the potato and the milk business. As you look at the new agriculture, how will the activities you're involved in change over the next ten to twenty years?

RO: Agriculture today is experiencing some of the best of times, but also some of the scariest I've seen. Agriculture worldwide is putting in the most expensive crop this spring that's ever been put into the ground. In three years, fertilizer has gone from $220 to $1,200. And Belmont Industries is more than doubling prices on their center pivot systems to $100,000. The price of steel and cost of galvanizing are the drivers. It's going to cost $7 million more to feed our dairy cows than it did a year ago. Does that change the way I think about prepricing our production? Not necessarily. But we need to rethink how we protect ourselves against inputs with wild run-ups.

RG: Do you think contracting over long periods of time will become more commonplace? A Department of Agriculture study determined that half of what's sold today is under contract, mostly with large farming operations like yours. Will these contracts have clauses protecting buyers and sellers from extreme price volatility on inputs?

RO: I'm not sure about escape clauses per se, but there'll be energy clauses which will allow both parties to raise or lower prices based on outside forces. But I don't think there'll be clauses that shift, say, potato prices based on whether corn goes to $6 or falls back to $3. It'll be input specific.

RG: Many people complain that our food policy only helps large-scale farmers get larger and small-scale farmers get smaller. Is that an inevitable trend, or will it change?

RO: Our operation, because of our size, isn't really affected by farm policy. We're too big to qualify for most government payments. While it's an excellent time for the government to exit the farm policy business, when commodity prices eventually fall, how do we rebuild a safety net if the industry needs one?

RG: There's roughly 570 million farmers in the world. Five hundred million of them have less than five hectares of land, and maybe one million of them have more than two hundred hectares. The world is concerned about poverty and malnutrition, much of it in rural areas in the developing world and even in our own country. You grew up post-Depression, but your father grew up in the Depression.

RO: Yep, yep.

RG: We lost half our farms in this country in a two-year period. We had six million farms in 1931 and six million in 1933, but three million of those were owned by different people over a two-year period. No sector of our economy lost half the ownership of a major industry that's also their home in two years. Here we are in 2008 wondering how to develop a safety net that doesn't interfere with the market. It's not a Republican or Democratic policy. I think it's a national policy.

RO: I agree. I don't have the answer, but we don't talk enough about protecting the segment of agriculture that looks at farming as a way of life.

RG: We need a two-segment policy. Europe does it that way. Many farmers are beginning to invest in other countries. We have global supermarkets, global food processors, global input suppliers, and now global farmers. Will that continue?

RO: Very much so. You already see it in Brazil, Argentina, the Ukraine, and, to a lesser degree, Russia.

RG: What's the education of the farmer going to be like in the future? Many of our farmers today are college educated. Some of them have master's degrees. What's the appropriate training for our future farmers?

RO: Farmer education will mirror business. You'll have the technical people—the agronomists, veterinarians, and nutritionists. And you'll have the businesspeople and also the marketing people who straddle the business and technical production side. Will all this be done inside major companies? Not necessarily. I think much of the ingenuity will come from farmer producer organizations.

RG: Historically farmers distrusted both the market and their supply system. They created cooperatives to protect themselves. Today's cooperatives are much more sophisticated. Some of them have spun off parts that are publicly traded. How do you see farm ownership through cooperatives changing over the next several decades?

RO: I think there'll be a hybrid of cooperative, farmer-owned assets jointly owned by a marketing company like Cargill. Right now in Wahpeton, the farmers own the plant. Cargill manages it and sells the high-fructose sugar. The producers want to participate in the value added. By the same token, a lot of capital assets with value-adds don't earn the return many publicly traded companies need or their financial engineers want. So I think it'll be a hybrid of corporate America and the co-ops.

RG: You're a family-owned business. How do you see succession planning for yourself?

RO: I'm lucky. My daughter is involved and has a passion for the equipment business. On the farming side, my son-in-law has a real passion and operates our farming side. So from a succession standpoint, right now I'm blessed. Could that change? You bet. But if I checked out now, I could check out peacefully and know it's okay.

RG: What will the role of the farmer be in the next ten or twenty years? The Industrial Revolution separated functions throughout the food system. Slowly, they're coming back together. But where does farming fit into the future? You say it's both a way of life and a business, with the way of life being partially supported by off-farm income. As you know, over a million farmers in the United States support themselves with income off the farm. Essentially, they work to live on the farm. Will the farmer play a different kind of role in society, because he or she is a farmer, or will it be just another business?

RO: There'll be a continuum of consolidation on the agricultural side. The producer and the value-added manufacturer will get tighter and tighter, both having greater and greater respect for each other. They'll both have to get a return on their equity and the dollars and get paid for the risk-reward ratio.

RG: You're basically saying the farmer's becoming more of a partner in the total food system.

RO: Very much so.

RG: Thank you so much. I really appreciate your thoughts.

RO: Thank you, Ray. I've enjoyed it.

JOSEPH LUTER III

Chairman, Smithfield Foods (2014)

Chairman of Smithfield Foods, Joseph Luter III turned his bankrupt family firm into the leading pork producer in the world through acquisitions, improving the taste and consistency of the product through better breeding, improving relations with farmers by inviting some to join his board, and global expansion. He became chairman of the company at twenty-six, and admired his father's willingness to do business without contracts. The firm was eventually sold to a leading Chinese firm to improve the market for Smithfield and to improve the domestic operations of the Chinese firm.

RG: Joseph Luter III is chairman of Smithfield Foods, the largest pork company in the world. Smithfield was founded by his father and his grandfather. You became president at the tender age of twenty-two. It's a unique company. How did you come to focus on the strategic importance of the supply side and the technology of that supply side?

JL: I spent a lot of time traveling the world during my younger days. In Europe, the quality of pork was much more consistent than it was in the United States. It was a lot leaner, the moisture content was tightly regulated, and both the external fat and color were very uniform. By contrast, in America our product was very inconsistent. The reason was simple. Our farmers were too removed from the end consumer. Their customer was the meat packing plant, not the retail store and not the individual consumer. The American farmer had the attitude that, I've been raising hogs this way my entire life. No one is going to tell me how to raise hogs. The result was an inferior product, so at Smithfield we said to the farmer, We have to give American consumers what they want, not what you want to give them. We began working closely with four large producers in North Carolina. We added our own farms and together came up with consistent genetics, consistent feed, and the end result was a consistent product that was far superior to what existed in the United States.

RG: Historically, the farmer and the processor were considered competitors, not necessarily friends. How do you—

JL: Adversaries.

RG: That's a better word. How do you get people to think differently about the person that they're supplying?

JL: First, I said what I just said hundreds of times to lots of individual farmers, and it began to sink in. Second, we developed a pricing matrix which rewarded hog producers if their product met our specifications, and the only way you could do that is to have consistent genetics and consistent handling and feeding of the hogs.

RG: But trust has to be there somewhere?

JL: Certainly. I spent an awful lot of time with four very large hog producers in North Carolina and developed trust over many years. Today they sell their entire production to Smithfield Foods.

RG: You were also one of the first firms to bring farmers onto your board of directors.

JL: There's always been an adversarial relationship between the meat packer and the farmer. Neither trusted the other. By bringing them together, I encouraged farmers to take a financial interest in Smithfield Foods through purchases of our common stock. Three farmers joined our board, which helped develop trust and at least some empathy for the problems we have and vice versa.

RG: You also developed a relationship with a genetic hog company to develop a unique kind of hog for Smithfield.

JL: Yes. I went to England, which has been a leader in this area—cattle and pigs—for a long time. We developed a very close working relationship with the National Pig Development Company (NPD), which had the best genetics. Today, we own those genetics for the United States.

RG: How do you work with firms that don't have this vision, and how do you eventually invite them to be part of your company?

JL: Most of the competitor firms we've bought didn't think it was possible to put something together on this large scale, but they saw us do it. Most of our competitors have a deep respect for what Smithfield Foods has accomplished. When we buy these firms, we impose our vertical integration concept on them, but it hasn't required much effort. They see the good that's come from working with us.

RG: Other firms have tried to develop independent operating companies, then tried to integrate them, but they haven't been successful. Con Agra is an example. They had ninety independent operating companies and just couldn't put them together. What do you do that enables firms to be both independent and part of a cohesive whole?

JL: Mike Harper built Con Agra, and allowed those individual companies to remain independent. Management has changed at Con Agra several times since Mike Harper left, and the new management believes in centralized control. We'll see whether they succeed. This business is so big, so dynamic, so fast moving, and this is a very large country with different cultures and different policies in different parts of the country that it's a mistake to centralize, because no one person or any one group is smart enough to adapt to today's fast-moving environment in the United States.

RG: Early on in your company, you encouraged people to be performance oriented, and developed pay for performance long before people said,

You ought to pay for performance. And you live in a small community. How do you attract the men and women who are entrepreneurial enough to want that kind of opportunity but still see the big picture you just talked about? How do you get those kinds of people?

JL: It's awfully hard to find top people that are entrepreneurial. You have to give them authority and know they're going to make X number of wrong decisions. You can't be too harsh when wrong decisions are made nor too quick to support people when they make good decisions. We try to encourage all our people to make decisions.

RG: This is not only an entrepreneurial industry and an entrepreneurial firm; it's also a volatile industry. The hog and corn cycles, consumers' attitudes change, new kinds of competition, both domestic and global—how do you manage risk in such a volatile environment?

JL: Sometimes we don't. But we recognize it's very volatile and we have ups and downs in our earnings. Many things are beyond our control, like weather. We have companies that will make $15 million in December and lose $5 million in January. A lot of people don't understand that, but we understand it and accept it.

RG: PE ratios penalize a company that's volatile. How do you live with those low PE ratios?

JL: We just live with it. Our investors have had a 26 percent compounded rate of return since 1975. We don't have a PE ratio as high as some Wall Street darlings, but when we think stock is undervalued, we've purchased substantial amounts of stock. We've bought back over half of the company in the last twenty-five years.

RG: When you look at Smithfield going forward and consider the global environment, how do you position yourself in terms of global competition? Do you have to be a global player?

JL: We don't have to be, but the gradual trend is toward freer trade in the years ahead. That's why we decided to go international. In addition, we're getting to a size in the United States that we might begin having antitrust problems if we continue to grow. We have a 30 percent market share in the United States in pork, so it's just to grow overseas, where we have a lot of opportunities, in particular Eastern Europe.

RG: Asia looms large. There was a recent announcement about an arrangement with a Chinese firm.

JL: Yes, COFCO.

RG: How do you see that playing out? Do you think that's significant, not just for you but for the industry going forward?

JL: It could be very significant. COFCO is owned by the Chinese government. We just received our first order. It was for sixty million pounds, which is sizable but not a giant order. Hopefully there will be others behind that. We believe there's a severe problem with disease with the hog producers in China, which is an opportunity to export substantial quantities to China.

RG: Do you think that the swine industry is more susceptible to disease than other protein areas or not?

JL: No. Asian bird flu has had a severe impact, and on the beef side there's mad cow disease. There seem to be major problems in poultry, beef, and pork, but we'll get through it, because our biosecurity today is better than ever.

RG: The world needs the kind of approach you've been able to provide Smithfield. Is what you do at Smithfield transferrable overseas or not?

JL: Somewhat, but each country has a different culture and political environment. Many companies have made [an] awful lot [of] mistakes trying imposing the American way on companies in other countries. Some have succeeded, but there've been some dramatic failures.

RG: How do you see Smithfield's approach, sort of country by country?

JL: Big corporate food companies such as Smithfield are not well received in France. They think small is good and big is bad, and we all know how much political power the small French farmer has. In Poland and Romania, the food production system was devastated under the communist rule, so they're more susceptible to the American approach.

RG: Some of these firms are owned by the farmers themselves. Are cooperatives becoming more important, and will they become more like partners rather than competitors?

JL: More like partners than competitors. I'm prejudiced, but you can't run businesses by a committee, and that's what cooperatives tend to do.

RG: If you could look ten years from now, what do you think Smithfield will look like?

JL: We'll be a global company that will probably be as big overseas as we are in the United States today. We'll be in all the proteins. We became the largest turkey processor when we bought Butterball from Con Agra last year and combined it with Carolina Turkey. We operate the world's largest feedlots in the United States—three times larger than our nearest competitor.

RG: Every executive I've been privileged to interview has a background—their family, their heritage, their environment—that affected how they manage their firm. What is there in your background that enabled you to become such an icon in our industry?

JL: That's a difficult question. I've said many times that only a fool evaluates himself. Having said that, I was raised by a father whose word was everything. He didn't require written contracts. Hopefully I've inherited that integrity. Ninety-five percent of our sales are based on verbal agreements rather than written contracts. Integrity is extremely important. You can have a short-term gain if you compromise your integrity, but it'll hurt you in the long run. It's a cliché, but if you treat people the way you want to be treated, you're likely to come out pretty well.

RG: Well, you've come out very well and so have the people you've worked with and partnered with. Thank you very much, Joe. It's been a real pleasure.

JL: Thank you, Ray.

ANDREW FERRIER
CEO, Fonterra (2007)

CEO of New Zealand's Fonterra, Andrew Ferrier is a Canadian who presides over one of the largest and most ambitious dairy cooperatives in the world. Under Andrew's leadership, Fonterra does 97 percent of its business outside of New Zealand using a business model that allows it to both compete and partner with some of the largest food companies in the world.[1]

RG: Andrew Ferrier is CEO of Fonterra, one of the largest dairy cooperatives in the world. You came from the noncooperative world. What did you find different from that world and the cooperative world you've entered?

AF: What really separates a cooperative from a publicly traded company is the deep connection your shareholders have with you as suppliers. Now that can also be a noose around your neck because they can slow progress. When Fonterra was created in 2001, an enormous amount of thinking went into ensuring that we had corporate disciplines as well as having the best of a cooperative. We have the skills of both our farmer directors and our outside directors, and we operate as if we were a publicly traded company.

RG: Looking ahead, a huge percentage of Fonterra's sales are global. You partner with many other firms, which makes you even more global. How are you able to do that?

AF: Yes, 96 percent of our sales are global. As we develop markets overseas, it's sometimes better to partner with someone who knows the market particularly well. We look for very knowledgeable players in individual markets, bring our global dairy skills to them, and try to make two plus two equal five.

RG: In the United States, you work with [the] Dairy Farmers of America (DFA), which is another very large cooperative. Do you prefer working with cooperatives, or would you rather work with the unique leader in the country?

AF: The answer is probably yes to both because often, the unique leader in the country is a cooperative. In the case of the United States, there's been a protected dairy market for many years, and there's a natural aversion for domestic players to do business with international players such as Fonterra. We were able to build a partnership with [the] DFA because we were both cooperatives. The farmer directors of [the] DFA and the farmer directors of Fonterra understand that the key drivers are the same whether you're an international player such as Fonterra or a local player such as [the] DFA.

RG: In the case of some partners, you're competing in one area and partnering with them in another. For example, Nestlé is a major competitor, but also a partner in Latin America. How do you manage that?

AF: As businesses globalize, the major global players have to line up with each other if they're going to maximize benefits. Nestlé and Fonterra both recognize that as global organizations we're better off working together than against each other. We ensure that the vast majority of activities of our two organizations are aligned, whether that's Nestlé as a customer of Fonterra—and they're our largest single customer—or it's Nestlé as a partner with Fonterra, where we have a very large partnership across South America. Nestlé is also a competitor of Fonterra, but we don't cross-subsidize to give Fonterra a competitive advantage. Our customers trust us for that.

RG: The farmers that own the cooperative are all from New Zealand. Do you plan to keep it that way?

AF: Yes. We haven't contemplated a cooperative structure outside of New Zealand.

RG: One of the constraints that's plagued cooperatives in the past has been capital formation, because all the capital comes from the farmer-owners. How do you see that playing out in your case?

AF: We've got a robust capital structure and quite a unique one in that we have a fair share value for our owners, who can see the appreciation through the annual share revaluation. However, the structure will always limit growth to an extent because all our equity comes into Fonterra through New Zealand dairy farmers. Over time that can be a constraint. We're currently exploring new types of capital structure that will support Fonterra over the next ten to fifteen years. But it's too early to suggest what those will be.

RG: Looking at the global environment, there's a lot of consolidation in our industry. At the retail level, it seems pervasive. Over 50 percent of the markets are managed by a handful of supermarkets. Do you find that difficult?

AF: So far, no. That's the reason Fonterra is split between our ingredients business and our branded consumer product business. The former is founded on building partnerships with customers. As our retail customers consolidate and grow, this is more of an opportunity than a threat.

RG: Another area that's been a major issue in all commodities, and especially in dairy, involves free trade. The WTO keeps looking at these commodity programs, and every country looks at their farm programs trying to figure out how to make them more market oriented. Do you think there's a chance to finally make milk a more market-oriented commodity?

AF: When you look at world trade reform, you look in terms of decades, not years. I believe very strongly that we'll increasingly see free trade in dairy products. But not in the short term.

RG: You talked earlier about an ingredient business and a branded business. Again, the retail trade keeps looking at private label as a strategic tool. How do you see private label versus brand for you?

AF: For Fonterra, we have to play both sides. We don't have sufficient brand equity to gamble on being uniquely just a branded consumer product player. Very few players in the dairy category can do that—Danone, for example, and Nestlé does a particularly good job. We want to leverage the supply chain into larger relationships with retailers, and that means being prepared to do both private label and brands. We play in both areas.

RG: Another aspect of a cooperative, at least from the outside looking in, is that historically, they haven't been able to attract people like yourself from the private sector. What's changing that will enable that to happen? How do the compensation committees of these cooperatives attract people when they don't have the stock options and other kinds of things that traditional firms have?

AF: Cooperatives have to evolve if they want to attract and retain world-class people. In Fonterra's case, we have a fair value share, so our compensation programs are similar to a publicly traded company in terms of fixed compensation, annual incentives, and long-term incentives built on total shareholder return. It's not as easy as if we were publicly traded, but it works in our case.

RG: Another area that makes your company unique is your unusual strength in R&D. You've made some unique discoveries, and not just in dairy, but in nondairy areas as well. How do you see that technology and your R&D going forward?

AF: We invest heavily in R&D and use our size and reach to support initiatives like splitting apart the compounds of milk into constituent areas, especially where they're enhancing health through nutrition. We continue to find ways to do that in dairy proteins. Consumers want more protein in their diet. Dairy and whey proteins used to just be in the muscle-building arena, but now they're going mainstream. We're taking things we've already invented and adapting them for our mainstream products—for example, putting whey into a clear beverage as opposed to a protein bar.

RG: Other companies in the beverage business have been looking at nutrition. They're focused on providing more balanced diets to avoid the obesity that plagues so many countries. How do you see that affecting your products?

AF: Worldwide, we see a trend towards healthier eating, and dairy products are generally viewed by consumers as healthy. So that's a very positive trend for dairy. We're focused on the positive attributes of dairy, for example, pulling good bacteria out of milk as probiotics. We are pushing to get [the] best attributes of our products to consumers in a multitude of ways.

RG: How do you maintain and improve your most important resource, your people?

AF: When I'm asked that question, I acknowledge we're not as good as we'd like to be. We're a global organization, so we have lots of opportunities for people around the world, and we don't hesitate to move very good people into new opportunities around the globe. First and foremost, we focus on finding good people who want to dramatically improve what they're doing, put them in increasingly responsible jobs in different parts of the world, and just watch them grow.

RG: If we were having this conversation ten or fifteen years from now, how do you see Fonterra?

AF: We are truly world class already, yet we have [a] huge upside. Today, our business is anchored in New Zealand, which will always be home base. But ten years from now we'll be substantially bigger, transforming dairy products from cow pastures to consumer products around the world. I think Fonterra will be three or four times the size of our New Zealand base. We'll leverage our strengths as a vertically integrated dairy buyer all the way—as we like to say, from cow to consumer.

RG: Thank you very much. You've provided a great view of what the dairy industry is likely to be, but more importantly, you've provided a point of what cooperatives can be that I think is important for our farming community. Thank you very much.

AF: It's my pleasure, Ray.

7

Small-Scale Farming and Economic Development

RAHUL KUMAR
Managing Director and CEO, Amul Dairy (2013)

Appointed managing director and CEO of Amul Dairy at age thirty-three, Rahul Kumar started working at the number one dairy farm cooperative in India when he was twenty-three years old. His goals have been to maintain Amul's leadership, improve farmers' education, improve the nutrition of the country, and make sure the company has strong leadership in the future. Kumar has grown Amul into one of India's leading companies, serving twenty-five million small farms throughout India. Son of a hardworking school teacher, he credits his family with instilling in him the honesty and integrity needed to work with farmers.[1]

RG: Rahul Kumar is the managing director of Amul Dairy, a shining light in the global food system that has both reached out to small-scale producers and let them play a leading role in developing a cooperative. As you look at the next ten years, how do you see Amul Dairy developing, and, even more, how do you see India developing?

RK: India has great potential in the dairy industry. Per capita milk consumption is increasing. We produced about 113 million metric tons of milk in 2012–2013 and, by our estimates, will consume about 210 million metric tons by 2020. That means that we have to add 10 million metric tons of milk per year, a huge task considering our resources.

We have an 80 percent or so share of all the dairy products in India. Growing demand puts lots of pressure on scarce resources like water, fodder, and feed. We export our raw protein to countries like China and Vietnam for poultry feed or Brazil and Argentina for biofuel, and then risk a milk shortage as a result if the cost of cattle feed rises.

There are other challenges. People are finding jobs in cities, and nobody wants to do agriculture as a prime occupation, especially in the young generation, which has an impact on milk production. We have to ensure that the next generation goes into milk production and maintains our membership base. As an agriculture system, the milk system in India is going to play a very important role, especially for employment at the rural level and supporting nutrition for both the urban and rural consumer.

RG: Is there much consolidation going on at the farm level? The average herd size used to be 1.5 buffalo. Is there much consolidation going on?

RK: Yes, farmers are consolidating. In my opinion, by 2020 about 40 percent of milk in India will come from the big farms.

RG: What about landless laborers? You were the first cooperative that took landless laborers into a cooperative, because they owned a cow. No land, but they at least had a cow. What's happening to landless laborers?

RK: We still have many landless laborers involved with Amul. Seventy percent of our milk comes from landless laborers and marginal farmers. They would like to add more animals. Perhaps that's a better option, because they don't have any land. They'll always be at the core of Amul.

RG: Are larger farmers and these larger landless cattle owners better educated today, and if so, how?

RK: Yes. They're better educated. At Amul, our educational emphasis is on dairy activity, including animal husbandry. We bring them to our modern farms so they can see how animals are kept, how the temperature is controlled inside the shed, the importance of water for the cattle, how fodder should be cut by the chaff cutter, and how calves should be housed.

RG: The veterinarians were very important in the beginning. Because of artificial insemination and other activities, they were able to increase the quality of the animals. Is that still going on?

RK: Yes. We want to double our animal productivity. We've designed two schemes—the first is a web-based, fertility improvement program. We found that about a quarter of our animals are infertile, eating but unable able to give milk. Our veterinary doctor treated those animals and 68 percent of them became fertile and started giving milk. Our second mega scheme is a productivity improvement program based on three pillars: breeding, feeding, and disease management.

RG: In addition to all that, you have a reputation for quality. You don't have a lot of the problems that China had with adulteration. You don't have a lot of problems with bad material being put into the milk. How do you constantly upgrade the quality? How do you see quality changing in the future?

RK: Basically from two angles. First, we quickly chill the milk, so there's no bacterial growth, and the milk is of world-class quality at the farm level and at the village level. We have put bulk milk coolers in almost 100 percent of Amul districts, and now essentially none of our milk goes bad.

Second, we check for adulteration, and continuously teach our farmers that it's against the law and unethical. We also send mobile testing vans to the villages without telling them, and take random samples from the bulk chiller to check for possible adulterants.

We have to be very supportive of the farmers, and education is the best way to eliminate adulteration. Amul is their own organization. If they put adulterated milk into the system, Amul's losses will be passed on to them only.

RG: Do some of the farmers become executives in Amul?

RK: Their kids do if they're educated and qualify. We offer scholarships for professional courses like engineering and medical or hotel management. We provide technical and financial assistance to them.

RG: Public policy has always been an important part of Amul. Dr. Kurien really got started by being friends with the prime minister and making food a major policy decision at the very top of your country. Is that still true today?

RK: Yes, but it's not dairy alone. It's our entire agriculture system in India, because whatever we feed our animals comes from the agriculture system. We also need more wheat, rice, and oilseed production in order to increase our milk production. So government policy will always be very important to us.

Although milk is our largest crop in India, it's not given agricultural status. We think it deserves the same support as other agriculture commodities, like wheat or rice or pulses. About ninety million people are involved in milk production in India, so supportive policies will be very good for a huge number of people.

Because of trade agreements, too much agricultural raw material goes out of the country, which can create shortages of raw protein or raw fat, and makes cattle feed prices very high. Cattle feed represents about 60 percent of total milk cost, so if feed cost grows by 10 percent, milk cost will grow by 6 percent. Exporting agricultural products hurts our dairy farmers.

RG: In the global scheme of things, you've been looking overseas. In fact, you're talking about having a manufacturing plant in the United States. Why?

RK: Amul is the number one dairy brand in India, and thanks to the IT revolution, a huge Indian population now lives outside India, nearly four million in the US. They have strong purchasing power, but still look for Indian products, especially Amul. Two decades ago, we started sending our cheese to the US, because everybody wanted cheese with vegetarian rennet, which only we had available in the entire world.

There was demand for ghee too, so we export [a] lot of ghee to the US for our Indian and other South Asian consumers. We then thought, Why not create a manufacturing base in the States? There are a lot of fresh products with short shelf lives like paneer, which Indians in the US want, so the manufacturing base made lots of sense.

As MD of Amul, I want our dairy industry to learn from developed countries about processing and hygiene, because we have to follow FDA regulations here. It was a very strategic decision based on cross-learning.

RG: In the United States, cooperatives have also tried to follow your example of creating their own brands and managing dairy products in the cases of supermarkets. As supermarkets come to India, do you believe that Amul will be in the business of trying to provide category management of the dairy case in these supermarkets?

RK: We are uncomfortable with the supermarket system, because they tend to exploit the local brands. They want to get more margin and that's disadvantageous to consumers, because the margin is ultimately paid by the consumer. In the future, there will be more supermarkets and we may have our own retailing arrangements—Amul Parlours or Amul Preferred Outlets which will sell only Amul products. People like to have fresh products from nearby shops, so we've targeted setting up around a hundred thousand beautifully designed shops to sell all our products. We already have about twenty thousand stores.

RG: How are they doing?

RK: Almost all the shops are doing very well. People appreciate the concept, because when they want Amul products they can go to Amul shops and find them at the best price.

RG: Around the world, there's a lot of competition, but also a lot of cooperation between people who compete with one another. For example, Fonterra and Nestlé work closely together. Fonterra does a lot of the marketing for Nestlé in Latin America. Do you see more of these kinds of corporate cooperative joint ventures taking place?

RK: We've not come across such collaboration, so I cannot comment.

RG: In the United States, this has happened fairly recently. CHS, which is a major cooperative in the upper Midwest, thought of Cargill as a competitor, actually almost their enemy. But ten or fifteen years ago, they sat down with each other and decided they had more in common in their flour milling industry than they realized, and that the farmers' cooperative and Cargill could help each other better than they could in competing with one another, and so they created their own flour milling company.

RK: Yes, that's possible because, as a principle, we should cooperate with the cooperatives, perhaps initially through technology transfers.

RG: How did you grow up, and how did you end up where you are?

RK: I joined Amul when I was only twenty-three years old. Ten years later I became managing director. That shows what kind of organization we have, because if you work hard and want to show your talent, you can be given more and more responsibility. Dr. Kurien gave me that opportunity.

I get great pleasure and satisfaction working for the farmers. I spend lots of time with them, and don't think my business is simply purchasing milk from them. I want to contribute to the overall development of their social life. They are good people and very hard-working. They are giving milk to our dairy, but they don't have proper sanitation, so I decided that no farmer should go to an open toilet, which was true for about 30 to 40 percent of them. Until they have their own hygiene, they cannot understand the hygiene of milk.

We are talking about a new generation in India, which is going to be the most developed country in the world in twenty or thirty years. But if we lack basic amenities at the farm level, it won't matter.

I also want to get the latest technologies to the grassroot level—solar and biogas systems, enterprise software like SAP, common accounting and auditing. Whatever advantages I have, it's a real satisfaction when I see a smile on a farmer's face.

RG: That value system is wonderful. When you were a little boy, did your parents provide that kind of value system for you?

RK: Yes, absolutely. Whatever we do, whatever way we think, it's all because of our parents and upbringing.

RG: What were their backgrounds?

RK: My father was a very honest teacher and very hard-working. He knew the value of money, and was very down to earth. Given our moderate circumstances, we knew how to manage the little money we had. Perhaps that's why I think like this. I also inherited the most important ingredient in my personality which is honesty and integrity, which is even more relevant when dealing with farmer—for the farmers.

RG: Amul's very lucky to have your leadership. Thank you so much.

MARK CACKLER

Manager of Agricultural Global Practice,
The World Bank (2015)

As manager of the Global Agricultural Practice of the World Bank, Mark Cackler has been actively involved in developing multisector approaches to promote agricultural development in poor countries. The World Bank's goal is to boost prosperity and eliminate poverty by 2030. Cackler believes that the world's five hundred million subsistence farmers are the biggest group of private sector actors in the world, and they need help to become part of the commercial global food system. Descended from a long line of farmers, Cackler grew up in Moline, Illinois, the headquarters of John Deere, where he worked before entering Harvard Business School.

RG: Mark Cackler manages the Global Agricultural Practice of the World Bank. Would you explain your department and its role in the World Bank?

MC: The primary role of the World Bank is to help eliminate poverty by 2030 and to boost shared prosperity. To do so, we need to work on health, education, transport, and, especially, agriculture, since 75 percent of the world's poor are rural, and most are engaged in farming. If we want to help poor people, we need to invest in better agriculture. Our group helps countries design and implement agriculture projects.

RG: In attacking poverty in a way that reaches the greatest number of people, certain countries have been making faster progress than others—China, for example. Why has China been more successful than other countries?

MC: The Chinese government made a decision, nearly a generation ago, to invest in agriculture. Investing in agriculture and the land was absolutely essential to lifting hundreds of millions of Chinese out of poverty. The good news is more are recognizing that agriculture isn't a nineteenth- or even a twentieth-century business. It's fundamental to eliminating poverty and creating growth in the twenty-first century. The Chinese recognized it before some of the other countries where we work.

RG: India is the world's second-largest country, and has a great deal of poverty. How do you see their approach?

MC: India is especially close to my heart. I lived there for four years and worked on some very important programs, like Operation Flood, in the dairy sector. India is a special country. A fundamental difference it has from many other countries is the importance of individual states relative to the national government. Agriculture is a state-dominated sector, which makes it more difficult to take a comprehensive approach toward agricultural development. Nevertheless, successive Indian governments have recognized that eliminating rural poverty is indispensable to achieving their overall economic goals.

RG: Years ago, I had the privilege of teaching by the case method in the World Bank, and I was always amazed that some of the participants thought the private sector wasn't really necessary. Has that changed?

MC: I certainly hope so. We need the private sector, the public sector, academia, and civil society. People mistakenly think of farming as outside the private sector. In fact, the world's 570 million farmers are the largest group of private sector actors in the world. Farming is fundamentally a private sector activity. The agricultural food value chain, going from inputs on the farm all the way to our dinner table, is a fundamentally private sector activity.

RG: The food system is also a quasi-public utility, because what people get paid for producing food and what people get paid for consuming food are political questions as well as economic questions. How do use your creative resources to encourage the public and private sectors to work together?

MC: The dirty little secret is that many wonder if there's any role for government in farming. The answer, of course, is yes, because what government does at the policy level from land tenure to international trade is crucial. At the World Bank we have two overlapping, but distinct parts. One part deals mostly with governments, but we also have the International Finance Corporation (IFC), which deals mostly with the private sector. Since the food price spikes of 2007–2008, there's been increased collaboration within the World Bank between the public sector where I work and the IFC.

RG: Jain Irrigation used irrigation as a way to get people out of poverty and farming and into commercial agriculture. The two biggest investors in Jain Irrigation are [the] IFC and Rabobank. Do they consider this investment as a development vehicle or as a real investment?

MC: Yes, to both questions. Both [the] IFC and Rabobank are in business to make money. Rabobank is a bank, and the International Finance Corporation generates profits. At the same time, they both have development mandates and want to generate public goods as well as financial returns. You referred to agriculture as a quasi-public utility and mentioned Jain Irrigation. When it comes to public policy, there are few things more sensitive in the political arena than water. Although Jain Irrigation is private, the government's role in regulating water use was absolutely essential to their ability to operate.

RG: The management of water as well as the management of land have become increasingly important. The original water rights that farmers had, say, in California, are being questioned when water needs to be rationed [for] competing uses. How is that going to be resolved?

MC: These will be political decisions, which gets back to the relationship between the public and private sectors. Water is one of the most sensitive subjects, and will only get more sensitive with climate change. Even without climate change, household, industrial, and commercial demand for water has increased, so the share available to agriculture is dropping. We need to be much more rational about how we consume and conserve water. There are many adverse implications of climate change on agriculture, having to do with heat, and pests, but the single scariest one is water, and how that will affect farming. We need a reasonable public policy environment so the private sector, in this case the farmers, can continue to sustainably produce the food we all need.

RG: And water doesn't stop at national boundaries, which is why we have an agreement with Mexico. Even though we're good neighbors, it's been very difficult to balance the water resources of both nations. How are we going to find a common water policy for the world?

MC: You raise a scary subject. Some people say the twenty-first century will be a century of water wars. Water stresses were going to be a problem anyway, but it's being exacerbated by climate change. Water stress leads to political stress, which can lead to conflict. Some observers consider Darfur the first water war. Unless countries come together, the potential impact of not managing water goes beyond growing food sustainably and becomes a matter of war and peace.

RG: The World Bank is sort of the secretary of agriculture for the world. How do you play a role in keeping the peace among competing nations?

MC: If the World Bank had one-tenth the influence people think we have, it would be a very different place. We're unique, because we are one of the few global institutions that is multiregional and multisectoral. If we want to deal with agriculture, we can't just look at farming. We have to consider other sectors, because agriculture is related to so many of them. Take human health. Food safety is a health issue as well as an agriculture issue. Zoonotic diseases like avian flu are health issues as well as agriculture issues. And there's transport and energy. There's an old saying that war is too important to be left to the generals. Well, agriculture is too important to be left to aggies like me. In addition to providing financing and creating and sharing knowledge, the World Bank also provides a place for people to talk. We look for areas where a multilateral, multiregional, multisectoral perspective can be helpful.

RG: If we were having this conversation in ten years, will your goals have been met?

MC: Not unless we do a better job of including women in the process of agriculture development. The amount of hunger in this world—eight hundred million people go to bed hungry—should be intolerable to all of us. There's some reason to be optimistic. A few years ago, the number exceeded one billion. If we gave women the same access to agricultural inputs and markets as men, we've estimated agriculture production and incomes in East Africa would rise 20 to 30 percent and national GDP would rise 3 to 4 percent, which is big. If we're able to do that, then actually I'm very optimistic. You know, my ancestors came from Ireland, and most people know the Irish story. Ireland today has fewer people than it had in the nineteenth century because one million died of starvation and another one million had to emigrate. Ireland has become a champion in promoting agriculture and food security. When I see my cousins sustainably farming the land from which my father's grandmother emigrated, I'm filled with optimism. Poverty rates have fallen in places like China and Vietnam, and that's cause for optimism. We have new challenges like climate change and old challenges like bad trade policies. Yield growth has been declining, and we need more resources for agricultural research. But it's helpful to remember how far we've come.

RG: What will it look like in ten years?

MC: My vision is that every farmer, whether female or male, would have secure access to her or his land, would have the inputs they need and the right kind of seeds for her or his local area, especially taking into account climate change. Another dream would be to improve fertilizer efficiency. We need game-changing innovations; let's call it "an electric car for agriculture." We need to embrace the idea that we're really one market. We can't hide behind trade barriers. We need to make progress on cultural and societal issues, like how do we educate rural youth.

RG: I've never seen a greater interest in the food systems and policies of nations. Cross-registration in all of our food-related courses is at the highest level in Harvard's history. There's a keen desire to make a difference in the world, and students believe that the food system offers promising opportunities. How do you attract the kind of people you want in the World Bank for that?

MC: We need people who understand there are no magic beans, as we call them at the World Bank, or magic bullets. A multisectoral, multiactor approach is essential. Technical skills are also necessary. Aspirations aren't enough. My advice to students would be to develop specific expertise to make a real contribution while developing a broad approach to development. Engineering, agronomy, medicine, and law are examples of technical skills that can make a real difference.

RG: Consolidation in the food system has created the highest level of distrust I've seen in my lifetime. Many don't think companies or institutions care about nutrition, resource use, or people. How do we re-establish trust in the global food system?

MC: The world needs trust and the world needs the food system, but I'm not sure I agree that there's more distrust than ever before. Any time there's change, there's suspicion, and suspicion breeds distrust. Maybe what we're observing is that as change accelerates, anxieties and suspicions accelerate and so does distrust. We need to do whatever we can do reduce the anxieties and reduce the distrust. We need to bring people together to build trust. The World Bank has been working with the public and private sectors on the Global Food Safety Partnership, which, in addition to focusing on healthy food, has been building trust across the different sectors in different countries.

RG: What in your background led you to do what you're doing, and why?

MC: I'm just a boy from a small town in the Midwest, Moline, Illinois. My family descended from farmers, which is true of most of us. Moline is a company town, headquarters of John Deere, the agricultural machinery company. My first job after college was with John Deere. They sent me to Southeast Asia, which is where I first heard of the World Bank. Working in agriculture, it sounded like a really interesting organization. I then went to a place called Harvard Business School and had a professor named Ray Goldberg, and other good professors, and was convinced that improving the food system to make the world a better place was what I wanted to do. I joined the World Bank to do just that and I'm very glad I did.

RG: We're very glad the World Bank was wise enough to choose you. Thank you very much, Mark.

MC: Thank you, Professor.

JONATHAN TAYLOR

President, International Basic Economy
Corporation (IBEC) (2015)

The former president of Nelson Rockefeller's International Basic Economy Corporation (IBEC), Jonathan Taylor has been at the forefront of mobilizing resources to enhance the economic viability of small farmers in Latin America. IBEC helped create the Mumias Sugar Project, and Taylor believes that for small-scale producers to succeed, there has to be a structure similar to the one IBEC created. Prior to IBEC, Taylor headed Booker McConnell, which was similarly active in Africa and Latin America. A strong advocate for cultural initiatives, Taylor chairs the Man Booker Prize for Literature.[2]

RG: Jonathan Taylor is former president of the International Basic Economy Corporation (IBEC). He was one of the first executives in the agribusiness system to follow the concept that Nelson Rockefeller and his son Rodman pioneered of putting the private sector and the quasi-development sector together to try to improve the food system. From your perspective, was IBEC premature or on target? How do you view what they tried to do, and where we [are] in the food system today?

JT: That's a big question. As conceived by Nelson, IBEC was attempting something very difficult, which was to use the capitalist system to achieve social and economic benefits. It was an uncomfortable dual objective. On the one hand it was a for-profit business very deliberately a part of the Rockefeller for-profit side, unlike the foundation and the Brothers Fund. It was for profit but had social objectives. The two coexist with difficulty. You can have a great housing project in Iran or Puerto Rico which does a lot of social good but is losing money. The people losing the money can say, Look how many people we're housing, but the business cannot continue if it's not making a profit. The businesses making a profit are fine, and IBEC had quite a few of those, particularly in the agribusiness area. I came to IBEC and worked with Rodman Rockefeller, whom I admired. He wasn't the greatest businessman, but he was wise. My task was to sort out the sustainable bits—particularly the poultry breeding businesses and the seed breeding business in Brazil—and sell off the rest. Nowadays we've got different structures for not-for-profit organizations using the discipline of the private sector. It's easier now to achieve what IBEC was trying to achieve. IBEC was quite revolutionary in its way.

RG: It was revolutionary. You were CEO of Booker-McConnell and had a project in Kenya, the Mumias Sugar Project, which was written up in a book by Susan George called *How the Other Half Dies*. She was very anti-business. But the one saving grace was Booker in Mumias, because she thought you represented what the business community could do in terms of economic development. You were way ahead of your time when you did all those things. Today people expect more of that. How do you see the future?

JT: Mumias was a success in part because it had to be a success commercially. We had to make sugar economically, and were a relatively low-cost producer because of favorable soil and climate conditions and so on. We had a practical way of efficiently growing cane, which employed a large number of small farmers. Small farmer agriculture has its place, not perhaps in the US, but at a certain stage of economic development with the small farmer owning his own land and organizing for economies of scale in harvesting and fertilizing. It's quite an efficient model called "outgrowing." There was one with the tea industry too. Mumias pioneered an agricultural production system which incorporated disciplinary structures that created some of the advantages of large-scale agriculture. Production capacity is now three hundred thousand tons of sugar a year, but over the last several years, production has been falling. It's a Kenyan problem—elements of corruption, and senior management and the board of directors are mostly lawyers and accountants with very few agriculturists or chemical engineers, people who actually know how to produce sugar. Politicians could get licenses to import low-cost sugar from Brazil, which created a problem for the domestic industry. While it's doing less well than it should, Mumias is still there, producing sugar, producing ethanol, contributing electricity to the national grid, recycling potable water. It's transformed part of western Kenya, and I think we can be proud of it.

RG: We have five hundred million small-scale farmers in the world, most of whom are in poverty. The majority suffering malnutrition are these small-scale farmers. Everyone wants to do something about it. Mumias was a pretty good attempt to do something about it. Amul Dairy, the food cooperative in India, is another example. Twenty-one years ago I was very worried about distrust throughout the food system. Everyone thought each other wasn't trustworthy, and the public in turn distrusted the science and corporate consolidation. I tried to put the private, public, and not-for-profit sectors together for an off-the-record discussion seeking common ground to collaboratively attack malnutrition on one side, obesity on the other, and corruption too. I got a phone call from Nestlé saying they're creating an institution in China called the Dairy Farm Institute. It's made up of all the stakeholders in the dairy industry that normally compete with one another but were willing to try to improve the dairy system in China, which has a terrible reputation.

JT: Quality problems.

RG: Terrible problems. For the first time they're all working together. They also have a university in Wisconsin and a university in China working with them. They have both the Chinese and US governments working with them. They're trying to change the whole dairy system collectively and on a win-win basis. Do you think that model will work?

JT: That's an encouraging development. The key will be a disciplined structure. That discipline comes with Nestlé in production and marketing. In order for small holders to work as part of a business system, there has to be a structure. It can't be a free-for-all.

RG: So they need the discipline of trying to be the most efficient and competitive part of the system itself. You've watched all these changes over many years. You've worked on commonwealth development programs in your country in the UK and others; how do you see the next one hundred years of the global food system? I know that's an impossible task and an unfair question. But frankly you were kind enough to try to address it once before, so here we are a quarter of a century later asking the same question.

JT: The questions are the same, aren't they? It's about population and urban migration from rural areas and climate change and water resources and agricultural technology. On the technology side we can be optimistic, but on everything else we've got to be pretty pessimistic, particularly politics. Yes or no? I'm going to ask you a question.

RG: Well I think that we've made more progress in technology than people recognize and universities now look at these problems in a multidisciplinary manner.

JT: Absolutely. And that's partially thanks to you. You can have a compliment.

RG: Thank you. Two months ago we had twenty-seven professors at Harvard from about eight departments—the medical school, the school of public health, the business school, the government school, the biochemistry department, the forestry department—talking about their discipline and their research. It amazed me that they were addressing problems you and I never thought would be addressed.

JT: Over ten years, there's been progress. But when you look at feeding the world, the agenda hasn't moved very much, has it? It's still about water and storage and distribution, climate—

RG: It is. But the numbers are working in our favor. We had a billion people going hungry a decade ago. We're down to eight hundred million. We have targets, and they're trying to meet them. My greatest concern is the leadership necessary to get the job done. In my most recent class I had sixty students from forty different nations, like a miniature United Nations sitting in front of me, and when I saw what they wanted to achieve and how they wanted to achieve it, I guess, that I became more optimistic.

JT: Are they going into agricultural and food production?

RG: Some were from the medical school with a health perspective, some were from the school of public health with a nutrition perspective, some had an agricultural production perspective, and some wanted to go into government. They care more than any generation we've ever had in a classroom. We have to find a way of getting more of them into positions of responsibility so they're the ones people look up to rather than the corrupt leaders.

JT: They can be real leaders. For well over a decade I've been very involved in literature. I run the Booker Prize and the Caine Prize for Africa and a prize for Arabic literary fiction. I've come to the conclusion that we neglect the development of civil society. We're not talking about per capita national income, but the communal culture of reading, music, dancing, theater, literature—I'm very concerned with the literature. Bilateral and multilateral development agencies have totally neglected this area. If we're going to create successful societies, we neglect the cultural area at our peril. Per capita income means a lot, but it's not the whole story.

RG: I couldn't agree more. My late wife was very active in the Boston Symphony and my youngest son is involved with a German opera house, so I couldn't agree more. It's an area where people can work and perform together. How are we going to get the arts and the literature and the music and the culture and the value system together? They've debased religion by making it an attack agent.

JT: Religion could have been part of the answer. Now it's part of the problem.

RG: It's part of the problem because it's no longer religion. It's something else. You've had more experience through your academic relationships with Oxford and the Royal Agricultural University and through your cultural leadership and the Booker Prize. How can I have a positive ending here if you, who've spent so many years trying to bring people together in so many different ways, if you are so worried that we're not making the kind of progress we should? Are we moving the needle at all?

JT: We've made progress. In the technology area, in health, in plant breeding, in agricultural technology, we have made progress. Many cultural activities are now global, and that's all positive. The negative is the risk religions are creating, particularly in North Africa, the Middle East, and Central Asia. The resurgence of Russia with Putin looks worrying. I was a strong believer in the UK not needing its missile defenses, but that doesn't look very realistic.

RG: That could prove to the rest of the world that we cared and could provide the hungry leadership that everybody wants in this world.

JT: If there's no political leadership, life is difficult. I don't see it in Europe or—I don't know enough about China.

RG: I have students from China who were disrupted by the so-called Cultural Revolution. I have students from Africa who suffered under adverse conditions. Even they are optimistic. It cheers me up. But thank you. You've been a leader in our field in so many different ways, and I'm glad you brought up culture, literature, and music as they're so critical to development.

JT: And neglected. The World Bank and the bilateral agencies are not interested, but it's fundamental to human development.

RG: Thank you very much for the privilege of interviewing you.

JT: As always, great fun.

ROBERT ROSS

Past President, Latin American Agribusiness Development Company (2016)

Past President of the privately owned Latin American Agribusiness Development Company (LAAD), Robert Ross worked with the Agency for International Development (AID) to profitably develop local processing capacity for the benefit of small-scale local farmers. Ross believes that for the small-scale producer to succeed, one has to provide a market, and one has to invest in entrepreneurs able to put resources and people together. He also believes strongly in having independent analyses of projects. In retirement, Ross has advised other development firms and written about his experiences with LAAD.[3]

RG: Robert Ross was president of the Latin American Agribusiness Development Company (LAAD) for over thirty years. Would you mind explaining LAAD?

RR: LAAD is a private, for-profit corporation started by twelve, mostly American, multinational corporations in 1970 for the purpose of developing agriculture in Latin America. They felt agriculture needed a specialized development corporation rather than the World Bank's IFC, which works with all sectors of the economy. The shareholders wanted to help Latin American agriculture grow.

RG: What about your background and growing up made them want you to be their first president?

RR: It wasn't so much my education. I was working for a venture capital company focused on Latin America and headquartered in Lima, Peru. Salvador Allende was the socialist president of Chile, which expropriated two companies, one of which was Ralston Purina, a

founding shareholder of LAAD. Another shareholder asked me to re-
solve the problem, so I flew down to Chile and met with the Chilean
government. We negotiated a reimbursement value mutually acceptable to the company and the Chilean government. Ralston Purina
learned about the negotiation and hired me to do the same for them.
Once that was solved, the EVP of Ralston Purina invited me to St. Louis
to talk about LAAD. He offered me the job on the spot, and I accepted.

RG: LAAD stands for what?

RR: Latin American Agribusiness Development Corporation. What we
stand for is the development of Latin American agriculture. When
I was hired, we had no strategy. An equity strategy wouldn't work,
because there was no secondary market for shares in Latin America.
LAAD had only $2.4 million of capital, so there was no way we could
both invest money and pay our expenses. Our only practical avenue
was to fund agricultural projects.

RG: How did the Agency for International Development get involved?

RR: That was critical. Without AID no bank would provide us with medium-
term funding. We merged with a company or an idea for a company
developed by Thomas Mooney, who was the vice president of Adela
where I'd worked for many years. He ran Adela's Central American operations and was a former AID economist. He went to AID and said, If
I can raise $2 million, will you give me $6 million so I can set up a regional development company focused exclusively on Central America?
They approved the loan, but he was unable to raise the $2 million until
he met LAAD. We put in $2 million and AID made a $6 million long-
term loan, which is how it all started.

RG: What was AID's motivation to work with the private sector?

RR: USAID was organized regionally, and Latin America was the only
bureau working with the private sector. Adela and Tom Mooney had
created a dozen development finance companies in Latin America, so
in essence, Thomas Mooney was offering AID another opportunity to
invest in a regional finance company, in this case focused on Central
America.

RG: In order to understand how this works, could we look at El Cosa as
a specific example? Could you explain what El Cosa was, and how it
developed?

RR: El Cosa was a pioneering venture like many LAAD ventures, because
we only finance entrepreneurs. The company was a subsidiary of
Hanover Brands of Hanover, Pennsylvania. Their main business was

producing and selling frozen vegetables primarily for the American market. They were having difficulty producing all year and finding labor for very labor-intensive crops. They looked all over the world but wanted a place close to America, and settled on Guatemala. They sent a team down to analyze the soil and weather and to choose crops. They then hired different types of farmers to grow these crops. They tried small farmers and tried large farmers, and concluded that in most cases small farmers, almost all of whom were Mayan, were more effective with labor-intensive crops than the larger farms or Hanover itself. So they decided that Guatemala was the right place. LAAD had lent to a small mom-and-pop company which froze the type of Guatemalan vegetables that interested Hanover. So Hanover acquired the only frozen vegetable plant in Central America. We put up money to expand the plant. That's how it started.

RG: You also hired someone to evaluate the project at the very beginning. How did you happen to do that?

RR: Actually it was AID that hired a very resourceful academician from American University to oversee our operation. He flew to Guatemala and hired himself out as a truck driver to drive produce from the farms to the plant. He peppered farmers with questions and wrote the most insightful study about any of our projects to date.

RG: Why is it so difficult to get someone to do that kind of project evaluation? Having an independent person review what's going makes it much more credible.

RR: It has to be independent. The likes of AID or, say, the Ford Foundation want to know what impact these companies have on the real lives of poor people.

RG: What were you doing?

RR: Our task was to address rural poverty by funding agricultural projects. The projects had to do more than make money. They had to have a positive impact on poor people, and in the case of Guatemala it was the Mayan Indians who were the main farming population in the highlands. The sociologist showed that the livelihood of these farmers improved dramatically. Our program allowed farmers to grow crops worth much more than corn, which they'd always grown. A farm in the Guatemalan highlands might make $1,000 per hectare annually, but $10,000 or $15,000 growing vegetables. That's a fundamental economic change for a family. Farmers didn't do that in the past, because there was so much risk involved. If they lose their crop to a disease or weather, they starve. There's no safety net. But along comes a company that says, We'll provide you with seed and will teach you about the crop and, if you need them, will provide you with agrichemicals. We'll also pay you a guaranteed price for whatever you produce, which takes the market risk away from the farmer. What happened? Instead of using their children to take care of the vegetables, they hired somebody local and sent their children to school. They bought shoes for their children. This wasn't possible as a subsistence farmer. These were fundamental changes that took place in a very short period of time.

RG: Did it affect the whole family, the wives as well?

RR: The wives had worked in the fields too, but with vegetables they were able to take care of the family, and many worked in the processing plant, cleaning and classifying the produce their husbands produced.

RG: Was AID pleased with the report?

RR: Yes. For several years, we were the number one success story in their reports to Congress.

RG: Did they make more investments in LAAD?

RR: Yes. At one point, we were AID's largest private borrower worldwide. When Latin America had what's called the Great Debt Crisis caused by Mexico's earthquake in 1982, it was impossible to raise private money for the region—impossible. But AID rescued us by providing loans throughout the long crisis. They had confidence in us and were willing to take a big risk as bureaucrats, because they were pleased with how we were using their money. At one point, they asked our shareholders for a guarantee, but the shareholders refused, so they were making unsecured loans. As civil servants, they were taking a big risk. If we failed there'd be mud on their face, and if we succeeded there were no bonuses. It was extraordinary risk-taking on the part of some civil servants.

RG: Given the pioneering example of El Cosa, why is there so much distrust today when government agencies work with the private sector to promote development? Why don't they look at El Cosa as a way for the future?

RR: Latin America AID did. We became AID's largest borrower worldwide for a while, which certainly demonstrates a willingness to work with the private sector. But that was just the Latin American bureau.

RG: We live in a world that's not very trusting of the private sector. In this particular case the entrepreneurship approach seemed to work.

RR: The entrepreneurs in this case are 95 percent local. The bulk of our clients have been local, family-owned businesses. That largely explains why we haven't had a problem with lack of trust.

RG: Is the market always global, or is it domestic as well?

RR: That goes back to our beginnings and OPEC's increase in oil prices in 1973, which caused huge problems in Latin America, including devalued currencies. All of our loans were and still are dollar denominated. Our borrowers were selling in the local market for local currencies. We decided that as a matter of policy we would only finance projects which earned dollars through global exports. But they had to be nontraditional. We were not going to finance sugar. It was going to be high-value products like flowers and vegetables. High value implies lots of labor. Today half our projects are high-value, nontraditional, agricultural exports. We never focused on projects, because a government said they were top priority. We chose projects with a market that generated cash flow needed to pay the loan back. That's our model.

RG: Why aren't other parts of the world trying to duplicate this?

RR: They are, to a certain extent. It depends on how much control the buyer has over his market. Take the counter seasonal fruits in Chile. Nobody's going to guarantee the price. The price depends on a Swedish supermarket chain or a British supermarket chain over whom the seller has no control. Working with small farmers, you pretty much need a guaranteed price. You can work with a market price with the larger farms we typically finance. But that's very difficult to do with small farmers, because they can't absorb much risk.

RG: You did something else as well. You looked at a product that was seasonal in one part of Latin America and not seasonal in another part of the world and got producers to work together. How did you do that?

RR: Those ideas came from the entrepreneurial growers themselves. The Peruvian asparagus industry is a great example. When we were starting operations in Peru, the largest global supplier of fresh, frozen, and canned asparagus in the world was Taiwan. I didn't even know they produced asparagus. We found a man who believed he could grow asparagus in the desert of Peru, and control the harvest by controlling water. He timed his harvest precisely to windows in the main markets, mostly Europe and the United States. Today Peru is the largest producer and exporter of asparagus. But the idea came from them, not me.

RG: AID's mandate is to work with the poorest of the poor, and yet they still make loans to you, so obviously you were working with those kinds of farmers.

RR: Yes. I asked, How do you want us to work with them? They said, That's your problem. We'll tell you how to use the money. It has to benefit the small farmers. We came up with the idea of financing labor-intensive farms, for example, vegetables and horticulture, which use much more labor than wheat, corn, or soybeans. Secondly, we financed packing plants which purchased products from small farmers. That's the El Cosa case. There were many others. We found a number of businesses which bought their raw material from small farmers, and chose projects that employed a lot of women, often the wives of the producers. Those were the kinds of businesses that we chose to meet AID's mandate. And it worked.

RG: Why doesn't AID insist that all their projects be evaluated the way El Cosa was evaluated, and why don't they pay for it?

RR: I wish they would. One of my great frustrations is that I could never get an AID official down to see our projects. They said they visited problems, and we were always doing fine.

RG: We live in a world where people are very suspicious of international or domestic businesses working with international or domestic agencies, because they worry about the public sector and private sector working together. Here you have a perfect example of success, but you don't have the documentation to prove to the distrustful outside world that the business community can be constructively involved in development. How do we find a way for the outside world to trust both you and AID?

RR: When I retired I offered to write a book about the impact we'd had. But they didn't want to do it.

RG: The land tenure problem is pervasive around the world. And yet land tenure is important to you as a lender. How do you consider that when you're going to make an investment?

RR: We evaluated projects on a case-by-case basis. We needed a viable cash flow to service the loan, and wanted to have a social impact as well. We also kept it simple.

RG: If we were having this conversation ten or twenty years from now, what would you like to see happen to programs designed to improve the livelihood of farmers around the world and enable the private and public sectors not only to work together but also [be] judged together?

RR: The LAAD model is a perfect model, but we don't need public participation, because we can raise funds from the private sector on acceptable terms. We needed the public sector at the beginning when the risk was highest, but once we proved we knew what we were doing, the private sector came around.

RG: When you look at the food system today with five hundred million small-scale farmers around the world, how can the private, public, and not-for-profit sectors find a better way of working together?

RR: I wouldn't look to the nonprofit sector. The solution in all cases has to be market based, which means for profit. Take the small farmers who were receiving assistance from the Ministry of Agriculture extension agents before El Cosa came along. They paid no attention to them, because they had no confidence in them. But they listened to the El Cosa advisers, because they were buying their crops. That's the market solution. I don't have faith in a nonprofit approach to a for-profit business like agriculture.

RG: How would you measure LAAD's success?

RR: I'd measure it by the income generated, the jobs created, and the value added to the sector. Some of these are measurable, some aren't, but everyone benefits if land becomes more valuable, because you make better use of it.

RG: Thank you so much.

RR: My pleasure, Ray.

BHAVARIL JAIN

Founder and Chairman, Jain Irrigation Company (2012)

The late Bhavaril Jain founded Jain Irrigation on the advice of his mother, who felt he could help more people by going into agriculture rather than the government. After convincing the Indian government that water scarcity would be a critical issue in the future, Jain adapted a sophisticated drip irrigation system to serve small-scale Indian farmers. He then helped develop markets for the producers and reduced the farmers' risk by guaranteeing a minimum price. Jain Irrigation trained farmers, provided financing for them, and became their bridge to the commercial food system. It is now the largest drip irrigation company in the world.[4]

RG: Dr. Bhavaril Jain is the founder and chairman of the Jain Irrigation Company, and this company is the second-largest irrigation company in the world. They've done more to help the small-scale farmer than any other company in the world. How did you get started?

BJ: It all started with my mother. I had a cushy government job offer, but I had to check with her as those are my roots. She said, Look, boy, I don't understand any of these worldly things. But I do understand if you work in a government service, you'll be able to feed yourself, your family, and maybe some relatives. If you go into business, maybe you'll take care of ten or twenty people you already know, and maybe a larger number as you grow. But who is there in this world to take care of the dumb animals? Do something to take care of them along with the people you want to serve.

My prime motive became [to] take care of animals. Only agriculture fitted that shoe. My mother inspired me to enter business.

RG: The technical knowledge of irrigation has expanded enormously in recent years. How do you stay on top of that technology, and how do you constantly improve it?

BJ: First, it's not a matter of improving the technology already available in the world. That technology is designed for large farms with thousands of acres. We developed it for the smallholder farmer with less than two acres. We had to manufacture a good-quality product, as well as install it, arrange the financing, and teach farmers how to use it productively. The technology was really an integration of these services, along with the product. We located the best technology in Switzerland and were able to adapt it for our own farmers in India.

That's the way we started working and continue to work. Even if I have a computerized farm, the computer must work for one or two acres. If I can reduce the cost of manufacture and manufacture it locally and adapt it to the local condition, I can make it inexpensive. And if I can make it inexpensive, I can make it affordable.

The third technology I had to work with was the public sector and government policy. Unless the government supports this kind of capital formation in agriculture, the capital cost of the equipment is prohibitive. If a farmer mortgages his farm, and it's not with a vision to purchase an irrigation system, the government had to step in.

When I started in 1987, they used to ask me, Since we're not importing any water, why do we need water-saving technology? My answer was, We may not be importing water today, but there'll be a time when you have no water to drink, so let's start today. The government of India was kind enough to understand this proposition, and in their collective wisdom decided our drip irrigation technology was the one to promote. They helped me to get our first technical fee, which was around $30,000.

Everyone else was working on large big farms. We were the only ones working for small farms. So that is what makes [it] a challenge for me. My challenges were affordability and the suitability of handing a sophisticated irrigation system over to a farmer who doesn't know how to write or read. I knew I needed a very committed staff to succeed.

The first farmer I wanted to sell the irrigation system to insisted on a special condition, a small condition. He agreed to buy the system on the condition that I come to his farm for a lunch. By my going there, he felt that, yes, the system may be worth it. He took the first system, which is the way we began.

RG: And he trusted you?

BJ: He trusted me.

RG: Did the agricultural banks help?

BJ: Most of the banks were defunct, but the federal government stepped in and offered to provide half the money to the farmer and as much as 80 percent to the very poor farmers. Not to me, but to the farmers. That helped propagate the whole idea, and created some faith in the technology. We also engaged in some rudimentary education, kind of like extension work.

RG: How did you pick which crops to grow, or did the farmer pick the crop?

BJ: The obvious crops for a drip irrigation system are horticulture and orchards, because they're spaced at regular intervals between two and, say, five meters. You need less plastic and fewer emitters to get the water out, so the cost becomes affordable. As time passed, we kept adding products, right up to tea and coffee. In a big way we now have groundnuts and cotton and—this will surprise you—we've experimented for two years with rice, and the results have been phenomenal. We're using 50 percent of the water and increasing yields, by 15 percent to 20 percent. There's hardly a crop we're not touching.

RG: Are you still worried about the shortage of water?

BJ: Agriculture uses 75 percent of the water, so anyone concerned with water security has to tend to agriculture, because even a 5 percent saving could supply most of the water needed by domestic people and the industry. But anyone concerned with water must also attend to the land, the entire environment. The whole thing is a circle.

RG: Do you get involved in the marketing of these products?

BJ: We purchase produce under a contract from many farmers. We guarantee him a minimum floor price, and if the market price is higher, we pay him more. We act as a buffer and absorb price shocks.

RG: You produce higher-quality products because of your drip irrigation. Where do these products go? Do you have a marketing arm that's constantly improving relationships with the rest of the food chain?

BJ: We sell fresh products directly to the stores, but in a somewhat limited way. We can add value to small farmers by selling their produce locally or sending it abroad for export. It's a small part of our business today, because we don't have the resources to create the whole chain from the farm down to the store. But we have a plan to do this through various acquisitions that we're making across the world.

RG: Do you think that the farmers will end up in cooperatives?

BJ: We're developing a model which is a substitute for corporate farming in [the] US, for example, or large farming. We want farmers to own their land. We don't want to buy their land or even rent it. Our role is to help them get the agricultural support they need, especially irrigation and engineering support more generally.

Can we reach everyone in this process? Unfortunately, no. Since 1987, we've served over two million farmers, but there are one hundred million farmers right in India. If you talk globally, there's an enormous opportunity for increasing agricultural productivity.

RG: If we were to look at your company in ten or twenty years, what will it look like?

BJ: We'll certainly be the largest irrigation company in the world, and I'd imagine the single largest agricultural company. As an agriculture company we'd be providing inputs, purchasing and processing output, adding value, and sharing part of that with the farmer and society. If you want great productivity, you also need to improve the potential of the seed planting material. We have a biotechnology division where we're conducting basic research and modifying products—not GMO, but transgenic. For example, if we could harvest a banana in ten months instead of eleven, we'd avoid high temperatures and water savings would be enormous.

We feel very satisfied in what we've done so far, not because we've made millions, but because we've been able to really achieve our purpose. Our corporate mission is to leave this world better than we found it.

RG: You're certainly to be congratulated for that. How do you relate to the global retailing and global food service businesses? Should you be in those businesses as well?

BJ: The globe is becoming a village, and villages have to start thinking globally. We have no choice but to get into that chain and to become a bigger part of it. It could be through an organic product, an altogether new green field project, through acquisitions or partnerships. We'll see.

RG: In order to do all this, how do you develop your people? How do you instill the philosophy that you have?

BJ: A difficult question. I can only instill the spirit in them as a role model. If I walk the talk, they buy the talk, or they don't. Creating trust is essential. If money does come, it will be shared with them. Not only that, but we are one for a higher purpose. Everybody wants to work for that. I haven't found it difficult to make such people. I think you make them rather than get them.

RG: What about stakeholders? Do you think they need the same sort of feeling?

BJ: The stakeholder is essentially an equity holder, a person who provides you with finance. They take almost unlimited risk by investing in your equity, so all my respect goes to them. They're co-owners. So a reasonable return on their investment has to be guaranteed. Our focus is on the farmer, around whom everything moves. If the farmer's there, I have a role to play. If I'm there, the shareholder has a role to play. And if the shareholder, the farmer, and I are there, then there are employees with roles to play.

RG: Thank you for the privilege of this interview.

ANIL JAIN

Managing Director, Jain Irrigation (2012)

Managing Director of Jain Irrigation, Anil Jain leads the largest irrigation company in the world, serving some five million mostly subsistence farmers in 116 countries. He took over as managing director of Jain Irrigation after his father's death. To create more reliable, less risky markets for small-scale producers, he has moved Jain Irrigation into processing and marketing. The World Bank's International Finance Corporation and Rabobank are major shareholders in Jain Irrigation.

RG: Anil Jain is the managing director of Jain Irrigation, a unique company focused on small-scale producers in the global agribusiness world. You've helped millions of farmers become a profitable part of the commercial agribusiness food system. As you look forward, how do you see both the challenges and the opportunities for fulfilling your mission to help small-scale farmers around the world?

AJ: Challenge and opportunity are flipsides of the same coin. We've helped improve the lives of only about 3 million of India's 120 million farmers. There are many more in Africa and other emerging markets. Many of these farmers don't have access to technology, knowledge, and/or finance. We work on multiple issues, starting with the view that small-scale farming can be sustainable, productive, and prosperous. Creating a distribution and delivery system for multiple farmers with multiple crops in multiple geographies and regions in different agro-climatic areas around the world is our goal. How do you do that? We must maintain our cash flow profitability because we are running a business.

RG: You are first of all an irrigation company, but you've become a food processing company, an energy company, and a total package company looking at the global food system. Why did you have to do so much to help the farmer?

AJ: The small farmer is fraught with risk. He has a small amount of land; weather goes wrong; diseases happen; water may not come; monsoons may not happen; the end prices for produce may crash. A lot of this is beyond his control. We want to create a business model for the farmer which is viable, so that ultimately it will create a sustainable society. We're helping with better planting material and micro-irrigation, which reduces input costs and grows output. How does the farmer get better value for his output? We decided to buy what he grows and give him a reasonable net return so he's willing to invest in the farming. That's how we got into food processing.

We're willing to buy from him, and he's willing to invest in an irrigation system. There may not be electricity, so we're working on solar water pumps. The whole idea is to create a virtuous cycle where farmers are less dependent on the outside world.

Once he's less dependent, risk gets mitigated, and agriculture becomes more sustainable. He can prosper not just for a season. Then, the next generation might also look at agriculture as something attractive. What happens if the next generation only wants to create software? If they don't do agriculture, who'll feed the world?

RG: Irrigation requires lots of power to move the pumps. How are you able to overcome the fact that they don't have power?

AJ: Lots of these farmers get barely two or three hours of power. Using a drip irrigation system, even if the power is available for only three hours, you can open one valve and irrigate the entire crop, something you can't do using flood irrigation. We have a further thought, which is to create a model at a village level where agri-waste creates energy for the whole village. We also create a community water tank to distribute water, and we've designed drip irrigation systems to have low pressure, so less water is required.

RG: The investment in irrigation is large for anybody, but even larger for the small-scale farmer. The government recognizes that, and they try to work with you. How do you see that sustaining the government involvement, or do you think there should be another model?

AJ: Government involvement is necessary now, but eventually, once this farmer becomes somewhat prosperous, he'll be able to manage [on] his own. Irrigation systems cost roughly $1,000 to $1,500 per hectare. When the farmer is doing flood irrigation, he only needs $100 to $200 per hectare. So this is a big decision.

Today, the government helps buy the irrigation system. The farmers are improving productivity by 50 percent to 300 percent, so the payback on the investment is two to three years. But the challenge for the farmer is capital. With government support, the payback is twice as fast. If the farmer has access to capital, he should be able to afford the system and become a sustainable farmer.

Over [the] past two decades, Indian farmers have become accustomed to government support. Changing that mindset will take time. We're going through that process now.

RG: Long term, you talk about creating some sort of a financial system yourself that will be beneficial to the farmer. How do you see that evolving?

AJ: We're setting up a rural credit institution, a nonbanking finance company, which would lend to farmers so they can invest in drip irrigation or other modern agriculture inputs that promote sustainable agriculture.

RG: Do you think [the] IFC and Rabobank and other financial institutions would like to partner with you to do this?

AJ: [The] IFC is partnering as a 10 percent shareholder, and we're talking to Rabobank and others about participating. Eventually it should be a rural credit institution, because in India, farmers borrow at between 2 percent and 5 percent per month interest, which is what keeps them in perpetual poverty. The next generation has to do the same thing so they can pay back the moneylender. If what we're trying to do works, we'll change the lives of millions of farmers.

RG: You went into processing primarily to make sure you didn't have a harvest glut. You also went into processing to stabilize pricing so you can afford to pay the farmer. How's that working out?

AJ: Initially, it was very difficult. We lost a lot of money. In the businesses we started—mango pulp, onion dehydration, and others—it was hard to produce consistent output. After ten years, the businesses are doing well, making money for both us and the farmers.

There's more pressure now coming from climate change. Civil society and the large companies in the food system want to procure more from small farmers, who use less chemicals. But the large companies are more focused on the marketplace, and when it comes to sourcing, they don't know much about agriculture. They rely on companies like us who know the small farmers and can help create fairer trade products for juice or soup they can sell to consumers, so everybody feels they're doing the right thing. The small farmer makes some money, and the consumer feels that the product is based on a fair value system rather than "capitalist greed."

RG: Are they willing to provide a minimum contract, so the farmer has less risk?

AJ: Some of that's happening now. For example, McDonald's is working with Indian potato farmers to set certain prices and quantities. Unfortunately, the produce markets vary a lot. Everyone's struggling with how to give a certain rate of return to the farmer while still ensuring that consumers get a good price.

When you work backwards—we looked at the last twenty-five years of the market price of onions—farmers were selling onions at a price below inflation. We talk of the government subsidizing the farmers, but the farming community has been subsidizing society for a very long time. This new approach would shift that equation.

RG: The value system you have for your company is unique, trying to help the small-scale farmer. And the value system of hiring people that have an identical value system, and work as hard as you and your family work, seven days a week, long hours—is it difficult to maintain and obtain those kinds of men and women to join you?

AJ: It's difficult, but possible. Not many people are able to grasp why we do what we do. For us it's natural. It's part of my DNA, so I never feel I'm doing anything special. It's our preordained fate. It's what we're meant to be doing.   But when you ask others to adopt the same value system, it's not necessarily in their DNA. So how do you educate, not in terms of knowledge, but in their ethos, their mindset, their value system? How do you create empathy in their heart for the farmer? Once you have that empathy, everything else falls in place. So that's a long-term challenge. But as my father says, the next generation of our family is already wedded to this concept, so from our side, we are safe.

But over the next fifty or so years, one family alone or few individuals cannot do this kind of massive work around the world. It's impossible. So we need a lot of committed people, sons of the soil, who have [a] similar value system. Knowledge transfer then becomes easy. We have seven thousand people more or less in line, thinking in the same way. The hard work they do has allowed us to reach where we are.

RG: Why are you so global when there's so much work to be done in India? Why are you developing plans for the United States and Africa and other countries?

AJ: Leadership at the global level means you must have excellence in everything you do, whether it's excellence in manufacturing, services, cost control, the quality of your products, your knowledge base, or your ideas. When you're global, you're competing in the best markets in the world and the best minds in the other companies. That's the best path to excellence, and one reason we're global.

Another reason is that we want to help the small farmer and make small-scale holding viable. Small rural agriculture can't do well without government subsidies. We're trying to change that by providing solutions that have never been thought of before. To do that, we synthesize the best practices and adapt them to the local conditions in India, or any other emerging market. And for that, you must have eyes and ears in all the agriculture markets in the world. And that's why we're everywhere.

Thirdly, we've been able to acquire products and technologies we didn't have through companies in the US and Israel, the two places where irrigation technology took birth fifty years ago. I want to give small farmers similar technologies available to a farmer maybe who has his own satellites. A lot of people say, OK, they're the bottom of pyramid; they need low cost. In terms of value, I want my farmer to have the best that any farmer in the world has. I can't do that sitting in India.

RG: Anil, you've been a wonderful friend, and a great colleague, and a wonderful leader. Thank you so much for being with us.

AJ: Thank you for bringing us all the way to Harvard. We are so grateful to you for coming all the way to Jalgaon. For all the people who came to Jalgaon for that agri-symposium, it was a once-upon-a-lifetime opportunity. There had never been a private sector gathering focused on what more we can do for small farmers. You provided the ethos and gravitas for that seminar. We will remain eternally grateful to you.

RG: Thank you very much.

NANCY BARRY

President, Enterprise Solutions to Poverty (2008)

President of Enterprise Solutions for Poverty, Nancy Barry spent fifteen years at the World Bank and was the second president of Women's World Banking, which serves twenty-three million low-income entrepreneurs. Barry has spent her life providing opportunities for small-scale producers to help themselves by partnering with the global food chain, thereby improving access to better production technology and new markets for their output. A graduate of Stanford and the Harvard Business School, Barry grew up "surrounded by people who were making a difference, and doing it from a very spiritual space," including an uncle who marched with Cesar Chavez.[5]

RG: Nancy Barry is president of Enterprise Solutions to Poverty. Would you mind giving us a brief biographical sketch?

NB: After graduating from Stanford, I spent two years working in the slums of Peru, came to the Harvard Business School, and was encouraged by my professor Ray Goldberg to join the young professionals program at the World Bank, where I worked for fifteen years and led industry trade and finance globally.

I then became the second president of Women's World Banking, which between 1990 and 2006 grew from serving twenty thousand low-income entrepreneurs to twenty-three million in Asia, Africa, and

Latin America. In 2006 I became president of Enterprise Solutions to Poverty, which was a new organization working with leading companies and emerging entrepreneurs in India, China, Mexico, Colombia, Brazil, and Kenya to promote competitive and inclusive business strategies in agribusiness, distribution, financial products and services.

RG: That's a noble profession and an entrepreneurial spirit. At the end of the day, what is it you want to accomplish with this institution and with your work?

NB: Poverty is a big problem, and big problems require big solutions. I've been blessed being able to spend my working life with a lot of low-income people. They want access to financial services and opportunities, not handouts.

I've devoted my entire life to creating systemic solutions, which engage them in global growth. We've helped many millions of poor people increase their income and their assets by giving them access to financial services and connecting them to the value chains of larger small companies.

RG: Many people want to address rural poverty, but few have been able to build an economic ladder to help the poor become part of the commercial world. How did you get started?

NB: Microfinance has been an important success story over the last twenty years. As you imply, much of development doesn't work terribly well. Many well-meaning actors simply don't understand how rural economies work. Microfinance has demonstrated that low-income people, whether in urban slums or rural areas, are responsible economic actors. If they get access to the right kind of financial services, they have a much higher propensity to repay than do the fat cats in those same economies.

We've shown the bankers how to bank with poor people. Mainstream financial institutions now have "barefoot" loan officers, who provide not just loans, but saving services, health/life/crop insurance, and micro-pensions—a broad array of products that really help low-income people.

Women's World Banking now has twenty-three million clients served by under a hundred institutions in Africa, Asia, and Latin America. Most of the leaders of Women's World Banking affiliates are leaders in microfinance in their country.

But financial services aren't enough. Poor people need and want access to higher value-adding opportunities.

Ela Bhatt—who's kind of the mother of microfinance, and a very Gandhian leader within India—told me last year that the only answer for poor people in India is the commercial sector. The private commercial sector represents the most powerful set of actors when it comes to solving poverty. Poor people need access to opportunities, and if they're part of the value chain producing wealth for themselves and for a company they're connected with, they'll be a good banking client and have access to better opportunities than selling oranges in the market.

As microfinance has grown, women tell me they've been able to send their daughters to high school and university, and they've become small entrepreneurs and, in some cases, aggregators of agricultural production. This new wave of enterprise solutions to poverty is the next stage of development.

Just as banks learned from micro-bankers that knew how to work with poor women, big companies getting heavily into fruit and vegetable exports—for example, in India, the Tatas and the Mahindras—they need to learn from the Amul Dairies and the SEWAs [Self-Employed Women's Association], an organization of self-employed women workers. And they need to learn from the farmers.

RG: In the world today with so much consolidation, countries want companies to be a change agent in their society. Companies are also recognizing that making a difference is professionally and economically rewarding as well. How can you help each other?

NB: I've been working with these large companies in the most attractive and major emerging markets—India and China, but also Colombia, Mexico, and now Brazil and Kenya. These six countries represent 60 percent of the world's poor making less than $2 a day. They also represent 60 percent of the GDP of emerging markets. That implies there are sophisticated companies in these countries that are positioned to connect poor people to growth opportunities.

We've mobilized 130 companies in these four countries, only three of which are US or European multinationals. They are what I call emerging market multinationals—Reliance; Mahindra; Nacional de Chocolates in Colombia; Exito, which is the Walmart of Colombia; and Bimbo, the world's second-largest baker. The larger companies like Nestlé or Proctor & Gamble are trying to learn from these local companies.

In four countries—China, India, Mexico, Colombia—over 95 percent of the farmers have less than a hectare. If a company wants to do agribusiness in fruits and vegetables, in dairy, poultry, or hogs, you need to work effectively with hundreds of thousands, even millions of small farmers.

You were the first to chronicle the success story of Amul Dairy, which deals with thirteen million small farmers. The dairy giants of China deal with over two million small dairy farmers. Reliance, ITC, and Tata Chemicals are building value chains to work with millions of small farmers. Local companies know that if they're going to succeed, they need to deal with large numbers of small suppliers. Those that are succeeding say the key is understanding rural economies.

RG: Practically all the companies you mentioned and their counterparts in this country recognize what you say but find it very difficult to identify the leaders so that these people can not only be helped by the corporations, but can help themselves. How do you do that?

NB: The successful companies, like ITC, call it cocreation. They know what they don't know and spend a lot of time talking to leading farmers and middlemen that, at very high cost, lubricate the system.

These companies do their homework, as Mahindra did in India with the existing grape cooperatives. Instead of going directly to the farmers, they reinforced the capabilities of the grape cooperatives and are now the largest exporter of grapes in India. This surprised me, because Mahindra is best known for tractors.

RG: It's very difficult to change people's attitudes and habits. If you have middlemen who succeeded because they took advantage of the people they're now trying to help, how do you regain the trust?

NB: I'm not sure these people view the middlemen as their enemy. They're more like the only act in town. What's fascinating is that the middlemen often owned the knowledge, especially about prices, and could manipulate the information so that farmers would buy high, sell low.

By providing complete price transparency, ITC broke the vicious circle of price information owned exclusively by middlemen. Transparency creates trust. The other thing is helping farmers with risk mitigation. When the avian flu epidemic came through India, Godrej Agrovet decided to pay farmers for the dead birds, because it was nobody's fault. Creating long-term win-win solutions across the value chain includes paying quickly and on time. Low-income farmers are just like us. They're looking for the best deal, not just for a particular crop, but over time.

RG: Ironically, the same thing is happening in the developed world. People who'd bargain over a cent a bushel are realizing their counterparts aren't just suppliers; they're partners. It's not easy moving people to a value-added partnership after hundreds of years of being confrontational. How do you make the change?

NB: Some companies recognize the depth of changes needed throughout the value chain, particularly at the interface with small farmers. They invest in people they already know and trust.

Some companies approach this as if they were simply building another fertilizer plant. Two years into it, those are the companies that come to us and say, We don't know what we're doing. They realize there's been a serious disconnect.

I'm very pleased that Enterprise Solutions to Poverty has been able to bring together CEOs from companies that are struggling with more successful companies willing to generously share their key success factors. Building trust with small farmers is key.

It's really a cultural change, because it's very different from dealing with large plantations, whether you own them or not. In the developing world the lion's share of production comes from small farmers. China produces 30 percent of the world's apples and 70 percent of the cashmere and a big chunk of all the honey. Most comes from small producers.

RG: Progress is definitely being made. But how do companies get beyond quarter-to-quarter earnings and develop long-term compensation programs for their employees, and the rest of the system for that manner?

NB: As I recall, when Nestlé entered China, they didn't expect to make a profit for ten years. That's unusual. Companies getting into fruits and vegetables didn't say they weren't expecting to make a profit for ten years, but that's what some of them are discovering. It all boils down to leadership. Interestingly, Abby Cohen, the principal US investment strategist at Goldman Sachs, says the single biggest predictor of future profitability is how well companies perform on sustainability indicators—how well they treat the planet and people.

There is an increasing recognition that if we want to succeed in a global world, we need to understand the local community in a much deeper way. Businesses need to engage the bottom 50 percent of the economically active population. If we leave them out, the chances are very high that we'll get Chavez-type governments. The poor want a piece of the action. The beauty of agribusiness, microfinance, and decentralized distribution and even the delivery of profitable health and education is that they lift lots of boats. But that requires a longer-term vision.

RG: What in your background led you to do what you're doing now?

NB: My father took me to work. He was a management engineering consultant. From the time I was twelve or thirteen, I was doing time and motion studies, connecting with machinists, or dry cleaners, or a whole host of industries. A classmate at Harvard Business School said to me, You're so annoying, because you've done something in an industry related to every case we studied. My father spent a lot of time finding jobs for Mexicans, and I had an uncle who marched with Cesar Chavez as a Catholic priest. My great-aunt ran hospitals in Southern California. I was surrounded by people who were making a difference, and doing it from a very spiritual place. That's what really motivates me, responding to, Why are we placed on this earth?

I've been blessed in terms of my education and my God-given talents. I've been extremely blessed at not having to work a day in my life on something I didn't love and believe in. I've been very fortunate to have platforms like the World Bank and Women's World Banking. Interestingly, each stage of my life is more entrepreneurial and I'm willing to take more risk pushing the envelope with Enterprise Solutions to Poverty. We think we can improve the lives of fifty million poor people by doubling their income and assets over the next five years. That's what excites and motivates me.

RG: Well, you've motivated a lot of people and you continue to make a huge difference. Thank you so much.

NB: You've been incredibly influential in my life, Ray. You taught me how agribusiness, health, the environment, and bioengineering need to be connected so we can make smart and human decisions.

DJORDJIJA PETKOSKI

Director of Business Competitiveness,
World Bank Institute (2009)

Director of the Business Competitiveness Program at the World Bank Institute, Djordjija Petkoski has been a leader in promoting cross-sector learning, focused especially on sharing what works and what doesn't in creating food system opportunities in poorer countries. Petkoski believes that the change-makers in the business world should pay more attention to the four billion poor people in the world, and that, through their operations in rural areas, these businesspeople have an opportunity to improve the lives of impoverished small-scale producers at the bottom of the food chain. Currently a lecturer at the University of Pennsylvania, Petkoski earned PhDs in economics and engineering, and was a visiting scholar at MIT and a Fulbright Scholar at Harvard in the 1990s.

RG: Dr. Djordjija Petkoski is head of the Business Competitiveness Program at the World Bank Institute. The paper that Kerry Herman, you, and I wrote about fighting malnutrition and poverty is important for the facts it assembled. The problem is still with us despite the millennium objective of reducing it 50 percent over the next several years. Why haven't we made more progress?

DP: There are several reasons. This initiative originated primarily from governments. I found that amazing— making commitments as if governments control everything. When we asked the question, Why aren't we making progress, we concluded that we should engage the private sector more. Initiating the work without the key stakeholders from the very beginning was a mistake. In addition, we never really tried to understand much about the people suffering from malnutrition and how malnutrition affects their lives and communities.

RG: Historically, what people get paid to produce food and what people pay to consume it are political as well as economic questions. It's understandable that governments would be involved and also understandable that there'd be riots when there's no food, which is why food security is so important to the stability of these governments. Why was the private sector so slow to recognize it's also their problem?

DP: Maybe they were too focused on quarterly earnings. They certainly focused too much on one segment of society—the higher and middle class—without seriously thinking about expanding markets. Companies simply had a nice life doing business with a relatively small portion of the society.

The global recession highlighted that it's no longer business as usual. Companies realized they had to broaden their market presence, something they couldn't do alone. They needed to collaborate with other key stakeholders, not just the traditional ones, but also NGOs. Companies had to establish real relationships with people living in local communities and look at them as a source of potential wealth creation.

RG: NGOs have also played a major role in promoting food security, as have churches. The Mormon Church, for example, requires that their members set aside a certain amount of food to support the poor. The

Swiss Army and the Swiss government have a food security program too. Why isn't food security at the top of the list for every society, every government? The United States was so concerned about surpluses, we created a crop reserve program with thirty million acres of land set aside to support the market. Theoretically it would be available for food security, but nothing is being grown. How do we get the private, public, and not-for-profit systems to create a global food security system?

DP: The oversimplified business models promoted by academia are a fundamental problem, because they measure what we've done in the six months or one year. The cost of not doing things two or three years later should be part of the equation. Food security provides critical stability and robustness for the system. A crisis is really an opportunity to face challenges in a far more organized way that emphasizes development and inclusion so we can address even bigger challenges in the future.

RG: We haven't discussed the recipients themselves, the people who are poor and malnourished. How can they get involved in the process of trying to figure out what to do, short term and long term?

DP: The bottom of the pyramid concept includes over four billion poor people. It's important to understand that. Unfortunately, there was a tendency to look at the poor as passive consumers. The poor need to be engaged in wealth creation—creating opportunities for jobs and entrepreneurship. We need to create space for local leaders to take the lead not only in their own communities, but to help us understand how all of us benefit.

RG: Despite all the negative perceptions, there are individual companies, governments, and NGOs supporting leaders of the poor communities which are making progress. Not everything is gloom and doom. For example, Nestlé builds factories they know won't be profitable for a decade. They build the factory to demonstrate a long-term commitment to people willing to start producing milk. Why don't more firms learn from positive examples like that?

DP: It's not for lack of examples, good and bad. The problem is how we share knowledge, and the criteria we use to evaluate projects. We need to bring the human face of both the poor and the decision makers, including the Nestlé people, together to communicate the story. We also need to emphasize the broader contributions too—the training, the financing, and the cross-industry cooperation.

How and who communicates is very important. Somebody from Switzerland telling the story in Africa about what Nestlé did in India isn't very effective. But if someone who benefited from Nestlé's engagement in India shares that experience in Latin America or in Africa, well, that's much more effective. That's a completely different way of motivating people to think differently.

RG: You're really asking who the change-makers are and what motivates them and how do they develop. President Lincoln created a land grant college system throughout our country that enabled extension agents in every state to help train farmers. During that period, most of us were just farmers. Lincoln was using education to create an economic ladder up and down the system. In every industry, there has to be a self-interest for the change-maker to develop. How do you identify the change-maker in a system and work with him or her to make things happen?

DP: Picking change-makers is very difficult. Providing more opportunities for them to take the lead in more natural ways is the best path forward. The challenge is to create these conditions throughout the whole hierarchy, from the local community to the presidency of the country.

RG: One group we haven't discussed is the educators. What role does education play in attacking poverty and malnutrition?

DP: Education has at least two principal components. One is the official educational system, which is very difficult to change on a larger scale. The other is the education that happens on the ground. For example, Unilever educated women about hygiene in small Indian villages, and who then educated other women in the village. Education isn't just educating individuals; it's societal learning too.

RG: Another area we haven't discussed is the industrial structure of the global food system. A handful of companies in one room would constitute the major decision makers for half the world's economy. It seems inconceivable that with so much consolidation, the leaders of these firms must realize that these issues are among the most critical ones facing them. Why don't they?

DP: This is the heart of the problem. I've been wondering why we're trying to optimize a system for only a billion of the world's people, and leaving well over four billion people behind. Unless we change, we won't solve the deeper problem of hunger and malnutrition.

RG: As an academic, I tend to be optimistic, because so many students are so concerned about the issues we've been discussing this morning. I also see the heads of our major firms beginning to recognize they have two bottom lines. One is the audited financial report prepared for the public and the Securities Exchange Commission. The other is the bottom line for society. The attitude change on this has been dramatic. I know a number of people who believe that a company's very viability depends more on the second bottom line than it does on the first. They believe companies need to serve people and society by improving community health, nutrition, food safety, traceability, food security, and the like. They believe companies will be held accountable if they don't. Do you think the second bottom line will have an impact?

DP: Yes, we're becoming much more tuned into the second bottom line. It's also important for societies to start understanding that companies are not detached from society. We created the companies. We need intervention from both sides.

RG: Your job as head of Business Competitiveness at the World Bank Institute is dedicated to cultivating that understanding, trying to get the private sector, the public sector, and the NGO sectors to collaborate on these issues. How do you see that role developing over the next ten or twenty years?

DP: There's been a fundamental change in the way our institute operates. Our former president, Jim Wolfensohn, realized that the main benefit we bring to the rest of the world isn't really the loans. It's our capacity to capture knowledge globally and disseminate it so our borrowers can use it to operate their businesses better and share it with their communities. We're moving toward centers of excellence and supporting research focused on the less developed world. We're also talking more about so-called South-to-South learning. We share good examples, say, from India with counterparts in Africa, Latin America, or other countries in Asia. We see our role more as connectors, and not necessarily as generators of knowledge. The critical knowledge generation has to come from the developing world and then be shared with the developed world because at the end of the day, we're all in the same boat. Mutual learning, whether North–South or South–South, has to be part of that. We employ people from all over the world, which makes it easier to generate and disseminate that knowledge.

RG: These issues are multidisciplinary in nature. At Harvard, the business school offers joint degrees with the schools of government, medicine, public health, law, and engineering. Given the multidisciplinary nature of what we're trying to address, can the World Bank Institute become less compartmentalized? You have the different Rural Bank sections, the Government section, and the Finance section. How do you integrate the pieces so people have shared knowledge inside and outside the bank? There's no person—no global secretary of agriculture—who puts all the pieces together. The only institution left is the World Bank. What are you going to do about it?

DP: The silo problem is not unique to the World Bank. Every institution in this world faces that problem. We are going through a major reorganization of the World Bank Institute, and the driving principle is to dismantle the sectoral approach. Our teams are very flexible, and shaped according to specific projects. We encourage multi-stakeholder combinations, because we want representatives from governments, civil society, business, and multilateral organizations to work together. That's the best way forward. Proper incentives are very important, not just financial incentives but the personal satisfaction of changing something. We're changing the way we think about the world outside the bank and the happiness inside ourselves.

RG: You put it very well. At the end of the day, it isn't just concepts or ideas or programs or platforms or silos or no silos. It's people. Our family, location, and heritage all influence how we think, how we end up doing what we do, and how we see the future. Could you tell us a bit about the more important factors in your life historically?

DP: My interest in agriculture comes from the simple fact that I was born in a very small village [in] the part of Yugoslavia that is now Macedonia. I come from an agricultural background. I lived through the full destruction of the country where I was born and spent most of my teenage life. I became interested in changing the world through engineering, so after I got a PhD in engineering, I was a visiting scholar at the best possible school, MIT. Coming to Harvard Square, you pass by Harvard University, and I asked myself about other forces shaping the world, so I got a PhD in economics. But that's too much theory, so my last step was studying government at the Kennedy School. I then had the destiny and luck to meet you and join your courses at the Harvard Business School. That fundamentally changed my understanding about how the world works, because there's nothing so important, complex, and integrated as the food system. If you understand something about the global food system, you're able to understand many, many other things. I also learned from you about the importance of creating opportunities for young people to get engaged. Working with ambitious, intelligent young people who honestly believe they can make positive changes in the world keeps me feeling very young and even more dedicated. Over the past seventeen years, I've been very lucky at the World Bank to keep my program global and not be limited to just one country or one region. That's made it easier to understand how dependent we are on the rest of the world and how important it is to engage the less privileged in developing solutions. I'm one of the lucky ones.

RG: We're the lucky ones. Thank you very much.

DP: Thanks very much, Ray.

JOHN ULIMWENGU

Senior Adviser to the Prime Minister,
Democratic Republic of the Congo (2014)

Senior adviser to the prime minister of the Democratic Republic of the Congo and senior researcher at the International Food Policy Research Institute, John Ulimwengu has worked on behalf of the prime minister to develop the agricultural sector to diversify the country away from its dependence on minerals. John has successfully coordinated his efforts with different government ministries, international aid agencies, private companies, and farmers to create hubs of interrelated industries such as transportation, agriculture, and energy. Not since Abraham Lincoln created land grant colleges in each state of the U.S. has anyone attempted such a massive agribusiness revolution with the aim of improving a country's economy.[6]

RG: Dr. John Ulimwengu is a senior adviser to the prime minister of the Democratic Republic of the Congo. Another head of state who used the food system as an economic development engine was President Abraham Lincoln. What made the prime minister choose the food system as a change-maker for his country?

JU: It has to do first with the structure of our economy, which is so dependent on the mining sector and was hit very hard during the 2008–2009 financial crisis. Firms closed and many jobs were lost. The president decided the Congo had to diversify, and agriculture would lead the way. Second, for the past decade the economy [has] grown at 6 to 7 percent, but growth in the mining sector hasn't had an impact on poverty or food security. It was natural for the prime minister to focus on agriculture, because the country has huge agricultural potential, and 70 percent of the population relies on it. The government couldn't do it alone, so we brought in the private sector and the development agencies. In addition to food, we needed education, health, infrastructure, road infrastructure, energy.

RG: You developed clusters as a mechanism for creating and monitoring this change. How were you able to get everyone to work together?

JU: Someone said, If you want to build a road to move medicine from one place to another, few will take you seriously. But if you want to build a road to move food from one area to the other, people pay attention. The key was providing food and creating jobs around agriculture.

RG: Are some of the clusters beginning to take hold?

JU: Six ministers were recently on the pilot site to receive the first batch of engineering equipment. The government has invested $70 million to $80 million to provide basic infrastructure: roads, energy, and water. The pilot will grow maize on eleven thousand of the eighty thousand hectares available. Why maize? Because from maize, you can produce feed meal, and with feed meal you can farm chickens, goat, or fish, which opens up a whole range of activities for the private sector.

RG: Where do the farmers fit into this picture? Are they going to be able to organize themselves into cooperatives? Do they have the education, and training, and leadership from the farming community? How does the farmer become part of the whole system?

JU: That's a major challenge. In 2012, we created a $23 million fund to support small-scale farmers by providing seeds, rehabilitating feeder roads and better drinking water. But they didn't have any storage, processing capacity, or transportation. The way we were planning to help might have hurt them. That's why we developed a hub for technical assistance, professional training, processing, and financial support. We focused on small-scale farmers through an "out-grower" scheme. We also focused on cooperatives. Instead of having big farms, we're organizing small-scale farmers and providing them with all that's needed—irrigation equipment, some seed money, and improved seed. It's a business-oriented scheme. We'll create a registered company that will have assisted management for five years before we hand it over to the farmers themselves. The challenge is to find educated farmers. We've been in touch with some schools at Harvard and MIT to set up an ag business training center to bridge the gap.

RG: You're really thinking ahead. The cooperative setup and the five-year hiatus while you're training farmers for self-government give them an opportunity to both increase productivity and develop their own skills.

I assume the people from Harvard and MIT will be on site to help. Do some of the input suppliers also provide technical training, in terms of fertilizer, irrigation, seeds, and things like that?

JU: Yes. Valmont, the irrigation dealer from Nebraska, will set up equipment for our first cooperative. On fertilizer, we've signed a joint venture with Triomf, which is based in South Africa, to build a plant here.

RG: Does the prime minister have an agricultural background?

JU: No, he has a BA in monetary policy, and completed master classes on macroeconomic analysis. He spent much of his time at the central bank, and then became head of a procurement agency before he was appointed minister of finance. I may be the suspect for his love of agriculture. In the aftermath of the 2008 food crisis, my institute, the International Food Policy Research Institute, received a grant from the US to develop policies to bolster agriculture in the DRC. I knew the prime minister—we were teaching assistants at the university—so when I visited Kinshasa I'd stop by his office and lash out with frustration that our country wasn't taking agriculture seriously. When he was appointed prime minister, he called me and said, Why don't you come back and help us with our agriculture? It's been incredible, because I needed somebody ready to take political risk and who does things. The minister of finance has also been incredibly supportive. The support of both the prime minister and the minister of finance has made a great difference.

RG: The world is watching very closely because everyone wants you to succeed. You have wonderful land and water resources. You could be the bread basket of Africa, at a time when that's desperately needed. Where do you need the most help?

JU: As you say and the prime minister keeps reminding us, we have land and water and we have the sun and people. So what exactly are we lacking? First, we don't have the proper institutional architecture to support modern ag business development. We need to strengthen our institutional and human capacity. Second, we don't have technology. But today, when I called the minister of finance who was at the launch of the first pilot, he said, I feel for the first time that innovation has come to agriculture, that we'll be moving from hoes and machetes to modern equipment. We need financing, of course. The government doesn't have enough resources to invest. We should stop doing piecemeal programs. That doesn't work. In my own research, I've been focusing on the links between health and agriculture. We need a joint program that puts together agriculture, health, education, energy, and infrastructure.

RG: That sounds very wise. You seem to be the orchestra conductor, pulling all the pieces together.

JU: It's why the whole initiative is under the prime minister's leadership. You can't leave this to the minister of agriculture alone because you often need the ministers of energy, finance, and infrastructure. That's why the prime minister is taking the lead.

RG: It sounds like you've been reading a history of Abraham Lincoln, because that's how he felt. We were a nation of farmers at the time. We had plenty of land and resources, but nobody was putting the pieces together. He created land grant colleges, and all sorts of things. Getting back to priorities, Africa as a whole has been in turmoil operationally. How can you make sure the DRC avoids the turmoil elsewhere in Africa?

JU: We're emerging from a long period of war and political turmoil, especially in the eastern part of the country. We've made tangible progress. The eastern part of [the] DRC is now secure. There are pockets of violence, but overall things have improved. We need security, because agriculture is a risky sector as it is. We don't want more insecurity. One of the reasons we started the pilot agriculture business park in the west is because it's safer here.

RG: Are your educational institutions aware of what you're doing and excited about it?

JU: Yes, but not all share the vision. Some believe that our institutions aren't yet ready to implement the strategy. I told the prime minister, Your Excellency, this is not easy. He backed me, and that's why we're doing the pilot.

RG: That's very wise. In looking at the problem, it sounds like you're taking a case study approach. It'll be important to look at what you have right now and then measure what you have after you're finished, so the before and after is documented.

JU: Sure. We want to do a baseline on every single innovation in this transformation, and be able to make assessments every six months or every year tracking progress against our targets.

RG: If we were having this conversation five or ten years from now, what do you think we'd be talking about?

JU: First would be the innovations that we're planning to assess the effectiveness of each innovation. Second would be the whole initiative to provide good food at an affordable price to address food security, create jobs, and increase household income. Those are my targets. I would love to see significant changes in yield and household income and positive changes in job creation and our poverty rate.

RG: Many governments are having a hard time maintaining the value system of the people that come and go inside government. What you're doing is outstanding, and everybody wants you to succeed. How are you going to sustain that value system, so it doesn't deteriorate into people taking advantage of the situation?

JU: That's a big challenge, and unfortunately, I don't have control over that. I'm pleading for at least two more years to build a strong foundation that can't be removed by whoever follows us. The prime minister often tells us, Don't worry so much about how long we'll be here. Focus on how much we can do while we are here.

RG: He's a very wise man. You're setting yourself up as an important example for everybody else. You are the second-poorest country in the world. You have wonderful human resources. You have wonderful natural resources, and you're finally getting a chance to put them together. Everybody is saying, We want you to succeed. How can the rest of the world help you to succeed without interfering with you?

JU: The head of the African region of the World Bank's Department of Agriculture came here to set up a project for the World Bank on agriculture, and I explained what we were trying to do. At the end of the meeting, he said, We want to be part of this, asking how they can help. We have a homegrown strategy. Instead of people coming from Brussels, Washington, or Paris to tell us what to do, they're listening to what we're trying to do and giving us a chance. We lack knowledge, technology, and human capacity. We lack many things. But we know what we want to do and where we want to go.

RG: What you say makes a great deal of sense. There isn't a person in this world that doesn't want you to succeed. I hope I live long enough to see that happen. Thank you so much, John. And thank your prime minister and your minister of finance.

JU: Thanks very much, Ray.

8

The Importance of China

FRANK G. NING
Former Chairman, COFCO (2008)

Former chairman of COFCO [Cereals, Oils, and Foodstuffs Corporation], Frank Ning led the company's transformation from a state-directed trading company to a more market-oriented, full-service food company. As the number one producer and consumer of food in the world, China has more influence on the global food system than perhaps any other country. COFCO is the biggest food company in China and provides leadership in helping China develop its food system from raw material to consumer goods. The son of two doctors, Ning came of age during the Cultural Revolution in rural China, before eventually making his way to the United States and getting an MBA at the University of Pittsburgh.[1]

RG: Frank Ning is chairman of COFCO, the largest multinational food company in China. Could you try to describe COFCO?

FN: We were a pure trading firm before the Chinese economic and foreign trade reforms. COFCO was the only Chinese company trading with the world. We were a monopoly until the early '80s. Policies changed, the market was opened, and we had to find a way to survive and grow. We transitioned from pure trading by adding processing, distribution, and value-added services. In the past, we dealt with wheat as a commodity, but today we've added flour milling, bread baking, and brand distribution as COFCO provides 7/11 and the Starbucks in China. We used to simply trade soybeans, but today we do soybean crunching, refinery distribution, soy meal distribution, and the branding of edible oil for supermarkets. We're building a vertical value chain. The same is true for corn and barley.

RG: How do you look at the competitive environment in your country? Are you part of the government or something separate from the government?

FN: It depends on the sector. For consumer products, it's entirely market driven. The government doesn't interfere at all. They never interfere on chocolate. But for some of the trading in and out of China, WTO commitments are a factor. Annually, there's a minimum amount to import or export, so we follow the government's requests.

RG: As the number one producer and number one consumer of food, you have an enormous impact on how the food system develops. Over the next five or ten years, how do you see China's position changing in that food system?

FN: China is very clear about becoming self-sufficient for the whole system—production, processing, and distribution. Food security and food safety are major, major issues, particularly after the milk contaminant issue. We're going through a period in which business ethics, government regulation, and company practice are coming together. The milk contamination was a crime that people did for money. There are some other areas where these things happen, but in the food business it's people's lives and condemned by the whole nation. This milk thing could help improve our food safety system.

RG: It's very difficult to maintain a good food safety system in our world today. Everybody is dependent on everybody else. When you look at the food system you tend to look at relationships both internally and externally. For example, you recently invested in Smithfield Foods and now you're on their board of directors. How do you see that kind of partnering taking place in the future?

FN: We'll see more of these partnerships, because it's the most efficient way to improve our food system. Smithfield has years of experience simultaneously maintaining food quality and growing the business.

RG: Just-in-time inventory management is practiced throughout the world. Nobody wants to own inventories. They want to keep pushing them back to the original source. How much inventory should a nation or even a firm have on hand in today's world?

FN: Good question. We can lower reserves for two reasons. First, there are more types of food today. In the past, people relied mostly on wheat or rice, but today people rely on milk, meat, and other things. Secondly, reserves can be lower because transport from [the] US to China or China to [the] US or Russia to India is so efficient. We have a very interrelated food system.

RG: When you look at the world today and see the price levels, are we in a different farming environment? Are farmers going to rely more on the market and less on subsidies?

FN: Yes, to both questions. I think farmers will be better off when they rely on markets. Subsidies provided farmers with a minimum living standard, just enough to keep them on the farm, let them survive. Farmers have generally been poor. Today, the demand and supply situation has shifted with consumption getting much stronger. The balance between human beings and nature has changed a bit. I think farmers will be better off relying on the market, because the market will pay [a] higher value and [the] farmer will not be a low-income class in the future.

RG: Talking about the farmer, there were articles in the American and European papers saying that the government is trying to enable your farmers to have more control of their land going forward. Do you think that'll ever happen?

FN: That's happening and it's a big step for this nation. Farmers will be able to transfer title of their land. More farmers will leave the land for cities, and land will be concentrated with relatively large farm operators, and farm output will be increased. I think it's critical. Every year about twenty or thirty million people leave for cities, but we still have six hundred/seven hundred million people living in rural areas. That number will change. In the US in the late nineteenth century a lot of farmers left the land for the city too.

RG: One of the striking changes at least for those of us outside of China has been the development of a creative entrepreneurial, managerial group such as yourself. How do you keep training yourself and training your future people? Do you do it internally; do you do it externally; how do you keep ahead of the curve?

FN: We do both. More training is internal. Externally, people get a school education and can attend training programs. It's a routine process. Internally, you learn the organization, build a team, get a mission, create teamwork, and develop passion and skills—these all go together. We've spent lots of time on this. We've built a development center, and created our own courses. We try to teach every middle-level manager how to manage people. We create culture. We want people eager to communicate and exchange views, which is crucial. We want entre-preneurial managerial skills. Every company's different. You graduate from Harvard, from other schools; you get a very good, fancy educa-tion, but you go into a company and you deal with that culture. If you can't adapt, it's a big problem. We spend lots of time on organization development, which is why we can acquire and manage companies.

RG: An area that we worry about in the global food system is the environment—how farmers in our respective countries are managing our land and water resources from an environmental point of view. How do you address agriculture and the environment in China?

FN: China is trying to balance the agriculture capacity needed to feed our people with environmental issues. Today, agriculture production is our first priority. But China is developing a huge program to use water more efficiently and expanding forested areas instead of taking too much land for agriculture. It's a difficult balance.

RG: If we were having this conversation, say, ten years from now, what will COFCO look like?

FN: Quite different. Ten years ago COFCO was a monopoly. We had a New York office and took orders from the government to buy a par-ticular amount of, say, wheat. Ten years from now COFCO will have a much more sophisticated value chain. We'll be able to build upstream and match downstream. For example, our corn origination will match both our corn processing and downstream distribution. It will be more cost efficient and serve our customers better. It will help grow our economy, feed more people, create more food variety and better quality.

RG: We've had a genetic revolution and now have GMO crops of different kinds. China has been very good at its R&D and its genetic analysis. Do you think genetics will play an even greater role in the future?

FN: Yes. China just passed government regulations to allow more GMO crops in the future. Soybeans from Brazil, Argentina, and the US account for about 70 percent of Chinese consumption and virtually all are GMOs.

RG: Another major trend affecting our food system is health and nutri-tion. People have rediscovered food, not just as a part of their culture but part of their health, their wellness. How does China look at food in terms of nutrition?

FN: China is in a connoisseur stage, moving from eating grain to more protein. People consider protein more nutritious than wheat, rice, or corn. This stage will last for a while, say, ten or twenty years. Japan and

Taiwan, all the Asian countries went through a period of eating more meat, eggs, and milk, instead of only rice.

RG: You can talk about an industry or a firm, but at the end of the day it's an individual who creates the vision of the future. They do it with colleagues inside and outside the firm, but something in their background—where and how they grew up and how they thought— shapes the company's value system. Can you tell me a bit about your background—where you grew up and how?

FN: I grew up during the Cultural Revolution, which was a very difficult period for young people, but you didn't feel it at the time. Both my parents were small hospital doctors. After high school, I was sent to a rural area—you had to be a farmer first—and from there I joined the People's Army. The university reopened so I took the entrance exam and another exam to study in the United States. Linda Bergland at the US Embassy interviewed me and asked me what I wanted to do. I said something in business, and she recommended an MBA. I eventually went to Hong Kong for eighteen years, and for several years was CEO of China Resources. I moved to COFCO four years ago. I feel challenged and honored, because these companies are crucial to their sector. I was moved by how easily you can motivate an organized people in China. When I moved from Hong Kong to Beijing my friends in Hong Kong said, Frank, you're in trouble—how can you manage a company there? The second day I was at COFCO I gave a speech. Usually it would be two hours, about fifty pages. A speech had been prepared, but I said I didn't want to read it, which got a big applause. I called my Hong Kong friends and said it's easier to motivate people in Beijing than Hong Kong because they're looking forward to change and are willing to make sacrifices for it. That really touched me.

RG: Thank you very much.

9

Creating a Fair and Responsive Food System

WARREN MUIR

Executive Director, Division on Earth and Life Studies,
The National Academy of Sciences (2012)

As executive director of Division of Earth and Life Sciences at the National Academy of Sciences, Warren Muir is responsible for staffing and directing major scientific studies, including those focused on the future, safety, and nutrition of food. Many of these projects relate to the impact of life sciences on the food system, in particular assessing food safety and nutritional research in the future. Muir graduated from Amherst College and received a PhD in chemistry from Northwestern.

RG: Dr. Warren Muir is executive director of the Division of Earth and Life Studies of the National Academies. Would you please describe your work and where the National Academies fits into the food system?

WM: The National Academies is a really unique institution set up at the request of President Lincoln and chartered by the US Congress in 1863. The organization is the National Academy of Sciences (NAS), which established and oversees the National Academy of Engineering, the Institute of Medicine, and the National Research Council. The NAS has two missions. One is to honor the top scientists in the country with membership, which is a very high honor, probably second only to winning the Nobel Prize for a scientist.

The other is to serve as the country's science adviser by providing independent, expert advice to the nation. Currently the academy produces between 200 and 250 reports each year.

RG: The food system is going through a major revolution today. How do you see the genetic revolution, the information technology revolution, and the synthetic-genetic revolution changing the food system going forward?

WM: The life sciences are exploding in many different directions. There will be tremendous advances in health care and the plant sciences. Until recently, all of our knowledge in microbiology has been limited largely to organisms that we've been able to culture, but that's less than 1 percent of the microbes out there.

In addition, we can now study the genes of entire communities of microbes in environmental samples. We're beginning to identify previously unknown organisms and determine their functions—most of which are beneficial—for 99-plus percent of organisms in our soils, in our plants, in our gut, elsewhere in our bodies, and the like.

The transformational capacity of the life sciences raises a number of social questions. What is human, what's living, what's dead, what's right, what's wrong, the basis of our criminal justice system, what's willful and what's not? It's disruptive in many respects. We've seen a preview of such concerns in the discussions over genetically modified crops, concerns that will spread in the future to various aspects of nutrition and other forms of genetic engineering.

Another dimension of the life sciences revolution is epigenetics, a field that didn't even exist a few years ago. It entails an understanding that mutations in our genes are not needed to affect what the genes are doing. In some cases, chemicals on the outside of our chromosomes can influence the function of the genes they contain, without the genes being altered. The influence can pass from one generation to [the] next, but in some cases the chemical can be removed and the effects reversed. These epigenetic effects have profound implications.

The life sciences revolution is an area of enormous opportunity and benefit, but public engagement is needed in deciding how far, how fast, and in what ways we move forward. There are large implications for the whole food system, and health as well.

The information technology revolution is another extraordinary revolution. People are more familiar with it, because it's been around for a longer period of time. Smartphones are proliferating all around the world. The combination of their communication and computing capabilities, with new sensor technologies, data availability, models, apps, and so forth, is fundamentally altering the relationship between individuals and institutions and to their government.

Many of our future social goals will be achieved through bottom-up approaches, as opposed to traditional, top-down mandates that depend heavily on international agreements, or federal regulations, and the like.

I hope the academy can be trusted as an independent evaluator and can provide honest assessments of various scientific and social developments as they come over the horizon.

RG: If you look at the value-added food chain and the functions performed at every level in that chain, it seems to me that the revolutions you're talking about are going to change the operations up and down that structure. If you're a retailer, what's going to change?

WM: Wegmans and other retailers have talked about how they represent the consumer. They're very sensitive to consumer desires and preferences.

But in the future, consumers will be able to test retail products much more easily. For example, they'll be able to determine whether or not a product has a GMO, without relying on labeling.

If you're a restaurateur, you're not going to be able to serve an endangered fish, because your customers will be able to quickly determine what they're being served. There will be more accountability, and public values will be the driving influence.

RG: This revolution also enables the customer to look at food in terms of nutrition and health. How will that affect the food retailer and the restauranteur?

WM: I foresee big changes with respect to our health. We'll have access to all our medical records, and will be able to access tools to help interpret our lab results. Our own genetic code will be available to us, and we'll have trusted sources of information about various diseases or symptoms. The doctor-patient relationship is going to change.

Federal policies will be less generic than they've been to date. For example, the EPA currently bases its drinking water standards using the generic assumption that the average adult drinks two liters of water a day. In the future, people aren't going to care about the norm. They're going to care about themselves. Care is going to be more personalized than before, and personalized information will have profound implications for the whole field of nutrition. Retailers are going to have to accommodate customers purchasing foods and supplements tailored to their own personal needs.

RG: Moving down the value-added chain to the processor, and brand, and private label manufacturer, how is their life going to change?

WM: They'll need to provide what consumers want and will be more accountable than ever, because people will know what products contain. Many people are concerned about food safety and federal inspection, but we're not that many years away from people being able to determine for themselves whether their food is safe to eat. If a brand isn't safe, consumers and retailers will find out.

RG: Do you think this will change the kinds of foods we eat?

WM: Yes. Some of it will be what we consider enhanced food. In other cases, people will move away from foods with less nutritional value. I'm optimistic because I think we'll achieve real progress toward our social goals, be they in the food system, in our economy, in our health, or in other important social values from a new bottom-up revolution.

RG: Where does the farmer fit into all of this?

WM: Farmers are going to benefit. They'll practice an extreme form of integrated pest management, using sensors in place of people to detect the state of plants and pests. Farmers will be more accountable, but will have more tools to farm effectively.

RG: On the input side, what's going to happen to the Monsantos and the Duponts and the John Deeres of the world?

WM: They're pursuing new technologies that will play an important role in the future. Examples include new technologically based services, microbial products, new genetically modified crops, and new forms of pest control based upon new knowledge about microbes and pests.

RG: As this is a scientific revolution, won't scientists have to be more proactive than ever before?

WM: The three most important things scientists can do are [to] be honest interpreters of the science, provide objective analyses, and communicate the results as effectively as possible. Scientists need to engage the public much more in plain English.

   The role of a scientist as a scientist won't be to weigh scientific considerations against other social values. The role of a scientist should be limited to interpreting the science.

RG: When we look at the global food system, we have 500 million small-scale farmers with one or two hectares of land. How is this huge revolution going to affect them?

WM: It's already happening. Villages, and in some cases individuals, are getting cell phones. They're getting information about market conditions, about impending weather, about practices they can employ to increase their yields.

Because so much of social advancement is occurring in cities, it may be that more people will choose to move off small plots and move into the cities to get ahead. But in every case, these pending revolutions are going to have profound impacts on both rural areas and in the cities.

RG: Some of our problems in the food system are socially driven, especially in the case of malnourished people who don't have the resources to feed themselves. How is this enormous revolution going to help them?

WM: In China, India, and Africa, we've seen some significant advancements over the last couple of decades. Some of this is due to the technological developments we've been discussing. Thomas Friedman's *The World Is Flat* sees rising boats all around the world. I agree and think these revolutions could help advance people all around the world, not just particular companies, not just the United States, and not just advanced economies.

RG: The structure of the food system is changing and becoming more concentrated both domestically and globally. If you look at each of the world's major commodity systems, a handful of processors, a handful of retailers, a handful of other kinds of firms have half or more of the market in these industries. Will that change?

WM: Maybe. They're certainly going to be more accountable. It's worth noting that a number of multinational corporations are global change leaders. For example, Walmart probably has a greater environmental impact than the EPA, because they set standards for their suppliers.

RG: The science also makes people wonder whether they're going to be more vulnerable to bioterrorism and other kinds of threats.   If you were looking at 2050 and we have nine billion people, what's our food system going to look like?

WM: We're going to produce food more intensely, not only because of an increasing population, but also because of environmental concerns. On the one hand, people value farming and low-intensity agriculture. On the other hand, the environmental footprint of agriculture is very large. If we can feed nine billion people with a smaller footprint using less water and less land, we'll hopefully be able to preserve aquatic and terrestrial species, and ecosystems that people value. We may end up producing food on lands that are nonarable right now using technologies that will make plants more salt and drought tolerant.

RG: Could you share something about your background and value systems, where you came from, how you ended up at NAS, and why you enjoy doing what you're doing?

WM: I was born in New York City and grew up just outside the city in Pelham, NY. My mother was a housewife and dedicated mother. My father produced the *Howdy-Doody Show* and was one of the pioneers of early television. I went to public high school in Pelham and then Amherst College, which I'd been introduced to through my grandfather's reunions. I went to college thinking I'd be a minister, but became disillusioned when I learned about the role my local church played in housing segregation. I majored in chemistry and then got a PhD in chemistry from Northwestern during the Vietnam War. I got involved with a campus-based environmental organization that was mostly graduate students in science and engineering. My research was in physical and organic homogeneous catalysis chemistry, but I learned a lot about environmental issues. I completed my doctoral research in four years and was offered a position in Washington with the President's Council on Environmental Quality.

I wasn't sure what I'd gotten myself into, but the people I met were working on important things, and were very sharp and energized. I went from being a graduate student to being one of the first scientists in the White House working on environmental policies in the '70s. That's when environmental protection policies were mandated by large, nationwide events associated with Earth Day—a happening that people not living then would find hard to imagine. I eventually joined the EPA to help implement the Toxic Substances Control Act.

In the early 1980s, I was teaching at Johns Hopkins and established my own nonprofit research institute, Hampshire Research.

During eighteen years at Hampshire Research and teaching at Johns Hopkins, I served on five National Academy studies, chairing two of them. I was very familiar with the National Academies and its study process, so they invited me to become executive director, which is what I've done for over thirteen years. My position at the National Academies has allowed me to address a broad range of topics, and to bring to bear my background and interests in policy.

RG: I appreciate all you do for the whole food system. Thank you.

WM: Thank you.

PEDRO de CAMARGO

Former Secretary of Trade, Ministry of Agriculture,
Brazil (2004)

Former secretary of trade in the Ministry of Agriculture for Brazil, Pedro de Camargo led influential and successful WTO cases on cotton, against the United States, and sugar, against the European Union. The cases brought by Brazil helped a number of African countries who had legitimate trade complaints but lacked the political stature to make them against the United States and Europe. Trained as an engineer, de Camargo and his wife inherited several cattle farms, which he went on to run before entering the Brazilian government.[1]

RG: Dr. Pedro de Camargo, former secretary of trade in the Ministry of Agriculture for Brazil, is the architect of a WTO case on cotton in which the United States was found violating the WTO trading rules. Dr. de Camargo, did you ever think that you would win that case?

PC: When you start a case, you never know if you're going to win, but if you believe in your case and it's consistent, you should try it. We had a case we believed in, but we won more issues than even we expected.

RG: What were the various issues involved in the dispute?

PC: The simple one, which could've been done years ago, was the so-called Step 2 program, which is an export subsidy that the United States used in a manner that distorted international trade in prejudice against Brazil. That was the easy one. The difficult one involved direct payments. We weren't sure how this would be analyzed, but we also won that.

RG: You also had an ally in the African nations. How were you able to convince them to join you?

PC: What helped politically is that while Brazil suffered injury with the American cotton policy, the African countries were destroyed. The United States policy was very bad for Africa. When we started the case, we didn't know that. When we saw what was happening in Africa—Benin, Mali, Chad, Burkina Faso, which are small and poor countries dependent on cotton—we knew there was really a big political upgrade in the case. The WTO system is member driven, and supposedly all members are equal, but that's not true. Benin and Burkina Faso have equal rights, but how can they challenge the United States? Fortunately, Brazil was in a position to challenge a major power. We played a leadership role for the developing countries, and Africa gave us political support which was very important.

RG: In addition to winning the WTO cotton case against the United States, you also won the WTO sugar case against the European Union. How did that occur?

PC: We wanted a major case to expose the United States, and we wanted a major case with Europe. We also wanted a case with Japan, but we never got to it. Fortunately, we had a strong case with Europe on sugar. Sugar was an island of distortion in Europe, and cotton is one of the islands of distortion in the United States. So we constructed a case with Europe, and we won that also. They will now reform their sugar program, something they should have done twenty years ago.

RG: What were the issues they had to reform?

PC: One involves waivers to import sugar from their ACP countries—Africa, Caribbean, Pacific—their ex-colonies. We never challenged the waivers, but the footnote said they could re-export this sugar and not count it as a subsidy for re-exportation. We challenged that footnote, and won. The other issue involved cross-subsidies. It's a concept—a new concept—that the United States used to challenge Canada and won and we used the same argument about cross-subsidization. The United States won from Canada, and then Brazil won from Europe. It was jurisprudence.

RG: You used cases as a litigation tool to achieve change and point out wrongdoing in the WTO. Will this be a way of challenging WTO rules that are being avoided by various agricultural policies around the world?

PC: Litigation is not easy. It's complex. It takes time. If we can negotiate, it's much better. But there's no sense in spending ten years negotiating and signing an agreement, and then having it ignored. We're not creating these cases. It's the other side which is not following what they signed. On cotton, I heard the US trade representative Mr. Zoellick say these issues should be negotiated, not litigated. We have negotiated for nearly twenty years with minimal results. We're making sure that what's been signed is followed. That's the legal system. If it was against Brazil, we'd have been told to do that. So why not against the United States too?

RG: If you were secretary of agriculture in the United States, what would the WTO decision mean to you?

PC: Americans understand there's a distortion. What they did in cotton is wrong. Producers lobbied and received $4 billion, which is a major distortion. We have nothing against the United States. We're against the cotton which created a huge market distortion. The American citizen understands it makes no sense to give $4 billion to five thousand farmers. It's a route that was constructed by a lobby, but it's the wrong route. The United States imports more foreign products, more food and uses its money to export. They're losing the battle of food, because they're using their money the wrong way. Imagine if the $4 billion were used on a creative farm policy. A lot of sustainable things could be done that would be good for both the farmer and the consumer. I hope they understand that, and don't take as long as the Europeans took to realize they're on the wrong track.

RG: The United States tries to have a safety net under various groups. There's a minimum wage for labor and unemployment insurance. We have Social Security. The farmer really doesn't have any of that, and they tried very hard to find a safety net for the farmer. If you wanted to have a safety net for the American farmer that didn't distort trade, what would it be?

PC: A safety net for farmers is important. American farmers need a safety net, and Brazilian farmers need one too, particularly the small farmers.

RG: Politically, it's been very difficult for both political parties to change American agricultural policy. We've had very close elections. The rural vote has meant a great deal to both parties. Our food policy is largely nonpartisan. It isn't a Republican or a Democratic policy. It's a US food policy. As I listen to your analysis, it seems that you're recommending that the American public use Brazil as a scapegoat to build a more positive food policy. Is that what you're saying?

PC: That's exactly what happened in Europe. I don't see the United States using the cotton results to acknowledge they were doing something wrong. I have a different reaction for Europe and the United States. The latter is such a rich country that a good lobby can put $4 billion in the cotton program.

RG: From the WTO's point of view, this case is important, because it's a watershed case for validating the power of the WTO. Are you saying it's not only better for the United States to rethink their food policy, it's better for the WTO as well?

PC: Yes, it strengthens the WTO. WTO, the GATT, was developed by [the] United States and Europe. It's not a developing country idea. The

United States and developed countries have used the WTO to create and export ideas, concepts, and rules. They've done this with intellectual property and services and are trying to do it with investment. They've exported an economic system. No problem. But why not in agriculture? People said if the United States lost the cotton case, they might drop out of the WTO. That's ridiculous. The United States uses the WTO for intellectual property and for services, manufacturing, and trade, which are much, much more important than cotton. They'll never leave a system constructed for them.

RG: You've made your case very eloquently. Could you talk a little bit about your background and how you ended up doing what you're doing and getting involved in this case?

PC: Sure. I'm trained as an engineer—came to Cambridge, got a master's degree at MIT, then went back to Brazil, worked, got a doctor's degree in industrial engineering from the University of São Paulo and then worked as an engineer for fifteen years. I was a partner in a construction company, and we were doing well. We were surviving. But my wife and I are both from farming families, and we each received farms including a cattle ranch. So besides being in construction, I had farming—which I really liked. I would go to a farmer's association to check prices, check technology, meet other cattle ranchers, and then I got politically involved. I was invited to run for president, so I said, Why not? In 1990 I ran and became president of the Sociedade Rural Brasileira. I began going to Brasilia more, and learning about agricultural policy and trade issues. How did I get into trade and into GATT? The government opened the economy, and started importing food products, so we had to organize farmers against dumping. The subsidy and countervailing measures agreement, GATT, was law in Brazil, but had not been used, because we had a closed economy. This had recently changed, and Sociedade Rural brought the first countervailing duty cases in Brazil in '91 and '92 on beef and dairy. I started going to meetings in the government arguing, We should do this better; we should do that better. I was developing an Internet company to trade cattle. I was very involved in that and, like others, lost some money in the bubble. Then Minister Pratini de Morales invited me to join the government as secretary for coffee and for ethanol and sugar cane, but I said I'm really interested in trade and the WTO. He said, That's you also, so I entered the government, which I never thought I would. I've always been very critical of government. I mean, that's my job as a farm leader. So they're never going to invite me. I just criticized them. But then, I was there. I used the professionals from the Agricultural Ministry. I knew them. They knew me. I was always critical, but they knew I was consistent. One of the things I wanted to do was the WTO cases. When we brought a countervailing duty case on powdered milk from Europe, I said, Hey, we're against it. This is illegal; it's not fair. That wasn't clear in Brazil. They said, You don't want to compete with the European farmer. I said, No, we're much more efficient than they are. The powdered milk arrives here because of subsidies. I filed the complaint, and it worked out well. The United States has to change. They can use their money on safety nets. They can use their money on a more efficient system. The challenges of food are huge. The challenges of not feeding the American and world populations are huge. Let's not waste time and money with market distortions.

RG: Thank you very much.

PC: It was my pleasure.

JOSPEH GLAUBER

US Agricultural Trade Representative for the
Doha Round and Former Chief Economist
of the US Department of Agriculture (2009)

Former chief economist for the US Department of Agriculture, Joseph Glauber served as the US agricultural trade representative for the WTO's Doha Round of global trade negotiations. Glauber played a significant role in developing US food policy and represented the US in finding a mutually rewarding settlement for the cotton case brought against the country by Brazil. Originally an anthropologist and later an economist with degrees from the University of Chicago and the University of Wisconsin, Glauber taught math and physics in West Africa as a Peace Corps volunteer. He is currently a senior research fellow at the International Food Policy Research Institute in Washington, DC.[2]

RG: Dr. Joseph Glauber is the US agricultural trade representative for the Doha Round and also chief economist of the US Department of Agriculture. When you look at the food system as a system, many people call it a quasi-public utility because what people get paid for producing food and what people pay for consuming food are political as well as economic questions. Do you agree?

JG: Yes. I came to the USDA early in my career and thought agriculture was subject to the same economic principles as any other industry. Although that's generally true, politics plays a very big role. I'm often amazed that opposition to programs we propose is normally on political rather than economic grounds.

RG: Many Harvard students today have a keen interest in the food system. They recognize it [as] a vehicle for economic development, as something related to nutrition and health and the well-being of society. From the American point of view, how do you see the United States providing leadership for the whole world, not just for the United States?

JG: We look at our food system very differently than we did a number of years ago. We pride ourselves on its being efficient and safe. But those of us who take a global perspective know we should take a leadership role in crafting trade agreements and climate change treaties that affect agriculture.

RG: Those are lofty ambitions, but you acknowledged that politics plays a huge role in decision making. The rest of the world looks at us sometimes as being not objective enough, as not being true to the principles of the free trade we say we want.

JG: That's a valid criticism. As a country, we need to resist protectionism. If you take a political economy approach, you understand why those interests have so much influence on policymaking. But our leadership can promote good policies and convince the public that it's a good course of action.

RG: Do you think the WTO is moving in the right direction and providing leadership globally through the fairness of their decision making?

JG: I think so. The WTO is a misunderstood and in many respects antiquated body. However, it's still a place where a country can bring a legitimate trade dispute to other member countries and get an objective ruling. By and large, it's a fair process that has helped the world avoid the big trade fights that have plagued us in the past.

RG: The WTO cotton decision brought by Brazil against the United States went in Brazil's favor. How have we adjusted our programs in response to the WTO?

JG: That was a complicated ruling. When the decision was released, the US eliminated one export subsidy program, the so-called Step 2 program, but didn't adjust any of its programs dealing with price and income support, which is what the panel had found against. The panel then looked at the actions the US had taken and found against virtually all of them, except the elimination of the export subsidy program, which they applauded. Brazil now has an arbitration case with the US, to determine what damages should be applied towards US trade.

RG: The other decision that was made by the WTO was the Brazil sugar case against the European Union. In that case, they made an enormous adjustment at the producer level, the processor level, and so forth. How do you explain the EU's ability to be more responsive than we've been?

JG: Europe had already reformed a lot of their sectors, sugar being the one exception. They realized there were political problems with that. I doubt if any official would admit this, but some welcomed the challenge because it forced us to act because of the WTO. When we have a new farm bill, we get criticized by countries who say, When you change your rule, why don't you at least make them consistent with WTO rules?

RG: The nature of American agriculture has changed dramatically with consolidation at the farm level, the input level, and the processing and retail level. How has that affected the development of the food system in this country and our competitive position globally?

JG: It's enhanced our competitiveness in virtually every aspect of agriculture. The efficient production of high-quality durum wheat is a case in point. It's put on train cars right from the field and taken directly to port and shipped to millers in Italy or wherever. The efficiencies have been even more dramatic on the processed food side. I'm amazed that we still have some two million farms. Most of the production is on 15 percent of them. Thirty years ago some predicted we'd be down to a handful of farmers, but we aren't.

RG: Where does technology fit into this, especially genetic technology?

JG: That's been key to the gains we've seen, especially the bulk commodities. A lot of those genetic improvements were initially made to minimize producer costs for pesticide control or other sorts of cultivation techniques—for example, Roundup Ready soybeans or some of the Bt-corn varieties. The next generation of genetically modified seed will likely have traits with broader benefits—for instance, drought resistance—which may make the public more amenable to them.

RG: The proprietary development of these unique traits has led to more contractual integration. The farmer is now looked at as a partner, not just a supplier. How do you see that playing out?

JG: That's true. There's a move toward sharing more risk with farmers getting a higher share of the value added in areas like biofuel production and cooperative marketing.

RG: Contractual integration, even for organic farming, has become important too. People want to look beyond one crop season in order to develop strong supply relationships. As global population increases, people are concerned we're putting ourselves at greater risk. How do we provide food security in that sort of environment?

JG: I'm not sanguine about keeping more reserves, for several reasons. First, they're just not manageable. Essentially, we're telling producers, You need to grow at this price even though the market may be signaling something else. The notion of an ever-normal granary dates back to Henry Wallace, and the goal of stabilizing prices within some band. Another big problem with stock management is that it's quite expensive to hold stocks. Experience has shown that the private market does a better job. They know when to buy. It's also important for countries to be transparent about what stockpiles are out there, private or public. The US does a pretty good reporting, countries like India and China much less so. Lastly, there's merit to a humanitarian food reserve.

RG: What about the ethanol program? We used to look at a corn–hog cycle and anticipate whether you put corn through a hog or whether you sell it direct. But when you have a corn–hog–ethanol cycle, it's very difficult. People are concerned that we have to look at things differently. What do you think?

JG: Mandates that pay without regard to the market—the ethanol mandate, for example—eventually lead to trouble. At $100 and $150 oil, you can make money producing ethanol, but not at lower prices. Managing our ethanol program without distorting corn prices, and hence food prices, could increase the role imports play in meeting mandates over the long run.

RG: Another issue that's very political is water. How do we address the fact that agriculture uses 70 percent of all the water in the world, and we seem to be running out of water?

JG: From an economist's perspective, water isn't priced properly, particularly in developed countries. The most efficient way to reduce the waste is to price fairly.

RG: As you look to the future, do you think we're more likely to have more food crises in five, ten, twenty years? Do you think the kind of agriculture we have in this country today will be pretty much the same? How do you see the structure of agriculture changing?

JG: Those are interesting questions. Some of the policies we've put in place like biofuels have tied the price of corn much more closely to the price of oil. That wasn't true back in the '70s. When I was first studying agriculture back in the '70s, the Club of Rome was projecting dire emergencies only twenty years away, but we seem to have gotten through that. But there are certainly a lot more pressures. In the near term, we have to closely monitor the effect our energy policies have on agricultural markets. I don't think we're going to lurch from crisis to crisis.

RG: We've always looked at the food system to protect both the farmer and the consumer. In the case of the food stamp program, the agricultural budget is skewed more towards the consumer than toward the producer. It seems surprising that today between 10 percent and 20 percent of our population still uses food stamps. Why?

JG: There are a number of food programs that have been generally successful in improving health and nutrition and educational attainment, especially of children. But the food stamp program is an artifact of the '30s. There's a lot of debate over whether a payment program is the right approach. But some of the nutrition programs like the school lunch and school breakfast programs have had very good results.

RG: Some say, They've had good results, but not good enough. We still have too many people who are malnourished and we have a growing obesity problem. How do you address those issues, and work with other departments to find a common ground?

JG: We've made some progress on the health and assistance issues, but there's a very long way to go. Nutrition programs used to be dumping grounds for surplus stocks, be it dairy or whatever. That's begun to change, but we need to do much more and also work more collaboratively across the government.

RG: On food safety, for example, you've got the FDA, the EPA, and the USDA all trying to make sure we protect the consumer. How do you get those three groups working together on a common food safety program?

JG: We need a more integrated system. There's talk about a single food safety agency, but I'm skeptical about government agencies combining and getting efficiencies. You just get large buildings and a lot more supervisors. The critical thing is developing integrated plans. Consumers are going to demand it. They want to know where their food comes from. A lot of companies, the innovators, are moving in that direction.

RG: They certainly are, but we may have to mandate it. When an identification program is proposed, say, for the beef system, the cow-calf operator says it costs too much, and the person at the feedlot says he doesn't want the responsibility. Should the government mandate it?

JG: At some level, you almost have to mandate. In government we do two things. We either mandate or we encourage through subsidies and other sorts of things. You have to look at this in a broad context, and see what the public good is.

RG: Much of our food is imported, and we worry about that. We were worried when we had the tomato problem, and it wasn't a tomato problem. It was a Mexican jalapeno problem. How do we look at global safety in relationship to our food supply domestically and globally?

JG: We need to do more certification in the country of origin. Those sorts of things certainly are in place, but need to be improved. The flip side, of course, is grocery stores can offer blackberries year-round. We need a system that give consumers confidence, while at the same time not being exorbitantly expensive.

RG: The movie *Food, Inc.* attacks the industrialization of the food system. According to the filmmakers, we've lost our way. Eighty percent of our products have some corn derivative in them, which has added to our nutrition problems. And four firms control the whole food system. As an economist and as a government person concerned about competition, how do you react to that?

JG: That sounds a bit overstated. Most agricultural markets are fairly competitive. There are some very large companies, but take Whole Foods and organic agriculture. They figured out how to make it profitable, and now even mainstream food retailers like Safeway have big organic sections. There are disturbing trends in portion size and other issues, but I think adjustments will be made.

RG: You don't think that the food companies of today are the tobacco companies of yesterday?

JG: No, I don't.

RG: We used to think that food policy, trade policy, and health policy were essentially nonpartisan, neither Democratic nor Republican. As a professional economist working with a number of administrations, do you feel that our food and agricultural policies are still largely nonpartisan?

JG: They're nonpartisan, but very political. The ag committee votes pretty much as a block on issues of interest to them: price supports, whatever.

Occasionally, there may be a break on regulatory issues there, but when it comes to subsidy dollars, they're all in favor of it.

RG: If you were advising students to look at careers in business and government and not-for-profit, how do you see this generation looking at career paths?

JG: I'd say, Be open to a lot of different careers. Take myself. I thought I'd end up teaching and when I went to Washington never thought I'd stay there long. But I've really enjoyed public service—doing something that's not just good for you, but for others as well.

RG: What about your background led you to where you are today?

JG: It's a bit of a shaggy dog story. I got a degree in anthropology and went into [the] Peace Corps in West Africa where I taught math and physics for a couple of years. I entered a PhD program in anthropology with the intention of doing fieldwork back in Mali, where I'd lived. A small group at the University of Wisconsin was interested in land tenure issues in West Africa, and brought me up to Madison. On the side, I got a quick master's degree in economics, and discovered I really liked economics. My dissertation focused on mainstream economic issues: grain pricing, as opposed to, say, development work per se. Ironically, I'd been an undergraduate and grad student in anthropology at the University of Chicago, so I could've simply walked down a flight of steps to the econ department and not gone up to Madison. But I don't regret any of that. I had a very good experience.

RG: We're very fortunate to have a public servant like you. Thank you so much.

JG: Thank you.

ROBERT LANGERT

Vice President of Corporate Responsibility,
McDonald's Corporation (2008)

As vice president of corporate responsibility for the McDonald's Corporation for twenty-seven years, Robert Langert was instrumental in creating a multistakeholder partnership initiated with Greenpeace to protect the Amazonian rain forest from unsustainable soybean farming practices. Although cautious about Greenpeace, Langert studied the case, agreed that McDonald's and its suppliers were in the wrong, and worked collaboratively to address the problem. Among other programs, he worked with Dr. Temple Grandin to improve animal welfare in suppliers' meatpacking facilities. Langert started at McDonald's in logistics.[3]

RG: Bob Langert is vice president of corporate social responsibility for the McDonald's Corporation. Most people think of McDonald's as the number one company in supplying fast food around the world. But you're much more than that. You're a change-maker in our food system and are very responsive to consumer attitudes and consumer changes. Recently you were able to partner with Greenpeace, a consumer advocate group that to my knowledge had never partnered with a private firm. How were you able to do that?

RL: We were willing to sit down with Greenpeace, because we want to make a difference in the world and do the right thing. A Greenpeace campaign claimed that McDonald's had a role in damaging the Amazon rainforest and that got our attention. We knew we wanted to protect the rainforest—that's a policy we'd adopted in 1989—so we investigated their claims and discovered many of them were true. Their solutions at the time weren't practical, so we had to decide whether or not to work together. We only buy about half of 1 percent of the soya they were talking about, so we were a symbolic target, but even so we felt we should be part of the solution. We called up Greenpeace and met with them a couple of days after releasing their report.

RG: Not only did they release a report, but if my memory serves me correctly, they also entertained various people around some of your outlets in the United Kingdom.

RL: They showed up in around seventy restaurants wearing chicken suits, which got the media's attention. Our Brazilian soya goes into chicken feed that goes into our chicken products like McNuggets. They were leveraging us as a symbol. We could have reacted very negatively, but we've learned over the years if there's an issue we can be part of, let's address it.

RG: How did you look at your supply chain to help you address it?

RL: That's a great asset McDonald's brings into any solution. One part of the agricultural supply chain cannot be the main decision maker. We all have to work together. At McDonald's, we have long-term relationships with suppliers like Cargill that share our values. Corporate social responsibility is part of who we are and part of what we expect from our suppliers. We asked Cargill to help and they agreed to meet with Greenpeace. As we both engaged with Greenpeace, it was good that

Greenpeace changed. Greenpeace was not just campaigning against us; they had a decision to make as well. We told Greenpeace that the twenty sets of demands they were making were very unrealistic. To Greenpeace's credit, they became more pragmatic. And they don't always do that, do they?

RG: To my knowledge you're the first company that's engaged in a partnership with them. You're breaking new territory, both for yourself and for Greenpeace, and for that matter the food economy. So congratulations on being a path maker. Inside the company, you mentioned you look at the whole value-added chain as a system, not as segments. Inside the company, it's my understanding corporate social responsibility and the supply chain managers work hand in hand, is that correct?

RL: Corporate social responsibility is a core part of supply chain management. It's part of every discussion we have, and it's making us a smarter company. One of the main lessons from the Greenpeace soy issue is how our suppliers can impact our brand. One weak link in the supply chain can erode trust. Our main disappointment with the Greenpeace issue is the fact that it came to our attention from the study. Why didn't we learn about this beforehand from our suppliers? Why weren't they more knowledgeable about these issues? Why hadn't they come up with solutions before the campaign? That's the vision of where we need to be in the future.

RG: If you want your supply chain to have that vision, do you feel some responsibility in meeting with them and helping them to develop that kind of framework within their companies?

RL: Absolutely, which is why we've been inviting suppliers in to understand what we want to do, so we're not alone. We've hosted symposiums on sustainability for our suppliers, and are currently reaching out to all our primary suppliers to understand how they view sustainability. And not just our suppliers—it's the entire stakeholder community, including NGOs. We don't want to be driven by public relations or false science or activist demands that aren't genuine. We have to be strategic, because as a big brand we'll always be a target.

RG: You mentioned Cargill as a very important partner in this activity because of their value system. They understand the issues well, but how did you get players other than Cargill who don't necessarily have the same perspective that Cargill has?

RL: That was one of the key strategies we discussed with Greenpeace. We said, It can't just be Greenpeace, McDonald's, and even Cargill trying to force change. We brought other stakeholders to the table and invited competitors to join our coalition. Cargill reached out to other traders, and to Greenpeace's credit, we said to Greenpeace, It can't be Greenpeace alone. You have a certain image, that's both good and perhaps not good. Bring in other NGOs. And so they brought in Conservation International, the World Wildlife Fund, and local NGOs from Brazil. It became very collaborative.

RG: This is an example of how to achieve cooperation with all stakeholders. Some people are skeptical when they hear this. They feel that part of the reason people go to McDonald's isn't just your good values, but your food, your quality, your cleanliness, your food safety, and also a reasonable price that a huge percentage of the population can afford. When you start adding on the costs of corporate social responsibility to the value-added chain and the supply chain, do you get concerned you'll add to the cost structure and weaken the responsible, effective, fair consumer prices for which you're famous?

RL: Not if you take a long-term view. Establishing systems takes time and resources, which is why we all need to work together. One company or one brand can't foot the bill for systemic change. If there is cost, it's a cost of doing business. That point is strategically important to me. It's like having clean bathrooms at McDonald's. It costs us money, but it's part of doing business. Doing the right thing in managing the supply chain, treating your people properly, protecting the planet, maintaining animal welfare standards aren't add-ons. They have to be core to what our suppliers do. You don't do that overnight. If you respond to activists by trying to solve a problem overnight you'll probably spend too much money too quickly, and what you do may not be scientifically sound. But if you take a long-term view, our experience is that the cost is very minimal because in general it's smart management, smart people, good training, and awareness. Working for the past ten years with a leading animal welfare expert, Dr. Temple Grandin, we've really changed how animals are handled at the meatpacking facilities. We treat the animals properly. We measure objectively, not emotionally, and now have a program that our suppliers accept, because it makes sense, and has been done economically. Our changes promoting animal welfare required changes in training and awareness, not in capital investment.

RG: Your former head of supply chain management commented that it's a win-win for everybody in the system, because at the end of the day the consumer really does factor that into their buying practice or their eating practices. How do you know that?

RL: We study the consumer. We're one of the most consumer-centric companies in the world, and know that environmental and societal issues are rising in importance. Our research shows that consumers are changing. Are they translating it all into purchasing behavior? Perhaps not today, but directionally in the future we see them making more and more of their decisions based on doing business with companies that care about the same things they care about. Trust is one of our key metrics. Do consumers trust McDonald's? As we gain more trust we gain more loyalty, and more frequent visits to McDonald's restaurants. You talked about a win-win. The win-win isn't only for our customers; it's for our people and the owner-operators and the suppliers that work at McDonald's. We want to work at a place we care about. There's more to the world than just serving hamburgers and French fries and drinks. That's good, we love it, we have a lot of passion for our business, but it's great to have a passion beyond that. And I think at McDonald's, many of us, including me, feel like we are part of something bigger.

RG: The Brazilian soybean industry tries to supply a lot of non-GMO soybeans. Does that factor into the situation?

RL: Very much so. One of the reasons this issue came up was that McDonald's Europe switched its soya source from the United States to non-GMO sources in Brazil. Low and behold the boomerang happens, and they realize how much that affects the Amazon. It's a very complicated issue. We think GMO foods have a place in the world. Done right, they benefit society. On the other hand, European consumers don't want GMO products. It's really complicated because segregation adds a cost factor that is quite different than protecting the Amazon.

RG: Do people pay a premium for non-GMO soy beans?

RL: Yes, in Europe.

RG: They say one billion people in the world are obese and another billion are suffering from malnutrition. You've been targeted by NGOs in the consumer world with respect to nutrition. They think that when you buy a thick milkshake and a hamburger and French fries that you've got a huge caloric meal. How do you respond to that?

RL: We have a role to play that starts with educating the consumer, and creating more choices. We probably sell more salads and more apples in the United States than anybody else. There's an area of personal responsibility for people to make their own choices. I want to choose how I eat McDonald's food. It's all part of a bigger lifestyle issue. How I eat my calories depends on how active I am, and that's a personal choice. I eat McDonald's food all the time. It fits into a balanced, active lifestyle. Just like with Greenpeace and the issue in Brazil and soya, we want to be part of the solution. McDonalds serves fifty-two million people a day, so we have a role to play.

RG: Do you give caloric information on your meals?

RL: We led the way on that and to my knowledge we're the only company that actually puts caloric information on our packaging. We're proud of what we do, and don't feel we should be defensive about it. We put choices in front of people so they can determine their own diets and lifestyles.

RG: You say you don't want to be defensive about it, but in the same breath you are sort of on the offensive by working proactively with consumer advocates and nutritionists. How do you get the nutrition community to feel that and understand you are responding to their concerns?

RL: You become very open and show that you care by engaging people. We have a global advisory council of fifteen world-famous nutritionists and experts in public health. We bring them to McDonald's a couple of times a year, share our research, introduce them to our leadership, talk to our CEO, and help develop new food choices. Coming up with those solutions is very difficult. Children only eat a few things, and we don't want to put things on the menu that don't sell. Working with these stakeholders, we develop solutions that work. I wish we sold more salads and more apples. The more we sell, the longer they're going to stay on our menu.

RG: What about veggie burgers, which you tried, but didn't seem to work. Why?

RL: They didn't taste very good. Plus we're not into niche markets. Ray Kroc had a saying: "I don't know what I'm going to sell in the year 2000, but whatever it is it's going to be a lot of it." Our model is to meet a consumer need where there's mass volume. If we can figure out how to sell a vegetable entrée, we can make a big impact.

RG: You also change your menu depending on the culture of your customer and the country of your customer. How has that evolved?

RL: We only have nine core products: the Big Mac, the Quarter Pounder with Cheese, French fries, and a few others. When you travel the world, you're going to see beyond those nine products a lot of variation. In India, it's nonmeat products. In Asia; it's a lot more fish and poultry.

In South America, it's more fruits and vegetables. We're going to reflect the local culture. We're run by individual owner-operators that are very close to their communities and their customers. We're not monolithic. We're one of the most decentralized, closest-to-the-customer companies you could imagine. Ray Kroc instilled values that included being community minded.

RG: How do you attract men and women to your company that will continue to add to those values and expand your perspective of how to respond to consumer needs?

RL: We look for flexible people who share our values, and are very entrepreneurial.

RG: Do you have an internal training program?

RL: We have fantastic internal training programs. We're famous for setting up our own university, Hamburger University, in 1963. We now have seven of them, and have just established a leadership institute. Our CEO says his top three strategies include people and people selection, leadership, and succession planning. It's a really big priority for us.

RG: How did you get to McDonald's?

RL: I wanted to work in a big company where I could grow as a person and stay in Chicago. I came to McDonald's through the back door in the sense that I was involved with logistics. That's what brought me to McDonald's. What's kept me at McDonald's is that I like working for a company where we can make a big difference. My job is to integrate corporate social responsibility into our business-like operations.

RG: You work more with the supply chain than any other part of the business?

RL: In my twenty years of working on social and environmental issues at McDonald's, at least half my time has been spent on supply chain issues. When we set up a policy on antibiotics or recycled paper or animal welfare, we're changing not just McDonald's' supply chain in general; we're changing the whole environment. We're helping to change the world.

RG: Do your competitors follow suit?

RL: Not really, but we don't look at it from a competitive viewpoint.

RG: When we discuss these issues with other firms up and down the value-added chain, they indicate that although price has always been important in deciding what you buy, the broader issues we've been discussing have become more important in the decision-making process. Is that true or is that just talk?

RL: Yes. At McDonald's, we have a supplier performance index that helps evaluate our suppliers.

RG: Cargill recently won the supplier of the year award. Is that due to this or some other thing?

RL: They won because they really look at providing a full range of services to McDonald's like animal welfare, the environment, and volunteering to serve on our various boards.

RG: How do you go forward with that model?

RL: We are actively engaged in the roundtable discussions taking place. Our accountability system requires proper assurances that soya doesn't come from Amazon rainforest areas.

RG: If we were having this discussion in ten years, what's the world going to look like and what's McDonald's' role going to be?

RL: Sustainable agriculture will be better understood, especially in the United States. Retailers, suppliers, and the whole food chain will collaboratively work together to establish standards, policies, and programs that are transparent and credible. As with Greenpeace, its economical partnerships won't be developed in crisis. We've had too much crisis management related to food and sustainability. We need to get other retailers to the table, because even though we're big, we're just one voice. We need more retail voices.

RG: Thank you very much, Bob. It's been a pleasure interviewing you.

RAJIV SINGH

CEO, North American Division of Rabobank (2016)

As CEO of the North American Division of Rabobank, Rajiv Singh actively engages the financial and analytical capacity of the world's leading agricultural bank to facilitate the funding of a wide range of food system companies and initiatives. The Dutch banking cooperative advises and funds firms in all parts of the world's vertical value-added food chain. Singh grew up in India, where both his parents came from farming families, and graduated from the Harvard Business School.

RG: Rajiv Singh is CEO of the North American division of the number one agribusiness bank in the world, Rabobank. Could you say a few words about how you ended up in this particular position, what your background was, and what your value system is?

RS: Maybe first a little bit about Rabobank: it's perhaps the biggest financial institution no one's ever heard of. Over a hundred years ago farmers in the Netherlands pooled their resources to lower their cost of capital. That mission has expanded, but the roots remain the same. Although we are a universal bank in the Netherlands, everywhere else we focus primarily on food and agribusiness. Our narrow focus on food and agribusiness makes us very well known to our chosen market, but generally unknown to other businesses and the general public.

I grew up in India, where both sides of my family had farming backgrounds. One side were smallholder farmers; the other side were big farming landlords. I studied engineering and had not been thinking about agriculture, but finance appealed to me, so I came to the Harvard Business School. We used to have an agribusiness club and I remember interacting with you.

The spark was there, but I went onto traditional banking jobs in the US. After the financial crisis, I thought more about the kind of institution I wanted to be associated with, and Rabobank jumped out because of its character. The stability of their platform, their mission, and their values really stood out, so I joined them in 2009. I became CEO of Rabobank's North American Wholesale Banking business about two years ago. And I'm so glad. It brings me back to my origins and the spark mentioned.

RG: Everybody in the food system recognizes Rabobank as the bank that understands the food system, understands the small-scale producer, the large-scale producer, and everything in between. But I'm not sure they understand Rabobank's value system and its commitment to commercial firms with broader social agendas. One of those firms is Jain Irrigation. Their two main investors are [the] IFC and Rabobank. Why take on a firm trying to help small-scale farmers with drip irrigation? What gave you the courage to do that?

RS: Examples like that inspire people at Rabobank. We began as a cooperative with farmers uniting to support each other. That mission remains our guiding light. Rabobank thinks of itself as a long-term financial link in the food value chain. It's rare for financial institutions to plan for five years. But Rabobank thinks in terms of fifty years. In 2050, what will the food system look like? How can we facilitate progress in developing a food system that meets the people's needs in 2050? That mission drives people at Rabobank and the decision makers and our board. It's a part of the culture.

We have to be profitable. But we also look at the impact we're having on the food system and in the world. The industry we work with is cyclical. We know there'll be ups and downs. We've got the industry expertise to help make sure we do things that support the long-term vitality of the food system in a positive way for society. But we do so in a way that's commercially sustainable over time.

RG: Everyone admires Rabobank for all those attributes. Your research division evaluates all the major commodity systems, not just on a year-by-year basis but decades ahead, trying to see how that system will change over time and how that relates to the financial success of the clients you support. As the industry consolidates, not just the corporations but cooperatives too, how do you see your role changing over time?

RS: We'll need a lot more cooperation, as there are clear limits to what a single institution can do. We want to create a network where we commit our capital but go beyond that to become a connector to other sources of capital. There's an appetite for the risks that the evolving food and agribusiness sector presents for pockets of capital that may not be able to fully evaluate that risk. We offer the knowledge, structuring ability, and risk assessment needed to support fresh sources of capital. It's a role we play quite well.

RG: That matchmaking role is essential for the global agricultural system. Many countries, including our own, have government financial organizations like our Farm Credit Administration. Do you joint venture with some of these as well?

RS: We work closely with the Farm Credit System already, and jointly finance a number of companies. We'd be open to discussing a more formal arrangement like a joint venture, but it's a sensitive issue because the Farm Credit System is supported by the federal government.

RG: The food system has always been closely related to government policy, because food is a critical security issue for society and food production is a critical activity for managing land and water resources. It's not surprising you relate to government policies and government institutions. You're also an educator, not just in the research you provide industries, but on specific programs for particular commodities. How do these activities reinforce the role you play?

RS: That's a very good question because we have to think about how all these activities fit together. Fundamental innovations created new food sector businesses in the late nineteenth and early twentieth centuries— for example, mechanized farm equipment and food preservation and packaging innovations. Today we need another set of innovations. Everyone agrees that to feed over nine billion people by 2050, we need to do things differently. We work with a lot of entrepreneurs whom we mentor to start businesses. We've been planning a moonshot campaign for food, where we pick a topic we think is important, invite people to address it, and help incubate best ideas in concert with investors and companies with whom we work.

RG: You're not just forecasting change; you're actively supporting it, which is wonderful and badly needed by our system. All the new technologies—data analytics, iPads, drip irrigation, different methods for gathering data, and precision agriculture—point to a higher cost structure for the farmer, even the small farmer. That makes them more dependent than ever on the end-user, so they're more at risk. Are the market people willing to plan ahead five, ten, fifteen years with these farmers, so there's a market they can count on? How do you do that?

RS: It's tricky. One thing that's different about the food sector compared to the technology sector is that it's not just an idea that can lead to success. Rabobank's the only bank that's been very successful in Africa. We have a unique way of working: we have made investments in some of the big banks, primarily in East Africa, to help move them towards lending to farmers, even small farmers. There are lots of these development programs directed at farmers in Africa that had some success but weren't sustainable. Any effort directed at an isolated segment of the supply chain is almost bound to fail. Working with farmers in Africa, we realized you have to work with every single part of the supply chain—suppliers of fertilizers and seeds, people who have storage or facilities or logistics, or people who deal with trade. You need to bring them all together up-front and ask for longer-term commitments. Everything we do is targeted towards the longer term, because we know this sector is different. Unlike the technology sector, the development cycles are not measured in days and months. We look for like-minded partners willing to invest for multiple years. It's not easy. Luckily, we have the credibility and trust needed to create some very encouraging examples. We work with companies like Mars and eComm in Africa on the cocoa side. Those successes would have been very difficult if these companies hadn't come together with us on a long-term basis.

RG: The world's changing rapidly with the genetic revolution, and people's attitudes toward the food system are changing too. People are realizing that food is more important than pharmaceuticals. They're connecting diseases back to the crops you've grown. So the complexity of what you're investing in and your knowledge base is changing dramatically. You're in the education business and the medical business and the pharmaceutical business and the nourishment business. You're also in the development business. To do all that, you need some unique men and women. How do you attract people like yourself and others to do that? And how do you constantly renew them when this industry is changing faster than any other industry I know?

RS: That's very true. One business that you didn't mention is risk management, because the stability of the food system has been under a lot of pressure and volatility can kill a lot of good ideas. In terms of attracting people, I see a lot of interest from young people in food. Our challenge—and the industry's challenge—is to take that interest and channel it in a way that will be productive in the future. We're looking to create an ecosystem that addresses the major challenges we're facing in a way that's not overly competitive, in a way that promotes cooperation between the key players. That mission appeals to a lot of bright people today. I'm hoping we'll do a good job creating programs, projects, initiatives, and career paths for these people.

RG: How do you look at Rabobank ten, fifteen, twenty years from now? Dramatic changes are taking place at a time when land and water resources are becoming scarcer and climate change is such an unknown variable. How do you plan the future of your bank?

RS: While it's very true that we face tremendous challenges and uncertainties, and there's no clear path ahead, we have to experiment and navigate our way toward success. There's a clear and present economic opportunity. I heard someone say that the food sector is the only sector where you're guaranteed to have higher than GDP growth. There's disposable income, and a need to manage the risks and volatility inherent in managing where food can be grown and where it's going to be consumed. There's a robust economic rationale for our clients to continue investing in the sector, and for us to continue on our long-term path. As you said, we'll need to play the role of educator and connector much more, and encourage longer-term investments. In the recent past, people have been very short-term oriented. And I'm encouraged by the science I see.

RG: Well that's a very encouraging way to end. Thank you so much.

RS: Thank you, Ray.

J. B. PENN
Former U.S. Undersecretary of Farm and
Foreign Agricultural Services (2006)

Former U.S. Undersecretary of Farm and Foreign Agricultural Services under George W. Bush, J. B. Penn has had a distinguished career as an academic and a policymaker. He helped broaden the department's focus from being primarily concerned with farmers' welfare to include the whole value-added chain, as well the malnourished consumer and the impoverished producer. Penn also stressed the importance of working more closely with interagency partners such as the FDA and the EPA. Penn coauthored *The Book on Agriculture* with Secretary Ann Veneman. He grew up on a small farm. Currently he is chief economist for John Deere.

RG: Dr. J. B. Penn is undersecretary of agriculture of the United States. The Department of Agriculture and Harvard Business School have worked together since 1955 on the agribusiness program. And we've had the privilege of working with every secretary of agriculture, from Eisenhower to the second President Bush. I would like to get your views of the future of our food system, but equally important, how you see the role of the USDA changing over the next several decades?

JP: The USDA is one of the largest cabinet agencies in the government, and it has a multifaceted role. But as it relates to agriculture and the food system, the functions are going to change, because agriculture and the food system are changing. We play a big role both in guaranteeing the safety of the food system and in ensuring that we have a viable and efficient farm sector.

RG: The department has been cooperating increasingly with the FDA and the EPA and other departments. How do you see that changing in the future?

JP: Interagency efforts are expanding. Globalization is a big factor, and the world is becoming more complex, so we cooperate more with the EPA, the FDA, and now Homeland Security. There'll be even more interagency cooperation in the future.

RG: Traceability is an important issue in our food system today. For example, avian flu is on everybody's minds as a potential threat. How do you see that affecting the food system and the USDA?

JP: The consumer is playing a much more important role in the food system, and traceability matters. We have new animal diseases like avian influenza, which can mutate and infect humans, and then spread from human to human. This will get lots of attention in the future as we prepare for an outbreak in the United States.

RG: Historically, the USDA has provided a partial safety net for the producer against the cyclical nature of the industry. Do you see that changing much in the future?

JP: Yes, we were primarily focused on the risk inherent in production agriculture and providing a safety net for producers. Our emphasis has shifted somewhat from food security to new concerns like obesity. We're playing a bigger role in ensuring that people eat properly and get the information needed to manage their food intake.

RG: As our industry consolidates, contractual integration seems to follow that consolidation. Higher percentages of crops, livestock, fruits, and vegetables are contracted, year by year or even many years ahead. How do you see that changing?

JP: There's been a natural progression over time. Independent producers brought their products to the farm gate at harvest time and that ended their involvement. Now we're seeing integrated systems emerge in response to greater consumer preference for quality and traceability. There'll be even more food chain integration in the future. Agricultural biotechnology will play a role as well.

RG: The genetic revolution has had an enormous impact on the food system. Farmers aren't just producing food and feed, but fuel, in the form of energy and even pharmaceuticals. How do you see that changing in the future?

JP: That's exactly right. Until very recently, farmers had only one market, the food market. They now have renewable energy as a market, and are also able to produce pharmaceuticals because of agricultural biotechnology. There's also a market for "place." Farms are being used for recreational purposes now, for scenic purposes. So there's more than one market available to agricultural producers today.

RG: The farmer also seems to be taking on more responsibility in managing our land and water resources. How do you see that changing in the future?

JP: Agriculture plays a major role in the stewardship of our resources. We have conservation reserve programs, wetland reserve programs, and a variety of other programs to safeguard our natural resources for future generations.

RG: If you were secretary of agriculture thirty years from now, what would you be worrying about?

JP: Agriculture is a dynamic industry that's changing so fast that it's hard to know what the concerns will be in thirty years. We'll all have a responsibility—in academia, the private sector, or in government—to focus on the future and orient our institutions to address those concerns, whatever they may be.

RG: Everyone seems to think globally today. We have agencies like Codex Alimentarius, the WTO, and so many global agencies with whom we cooperate. How does the department relate to those global institutions?

JP: These organizations are becoming increasingly important because of globalization, trade agreements, and the emergence of new pests and diseases. The department plays a big role in everything related to food and agriculture, including Codex and the world animal health organization, the OIE. On the plant side, there's the International Plant Protection Convention. As major food producers and food traders, we want these organizations strengthened and accepted as international-standard-setting bodies. And of course there's the WTO where we're actively engaged in liberalizing trade in food and agricultural products.

RG: You're not only an undersecretary of agriculture; you're an academic. You were in the Economic Research Service many years ago and that department had more research capacity than any other agency in the world, global or domestic. How do you see the Economic Research Service doing on a global basis what you've done so well historically?

JP: It's a challenge. Our resources are limited, and the problems seem to grow. Management has to be forward looking—identifying the problems of the future and reorienting the research accordingly. The Economic Research Service has done a good job at that recently.

RG: What kind of men and women do you want to attract for the Economic Research Service? Essentially, it's the intelligence system not just for the USDA, not just for the United States, but for the world.

JP: We've seen a big shift in the people we're attracting to that agency. Fewer have a farm background. We attract people interested in food and agriculture—lawyers, economists, people with a better understanding of the world and with more language capabilities. The mix we need is changing.

RG: Many private firms are finding the same challenges you mentioned on the public side. There's more personnel interchange with other institutions. Men and women are being sent abroad to work in another company or in another part of the world. Does the USDA try to do that with the OECD or with the FAO or the UNDP? Do you do that sort of exchange?

JP: We do, and we need to do more. We're paying a lot of attention to the international organizations, those we've just talked about, but also regional organizations. Then there's the Food and Agricultural Organization in Rome, a part of the UN system. We're trying to get Americans positions in these organizations. We want our people to experience working in a different environment, and then have them return and share that experience to us. We need to do it even more.

RG: There are many other international agencies or institutions, for example, the World Bank, where Dr. Wolfowitz just announced that poverty and hunger are his two major themes for the World Bank. The USDA could play a huge role there.

JP: Yes, we could. Poverty and hunger are interlinked and particularly afflict the developing world, where most of the people are occupied with agriculture and live in rural areas. We know a lot about the development process and could play a bigger role there.

RG: On the political side, agriculture is much more political than it once was. Our food policy used to be nonpartisan. It wasn't a Republican policy or a Democratic policy. It was just our food policy. In recent years, it's become much more political, yet it's still a fundamental policy for the country as a whole. As we go forward, how do we avoid the confrontation of red and blue states, and make them red, white, and blue? How do we find a way of making the food system less political? And second, how do we develop a different kind of support system that enables us to help farmers without the programs being capitalized into land values.?

JP: That's a real challenge. Agricultural and food policy weren't very partisan. The industry, the congressional committees of the Congress, the USDA pretty much organized the policy, and partisan politics played a very small role. But our whole system has become much more charged politically, much more partisan in recent years. Food policy has been caught up in that. But I do think the more forward-looking leaders in the Congress, in the agricultural and commodity organizations, and certainly in the department recognize that we need to re-examine the farm safety-net system. We need new ways of providing support to agriculture without shooting ourselves in the foot. We need to be more competitive in world markets, not less. When we have forms of support that make us less competitive, that's going in the wrong direction. So we have a challenge in front of us, as we try to complete a new trade agreement and write a new farm bill.

RG: What about your background enabled you to end up where you are?

JP: I've had a lot of help along the way. In various universities, there've always been people eager to give me guidance, taking a little extra time and pointing me in the right direction. In my various jobs, I've been fortunate to work with some really good people. By nature, I'm a problem solver, which led me to economics and trying to define problems and find solutions to them.

RG: Did you have an agricultural background?

JP: Yes, I grew up on a small farm. My family was farmers. But they also recognized the value of education, so they always encouraged me to continue going to school.

RG: Thank you very much. I appreciate it.

JP: Thank you, Ray.

Future Trends and the Impact on the Global Food System

LORIN FRIES

Associate Director for New Vision for Agriculture,
World Economic Forum (2015)

As associate director of New Vision for Agriculture at the World Economic Forum, Lorin Fries brings business, governments, farmers' organizations, and civil society together to promote more socially inclusive and sustainable agricultural practices. Fries is a graduate of Brown University and the Harvard Kennedy School. She was my teaching fellow, and had extensive experience working in Africa prior to joining the World Economic Forum.[1]

RG: Lorin Fries is the associate director for New Vision for Agriculture of the World Economic Forum. Could you tell us what you do?

LF: The World Economic Forum supports public/private collaborations on a range of key issues all around the world. My focus is the New Vision for Agriculture, which seeks to bring together businesses and governments, members of civil society, farmers' organizations, and others to promote sustainable and inclusive agriculture.

RG: Given the global problems we have on the environment, on sustainability, on genetic modification, and on hunger, are you optimistic or pessimistic about the prospect for progress?

LF: Overall, I'm optimistic about leveraging what we can learn from each other. But we're at a critical juncture. There are over eight hundred million chronically undernourished people in the world. That's morally unacceptable given the power of our food system. There are a number of grassroots organizations doing critical work on the ground, specifically civil society organizations partnering with businesses and working in line with government policies and visions. That gives me optimism.

RG: Historically, it's been very difficult to measure the success of these activities. At the beginning of a project, the Latin American Agribusiness Development Corporation hired a sociologist who wrote an excellent evaluation of what worked and what didn't work. Do you think we need impartial evaluators to independently audit these projects? I worry that without impartial audits, the credibility problem becomes apparent. How do you handle that?

LF: It's essential not only to have the right incentives in place but to have a certain level of neutral evaluation. Collaborators often have different agendas, different power relationships, and different access to information. It's always helpful to have a neutral set of eyes and a common set of metrics and standards to measure progress. It's critical to have experts lending not only their credibility but also their expertise in an evaluation. There are many companies doing extraordinary work on the ground and just trying to tell their story. An independent evaluation would help. In addition to doing excellent work on projects, companies need to have economic and environmental sustainability at the core of their business. That begins in the C-suite as a set of commitments and expectations, and has to run through the entire company and be reinforced by the incentive structure. Doing well by doing good has to be packaged into everyone's role driving the business forward.

RG: That's well said. Many companies haven't figured out how to look at both economic results and broad social results and create incentives that reward both. Accounting firms and investment analysts are so used to looking at quarterly balance sheets and operating statements that they don't factor in longer-term social contributions when evaluating a company. The measuring stick we all want hasn't really been developed yet. How do we do that?

LF: The quarterly reporting cycle certainly traps us in short-termism. Executives who have stepped up as leaders in this field have asked their companies and their shareholders to take a longer view. We need both a broader and a longer view. For generations we've valued what's economically measurable, say, the P&L. We haven't valued various assets used. Some executives have called for putting a value on water or carbon. An exercise like that would help us see balance sheets differently. If we measured consistently towards a triple bottom line rather than for short-term profits, we could change the incentive structure. Leading companies are increasingly looking beyond their shareholders to a broad group of stakeholders who are affected by their business. It's important to understand more fully whom we affect and how.

RG: Do you think the stock market will reward them the same way?

LF: That's an area where I'm both optimistic and pessimistic. I think my generation will start to demand it, but it hasn't happened in the past. Companies taking leadership roles in this space seem to suffer in the stock market, but also gain credibility. They recognize the new reality of constrained resources, and are gaining a competitive advantage that is rewarded by many customers and some investors. I think the tide is turning, but it's not an easy process and it'll be a long one.

RG: Your generation is considered a change-making generation. Many of the firms that recognize more responsibilities than they ever accepted in the past are now seeking people just like you, as the World Economic Forum sought you out, to try to change both their organization and their operations. Yet many young people are reluctant to join these companies, because of the way they've acted in the past and the way they're often perceived today. How do they hire change agents like you, and how do you decide what kind of a firm to join?

LF: This is an opportunity for my generation and for business to see each other in a fresh light. The dating has begun, but the marriage hasn't yet happened. Someone like me who is very mission driven, socially conscious, and environmentally oriented brings a certain amount of idealism to my work and a certain amount of energy towards social and environmental issues. Someone like me may look at a company that hasn't put a high priority on these issues in the past and ask whether we fit within the culture and the priorities of that firm. But there's also an opportunity to contribute ideas and develop a pragmatic point of view. You ask important questions about the stock market. How do we reconcile a growing trend towards greater social and environmental sustainability with the pragmatic pressures of growing a business? I look for pragmatic leadership and a commitment to moving into a new era and, of course, an opportunity to use my skills. Many businesses are focused only on the stock market, but the tide seems to be turning and my generation may have lots to offer in support.

RG: Last October Nestlé announced they were creating the Dairy Farm Institute in China to respond to the problems of unethical behavior in their dairy system, the melamine example where people and pets were killed. They discovered that in order to train farmers to think the right way, they had to work with the government, universities, competitors, and different parts of the value-added chain. Nestlé and their collaborators were surprised by the enthusiasm that emerged in the process. Can we take that one model of collaboration and use it as an example of what can be done without sounding Pollyanna-ish, as we would say in my generation?

LF: That's largely what we do at the World Economic Forum. We try to spark broad collaborations, and then help scale them. When policymakers meet with proactive business leaders and very rational civil society organizations, you get the same enthusiasm, especially in the agriculture sector. People recognize that a diverse group of stakeholders can have a real impact at scale in an economically viable way. Multi-stakeholder collaboration is rather new, and it's difficult. There's often distrust between government and business, and, in some cases, distrust between business and civil society. Bringing everyone together can overcome some of those barriers. After a while we may not depend on convening organizations as much.

RG: Why do so many people distrust the food system?

LF: Some of the mistrust is put on business, and some on government. The mistrust about business stems from concerns over whether firms have the right priorities. Some companies driven by profits alone may promote unhealthy products or pursue business at the expense of the environment or the livelihoods of a local community. There are certainly examples of that. But some of the distrust lies with government as well. The political economy of agriculture is very complex and sometimes policies and subsidies are established for electoral reasons that aren't in the best interests of the people. The distrust often stems from choices made for the wrong reasons.

RG: Does your generation think the food system is a good place to change the world or not?

LF: Many of us professionally engaged in the food system see it as a tremendous platform for change. We've seen agriculture, food security, and nutrition issues emerge on the global agenda not only as humanitarian and moral concerns, but also as economic and security concerns. Do we have enough to feed people? Can agriculture be the economic engine of society? These questions fundamentally relate to human progress. Some of the biggest companies in the world are agribusiness companies. The food system offers a powerful lever for change in the world. As a side note, there's a broad and important discussion underway about the future of farming, and who actually does the work. There's an opportunity to leverage technology and different opportunities to work within the food system well beyond working on farms themselves. We can look to regions like Africa, Southeast Asia, and elsewhere to engage youth as change-makers, but using less traditional platforms than farming.

RG: Looking at the food system from your generation's point of view, you're a breath of fresh air, but you also challenge your generation to leverage this powerful part of the world's economy in a way that addresses the environmental, social, economic, health, nutrition, and food security issues that are involved. Thank you very much.

LF: Thank you, Ray. It was a pleasure.

FAUSTO COSTA
President, Nestlé Venezuela (2016)

President of Nestlé Venezuela, Fausto Costa has successfully taken a long view by working with the government of Venezuela to boost local food production in a time of economic and political turmoil. The oil crisis devalued the currency to such an extent that food importation became very difficult. Nestlé realized that they had to collaborate with the government to find a way to create a functioning food system both for the citizens and for themselves. Costa had extensive experience in the food and cosmetics business in his native Brazil prior to his assignment in Venezuela.[2]

RG: Fausto Costa is president of Nestlé Venezuela. Could you tell us about your background and responsibilities?

FC: I've been working with Nestlé for fourteen years, and before that worked for three different companies, two in the food business and one in cosmetics. At Nestlé, I had different positions in Brazil, my home country, and five years ago become CEO of Nestlé Venezuela.

RG: When you were transferred was the country in crisis?

FC: Not yet, but the signs were there.

RG: What's it like today, and what are the primary issues you have to address?

FC: The situation is much worse than anyone predicted. We're in our fourth year of dramatically reduced GDP—some estimate more than

10 percent down over the period, so it's really a depression. The crisis was accelerated by lower oil prices, but that's not what started it.

RG: When you saw what was happening in agriculture, what changed dramatically and what did you have to do?

FC: Venezuela is an oil-dependent country, which had an artificially fixed exchange rate that made it more profitable to import things than produce them. Nestlé has always been linked to agriculture—to the farmers. Historically, we operate in different major value chains—milk, cocoa, and coffee. We know how to interact with farmers, how to stimulate production, and how to develop good agricultural practices. When we realized we wouldn't be able to continue importing the raw material we needed, we focused on stimulating local production and developing new value chains with agriculture, with farmers, with associations, and with the help of the government, because in Venezuela the government is very present in business. They interfere, and there's lots of legislation, so it would be very difficult for a company to do anything without government support.

RG: How do you get the support of a government that for the most part doesn't trust the private sector?

FC: Good question. We had to gain their trust over time. Nestlé is not a political actor. We've been in Venezuela for more than a hundred years, and producing locally for almost eighty years. We have a long-term commitment to Venezuela. We never leave a country, so we wanted to find a solution. We approached local institutions and the government with a proposal to work together on a solution rather than trying to blame whoever was responsible for creating the crisis.

RG: The government must have been surprised that you asked for their cooperation, or did they understand you were both in the same boat?

FC: The response wasn't unique. We wanted to work with a number of institutions. Some opened their doors more easily than others. Different sides of the government realized that we were working to find solutions. One initiative was developing farmers to grow vegetables around a Nestlé factory. We needed to process the vegetables, but we don't process raw vegetables at Nestlé. We need to have an industrial product like a vegetable powder dehydrated through an industrialized process. We succeeded and, little by little, built enough trust and credibility so that today when we approach the government, they know we are in Venezuela to work together to find solutions for problems we're facing in the country.

RG: Were people in the private sector—the processors—surprised that you were able to work with them?

FC: They were very surprised, because for many years the model in the country was to import everything. They were quite suspicious, and questioned whether we had a long-term commitment to them: maybe next year you'll find an alternative supplier. We said, No, this is a long-term commitment. We won't change direction. Our objective is to improve the level and quality of production every year and to create sustainable supply chains.

RG: Were you able to provide long-term contracts, so the financial community would provide funds for them to expand?

FC: Yes, we realized that long-term, contractual commitments were necessary. We created a third-party agreement, between our food processers—we now have sixty-eight—Nestlé, and a financial institution. The financial institutions are much better protected in terms of risk, because they know Nestlé will pay. There is no risk there. So the financial institutions liked these programs.

RG: The other part of the triangle is the farmer. How did they respond?

FC: That's a good point. Farmers were demotivated, so we needed to stimulate them and develop a good relationship with the farmer associations. We met to explain what Nestlé was developing in Venezuela, and, through these farmer associations, we looked for the pioneers who were really excited about the opportunity and wanted to work with us. As a group, farmers are well connected, so when they see a farmer in the group doing something different that works well, it becomes much easier to get more people on board. The program now operates in eighteen of the twenty-three states of Venezuela. It's a national program with different agricultural products and different suppliers. The farmer associations got very excited about working together with a company like Nestlé.

RG: Were the farmers able to get the financing to expand because they were working on these operations and presumably had contracts with the processers?

FC: Yes. Depending on the agricultural product, some farmers already had contracts with processers. Others didn't. We financed some directly and helped others through the third-party alliance program by finding financial institutions to specifically support the farmers working with Nestlé. We've done that with our milk and cocoa businesses.

RG: Looking ahead, the crisis isn't going to be solved quickly. Are the people patient enough even though they can't get food because the stores are empty? How do you make the people who are paying a huge penalty for this crisis feel like there's progress?

FC: That's a very good point. The crisis has transformed the economy. Everything was fully subsidized when oil prices were close to $150 a barrel. Nobody sees that returning. This is an opportunity for the Venezuelan economy to reduce its dependence on imports and develop a competitive advantage by producing locally. Venezuela has very good soil, and used to have a good agricultural base with good people that understand the business. The market is ready for the long-term commitment that Nestlé can make in different regions of the country. The farmers and food processers already see the benefit. Take coconuts. Venezuela used to produce them, but as an import economy they bought them from Thailand, which has coconut trees everywhere. We saw a big opportunity to process coconuts and generate products for Nestlé like coconut powder and coconut oil. It's a program with a big impact not only in the economy but also socially, because we're restoring the economic base of small towns and villages.

RG: Do the consumers understand what's going on in the food system? Do they see the progress that's being made, or do only the people in the food system see this?

FC: It's very important to communicate. We hold an annual "shared value" forum with farmers, food processers, NGOs, the press, and also the public. It's like a fair. We've also developed some small films that play in local theaters and cinema. Before the movie starts we play a short video showing what we're doing in Venezuela with the farmers.

RG: Do consumer activists see this as an acceptable model?

FC: Yes. It's a model that adds value to the people and to villages and small towns. We're improving conditions for people who otherwise would leave the countryside and move to a big city.

RG: Do the people employed by Nestlé understand what you're doing?

FC: Very important. We realized quickly that the first public that needs to understand what we're doing in Venezuela is our own employees. We actively explain what we mean by creating shared value at Nestlé and our program of agriculture industrial development in Venezuela.

RG: The employees become your ambassadors.

FC: Yes.

RG: In Chile, you were one of the few companies that wasn't privatized, because your workers said you were a responsible company trying to improve the economy, not just the company. Is this a model for the rest of Nestlé?

FC: For sure. It's a model that could be replicated not only by Nestlé, but other companies and institutions as well.

RG: Do your competitors applaud and cooperate with you?

FC: In the beginning they were trying to understand the impact, but other companies want to participate, which we encourage. We never said this program is only for Nestlé. It addresses the shortages in Venezuela. Other companies are developing similar programs at different scales.

RG: Historically, in most countries, including the US, the food system is considered a nonpartisan system, neither Republican nor Democrat, liberal nor conservative. Eventually, it became part of a tug of war. Do you think the food system is so important domestically and globally that your model will become even more important around the world?

FC: As you know, there's a high level of political tension in Venezuela. We've had some tense discussions with some people about the food system, and said, The food system should not be politicized. If it becomes political, it's a lose-lose game. There's a real opportunity for it to be win-win.

RG: In most every country, we put a safety net under both our producers and our consumers. Is what you're doing in Venezuela a way to engage both consumers and producers as part of the same problem and with the same answer?

FC: That's the approach we're using. We look at food as an integrated system, and we truly believe that doing the right thing, gaining scale, and having more people and companies on board will have a very positive impact.

RG: Throughout this whole program, you've relied on people who constantly had to upgrade their performance, and that requires education. Where does education fit into all this?

FC: Education is fundamental. Compared to other Latin American countries, Venezuela has a very good level of education in the countryside. We're building on this base by focusing on specific aspects of production and best agricultural practice and how to protect water. Water is a critical resource in the world nowadays, and we want to develop a food system that uses water efficiently. We have agronomists and engineers working on this together with universities. Education is very important.

RG: In addition, food is finally being recognized as more important than pills. People understand the problem of nutrition better. Do you think the kind of cooperation you're developing will also help the food system be more responsive to the nutrition needs of Venezuelans?

FC: For sure. When we start working with the community, we bring together our nutrition program and our "healthy kids" programs. Our objective with the "healthy kids" programs is to teach young people about better nutrition. It's purely education. We're not selling products. We're working with some farmers in the cocoa area. Their wives want to earn some income to support the family, so we developed an entrepreneurship program specifically designed for women in rural areas. We use other collaborative programs to create a social impact in these communities.

RG: Women are underrepresented and undervalued in agriculture. Is your program in Venezuela addressing that issue?

FC: We believe this is an opportunity, which is why we designed a specific program for women in rural areas. We're also talking about a youth initiative in rural areas, because we need to get millennials involved in agricultural production.

RG: In many countries, the off-farm income of a farmer is now more valuable than the on-farm income. Is that true in Venezuela?

FC: Yes. We need to add value to the food system so farmers have better incomes and don't need a second job. It's why entrepreneurship programs are very important. Education helps farm families improve their businesses and have higher incomes.

RG: The crisis in Venezuela has brought out the best in Nestlé and the best in Venezuela. But do we really have to have a crisis for people to think this way?

FC: Hopefully not, but, of course, a crisis can accelerate change. It's much more difficult to take a food system approach without a crisis. It's important that this be a long-term solution that will work with a crisis or without one.

RG: A wonderful interview. Thank you very much.

FC: Thank you for the opportunity, Ray.

JAMES BEAGLE
CEO, Grapery (2017)

CEO and co-owner of Grapery, James Beagle and his partner Jack Pandol developed an integrated system for growing and marketing healthful, flavorful grapes that had a consistent taste that kept the ultimate consumers—often children—coming back for more. They succeeded by patiently selecting appropriate varieties, developing thoughtful labor practices, and connecting with consumers. They believe the future of the industry is not simply about cost, shelf life, and nutrition. They've proven that taste matters. A California farmer, Beagle is a science graduate of UC Davis, and earned an MBA at the Harvard Business School, where he was my research assistant.

RG: Jim Beagle is CEO of Grapery. Tell us about your background and how you ended up being CEO of Grapery.

JB: A lot of my values stem from my early experiences, including working as your research assistant here at Harvard Business School after I got my MBA here. I'd studied science at UC Davis and farmed in California for several years. I worked with several companies that produce fresh produce for consumers. In 2006, I met Jack Pandol, the founder of Grapery and now my business partner. We are passionately committed to growing the best-tasting grapes in the world and to working closely with all our stakeholders to create a sustainably successful business. It's important for us to have a good relationship with all stakeholders—investors, banks, employees, customers, the environment, and the communities where we work.

RG: A recurring theme is that nutrition is more important than just eating food. Fruits and vegetables have become more important in our diets. Historically, it's been hard to eat the recommended portions of fruits and vegetables. That's partially tradition, and partially because people aren't accustomed to the taste or consistency. When you described your firm, you talked about taste being a priority. How do you get taste to be a priority, especially in the grapes that you produce?

JB: Step one is getting all our partners in the supply chain to understand that people really want to eat fruit that tastes great. Remember the best peach you've ever eaten, or the best plum, strawberry, or grape? It's some of the best food you've ever had. If you walk down the candy aisle in a store, half the candy is fruit flavored, because that's what fruit should taste like. People love great-tasting fruit. We serve it for dessert. We enjoy it, and it's very healthy. Over the last several decades there's been a lot of pressure in the produce industry to serve the supply chain, which pushes us toward low-cost food with a long shelf life. On the plus side, more people around the world have better access to healthier food than ever before. That's important, but along the way as innovative breeders and growers have focused on lowering costs and extending shelf life, flavor has taken a backseat. That's been true with peaches, nectarines, grapes, tomatoes, and many other commodities readily available in grocery stores. We began to focus on flavor without maybe achieving the highest marks in either shelf life or cost. But we found a few retail partners willing to take a big risk on our product. They paid more for a product with a shorter shelf life that tasted great, and put their jobs on the line doing so. We saw how passionate people were about the food they were eating, how much they enjoyed it. A mother wrote that she'd seen our grapes but never bought them because they're too expensive. Finally, she breaks down and buys them and her kids eat the whole bag in one sitting and ask for more. They're asking for our grapes instead of potato chips or candy bars or something unhealthy. We love seeing people enjoying fruit that tastes the way it really should.

RG: How difficult is it to produce grapes that have the consistent taste that consumers really enjoy?

JB: We had to rebuild our entire company making flavor a priority. There are three legs. The first is breeding grapes for flavor. We search the world for wild strains of flavorful grapes, cross-pollinate them with traditional table grape varieties, and get those flavors into the thin-skinned, seedless grapes that people enjoy eating. Our breeding program has a very long horizon, and it's very expensive. The second leg is how we farm the grapes. We harvest by hand, so we have big seasonal workforces. Not all the clusters ripen at the same time, so they have to pick the ripe clusters and only pick the ripe ones. We've developed a lot of motivational tools, incentive programs, quality control systems, and training systems that encourage workers to return to us every year. We also pay higher than anybody in the industry. The third leg is how we market our grapes, which are more expensive than others. Our grapes cost more to grow, but they look like regular grapes. So how does a consumer know they're special? Our relationships with our retailers are really partnerships. We create merchandising excitement that allows retailers to market grapes as a shopping event. We also work closely with consumers. We read every email and social media post, and respond to each of them within twenty-four hours. Jack and I still read every single post. If we ship grapes out and we don't get any response, that's a bad thing. We want people raving about our product.

RG: Was it difficult to get retailers to pay a premium and partner with you on the idea?

JB: Originally, yes. The food system in the United States is built around selling high volumes of reasonable-quality food at low prices. Retailers are very efficient at getting the best value they can from the supply chain. So, when I say I'm going to sell you expensive fruit that has a shorter shelf life, it's a big risk for you as a buyer. At the end of the day, retailers have found that our grapes generate higher margins and higher turnover. Consumers are willing to pay a little extra for something that tastes great.

RG: Do you have to give the retailer an exclusive to your product in a territory or not?

JB: We don't do exclusives in territories. As retailers grow and expand and move into new territories or acquire other retailers, that creates a lot of complications. We partner with retailers who differentiate themselves on service and quality, and who are best at positioning premium products on their shelves to stand out in their market. We don't work with some of the largest retailers in the country, nor do we work with the discount chains.

RG: Are many of your retail partners privately held?

JB: Many of them are.

RG: Why's that?

JB: Private firms tend to take a longer-term view of their supply chain relationships and their merchandizing strategies. We're in the fourteenth consecutive month of retail food deflation. They're selling the same amount of food, but for less dollars, so their sales numbers are down. That's a difficult dynamic for public retailers. The privately held retailers are generally holding up better. However, some privately held companies we work with don't really share their long-term vision, and some of our publicly traded companies take a very strategic, long-term approach.

RG: Do you have more than one-season relationships? Do you have long-term contractual relations with these companies or not?

JB: We don't have a single long-term contract. We have great relationships with the retailers and we get orders when we're ready to ship. Sometimes we'll get a verbal commitment three or four weeks out, but there's a spot market, fluidity to it. That makes it sound more short term than it is. We sit down with retailers in February, six months before we ship them grapes, and talk about floor plans and where the Grapery shelf is going to be.

RG: Do you find that these planning sessions, even though you don't have long-run contracts, assume you're going to be partners for some length of time?

JB: They do. Our relationships with retailers have really become partnerships. It's not transactional like most of the fresh produce industry. We work with the merchandizers to train their people at the store level, and we equip each store with the tools they need to let our grapes stand out and be recognized by consumers for what they are. We work with our retailers throughout the year, so 99 percent of the work has been done on both our parts by the time they give us purchase orders to ship the grapes.

RG: Are the chief executives of these firms aware of all this?

JB: In the smaller, more privately held companies we work with the CEO. Our grapes are pretty high profile. We've been featured on *Good Morning America*, the *Today Show*, NPR, and BuzzFeed. Even the largest retailers are aware of our grapes and put pressure on their purchasing divisions and produce teams to make sure they have a relationship with us. They want to offer the best mix of products they can, and we're growing grapes that people want to eat.

RG: Do you have to turn down business?

JB: Yes. We're growing as fast as we can, but this is a long-term business. We buy land, but it takes three years to develop a table grape vineyard. That takes capital and time to build the infrastructure we need without sacrificing quality. If we grow too fast and don't deliver on quality, we've messed up our whole purpose. We're very cautious and grow as fast we can, while maintaining quality and not risking our company financially.

RG: And you are privately held?

JB: Yes. Jack and I are the two owners of Grapery.

RG: How about labor? You talk about labor being better paid, better trained. I assume much of this is seasonal labor, therefore migrant labor. Do you have problems with migrant labor?

JB: Most of the people who work for us are not migrants. We're fortunate to live in an area in the San Joaquin Valley in California that grows a diverse range of crops. So most of our workforce lives there full time and typically works in citrus from November through May, and grapes from May until November. By working in a couple of different commodities, workers can stay employed year-round and earn a good living. The difficulty is that California is a highly regulated state. We've got the $15 minimum wage coming over the next five years, and it's gone up quite a bit in recent years as well. Roughly 60 percent of the cost of a box of grapes is the direct labor in the field. That's gone up by half, so our costs have gone up 30 percent. It's a challenging cost environment. I worry whether our labor-intensive grapes will continue to be affordable. We're looking at mechanization and automation, but that's not feasible in the near term.

RG: Are your laborers citizens or noncitizens? Any problems there?

JB: Most of our people have either been here for a very long time and are citizens or were born and raised here. We tend to have quite a few second- or third-generation natives, usually of Hispanic descent, whose families moved here to work for us in the fields.

RG: Do they feel that they're part of the company?

JB: They do. We pay better than others in the table grape industry. People can earn quite a good living working for us. We try to do a lot for our workers and make the Grapery a great place to work.

RG: Are the labor contractors aware of the relationships you've developed?

JB: Yes. We're actively engaged with our labor contractors, and treat their employees like they're our own. We make long-term investments in training at a lot of different levels, from the entry-level field worker up through the foreman and the supervisors, who have an active and important role in our company.

RG: Could you be a model for the industry? Or do only a handful of people have your value system and the patience to change the varieties, change the harvesting, change the soil, and all the things you need to change to produce a unique product? Is it too hard for people to replicate?

JB: It's not easy but it's very scalable to a lot of different commodities and a lot of different companies.

RG: Why do you say that?

JB: When we began talking to retailers about taste in 2008, it was like talking to a wall. They had no idea why we were focused on it. As we began proving ourselves with grapes, their mindset changed to include other fresh and flavorful fruit. Honeycrisp apples are a good example, and there's a company in Arizona whose melons taste like a cantaloupe ought to taste. Driscoll's and other berry companies are breeding for flavor, not just shelf life and seasonality.

RG: Is partnering up and down the food system becoming more of a win-win relationship rather than "I win/you lose"?

JB: It's becoming more common. The food industry is a very dynamic and innovative industry that's always been built on relationships. Supply chains are complex, and run poorly without trust. Being farmers, we're essentially at the beginning of the supply chain. Everything we knew about consumers from retail grape buyers was mostly wrong. Just listening to consumers and staying focused on them makes it easy to create sustainable win-win relationships as long as the whole supply chain works together to serve what consumers really want.

RG: Do you think farmers are now much more consumer oriented than they used to be?

JB: Yes, and there's lots of room to become even more consumer oriented. We put our personal email addresses on every bag of grapes we send to market. Our label has a "flavor promise"—that our grapes are the best grapes you've ever eaten. That's a bold statement. It can be scary to expose oneself to criticism. But there's tremendous potential for companies that really listen to consumers.

RG: People generally want to produce something unique, something differentiated, but historically they didn't trust the system into which they sold their product. That seems to be changing. More people are interested in creating shared value, not just taking advantage of one another. How have you built such successful relationships?

JB: You hit on the key, which is lack of trust throughout the food system. Fifteen years ago, GMO products were introduced that had the potential to benefit lots of people around the world, but they were very controversial. Five years ago, we introduced an amazing grape that tastes like cotton candy. People went crazy over it, but there was an unexpected backlash from people who assumed our product was GMO. Jack and I believe in the science and benefits of GMOs, but our product isn't GMO. We've focused on communicating with consumers about the differences between GMO and non-GMO, and created a dialogue with people. It was difficult at first. There were a lot of difficult conversations, but BuzzFeed did a piece on us that got 1.4 million initial hits. Mostly from millennials, the posts were about the pluses and minuses of GMOs and it was as intelligent as any exchanges I've ever seen. I came away from it incredibly optimistic about consumers and their willingness to engage the food system. I couldn't be more optimistic.

RG: I wish we had thousands of entrepreneurs like you who take the long approach—creating breeding processes from scratch that take years but lead to breakthroughs that are good for consumers across the board. I can't thank you enough, Jim.

JB: Honored, Ray.

Conclusion

I HAVE TRIED to represent as many participants at each level of the food chain as possible by selecting those that, through my teaching and research experience, I felt were some of the leading change-makers of the world. Some are former research assistants or students I had the privilege of having in my class. Collectively they are a forward-looking mosaic of that industry.

From the interviews I have done, I believe the reader will understand that these leaders have individually and collectively moved to become "solution institutions." I had thought that the experience of creating so many coordinating entities would result in a more collaborative food system, and ultimately it has.

What Business Are We In? Why Do We Exist?

Some fifty-seven years ago, one of my colleagues and close friends, Professor Ted Levitt, wrote a *Harvard Business Review* article that has stood the test of time, called "Marketing Myopia."[1] The focus was: what business are we in? The once-mighty railroad lines thought they were in the train business rather than the transportation industry; they were product oriented instead of customer oriented. Levitt argued that companies must define their industries broadly, focusing on their customers' needs and desires, or they will stop evolving and start shrinking.

The leaders in the global food system whom I have interviewed think of their missions in the broadest terms possible, and in a manner that Professor Levitt would approve of. For example, the Nestlé chairman and his colleagues think of Nestlé as a "wellness company"—and hired a health community leader, from outside the company, as the new CEO.

In his interview, the head of Cargill thinks Cargill's mission is "to nourish the world"—a far cry from the company's beginnings as a single country elevator in Iowa.

The food system is no longer a food system. It has become something much more. It's part of the health system, it's part of the economic development system, it's part of the environmental system, it's part of the waste management and energy systems, and all of these are interrelated. Because of the complexity of the food system, firms have to change, the people who manage them have to change, the public policies have to change, and the education of the leaders of this new complex entity has to change. The forty-seven interviews in this book show how each of these firms or organizations is changing the food system and in turn is being changed by it.

Perhaps the most important element of change is how the participants in this new complex relate to each other. Historically, the food chain consisted of decision makers who felt they were part of individual commodity systems, didn't trust each other, and focused on driving the best bargain with one another. They employed people who were good at trading and who understood the agronomics of all the commodities they dealt with, but who were not well versed in how those commodities affected the end product, nor how they affected consumer health. This has all changed.

We now have participants in the food system that have never existed before: who can produce animal-free meat via cell propagation (Memphis Meats, which Cargill has invested in),[2] edit the genes of pigs to produce human-useful organs, and produce pharmaceuticals in the milk of animals and in specific plants. Therefore, the types of men and women needed to work in and manage these areas are very different than the bargaining traders who were essential in the past. The academic community is developing multidisciplinary courses and joint degrees to give potential managers a broad enough education to prepare them for this new complex system.

Participants in the food system have rethought their purposes and the business they are in. This book is full of examples of this change. The food systems change-makers recognize their responsibility to improving the health, economic development, and environmental management of the world, as well as their own economic well-being; they realize that they have to be both food citizens and economic operators.

Overcoming a Climate of Distrust

A recent global poll[3] indicates that people very much distrust the global food system. There are unethical procedures and unethical people in the food system as there are in every profession, including my own. Marion Nestle, among many others, rightfully believes we have to do a better job in explaining ways to use our food system, our educational system, and our governmental support systems to feed people more nutritiously and to provide economic help for those who need it.

Nestle began our dialogue in this book by documenting food system leaders' unwillingness to improve the nutritional content of the foods they produced and the shortcomings of the restaurant business in not providing better portion control. However, even though there have been delays in government recommendations requiring the food service industry to label the caloric content of prepared foods, firms such as Wegmans have begun to do this without waiting for the government. Nestle's voice is being heard. She, as do I, has great faith in the millennials, the eighteen-to thirty-four-year-olds who are the largest generation in America. The millennial generation uses social networking to voice their views on what they want from the food system. Their influence is important in determining the food system's future.

Their influence seems to be working. Denise Morrison, chief executive of Campbell's Soup, indicated

> that the company will withdraw from the Grocery Manufacturers' Association (GMA), a major food association, by the end of the calendar year. The decision, according to Morrison, is not financial but rather driven by purpose and principles. Morrison's remarks focused on the company's goal of being the leading health and well-being food company, which includes an emphasis on transparency as a means of building trust with consumer, particularly Millennials.[4]

Other firms responded to Nestle's arguments against advertising candy to children under twelve years of age:

> On April 13, 2016, six new companies: Ferrara Candy Co, Ghirardelli Chocolate Co, Jelly Belly Candy Co., Just Born Quality Confections, the Promotion in Motion Company, and the R.M. Palmer Co joined

six other confectionery companies: the American Liquorice Co., Ferrero USA, the Hershey Co., Mars, Inc., Mondelez International, and Nestlé: all of these firms do not advertise directly to children.[5]

In addition, firms such as Mars are labeling their candy "To be consumed occasionally, no more than once a week."[6]

I believe that the changes that we are seeing in the food system, and new technologies enabling easier recognition of fraudulent activities, will result in a safer and more nutritious food system for the future.

George Church talks about the new scientific technologies that will improve the food system, but at the same time says that the developers of these technologies have to spend as much time on safety as they do on efficacy. Greg Page of Cargill talks about the importance of culture and a value system in a company when he says, "There are big moments in a company's history when you make decisions that visibly define your culture." But that doesn't happen often. Culture can't be shaped by decision points alone. Everyday treatment, who gets honored and who gets recognized, really matters in deciding whether the company will do the right thing when this is not in its immediate self-interest.

A Nonpartisan Public Issue

Nestle also points out that many academic and research studies are overly influenced by financial support from people who have a financial interest in the results. There has to be a way of blending funds from private, public, and not-for-profit sources that reduces that potential of undue influence by any one group. In addition, just as CPAs and auditors are expected to be neutral in their evaluation of firms' financial data, a group of individual firms should be developed that has both the scientific background to evaluate nutritional qualities and the independence to do so. Erling Lorentzen had to search globally to find such an independent firm to evaluate the harmful effects by the forest and paper industry of using dioxin to whiten paper. He had to avoid the academic community because of their ties to specific industry funds and their openness to bias because of them.

The industry is responding to the public's rightful concern about nutrition, health, the environment, and poverty, and the overriding focus of the new private, public, and not-for-profit leadership of the food system is: how do we create both a competitive and cooperative food system that responds to society's needs and priorities?

Public policymakers recognize that close collaboration among their departments, domestically and globally, and with the private and not-for-profit sectors, is critical. Farm cooperatives will become multinational in nature and in operation. Consumer activist groups will be partnering more with the private and with the public sector. Resolution centers such as the World Trade Organization will play a more important role in providing a level and fair-minded world trading environment. The World Bank will play an increasing role in bringing together this new complex system and enabling small-scale producers to become part of the commercial food system more easily and rapidly.

Historically, the United States has had a nonpartisan food policy. It is the one area that has brought political parties together. Even in 2017, "Legislation has been introduced in the Senate to target food deserts by incentivizing grocers, retailers, and nonprofits to help eradicate these areas. The Healthy Food Access for All Americans bill creates a system of tax credits and grants for business and non-profits who serve these low-income and low-access urban and rural areas."[7] Two Republican senators, Jerry Moran from Kansas and Shelley Moore Capito from West Virginia, and two Democratic senators, Mark Warner from Virginia and Bob Casey from Pennsylvania, introduced this legislation.

Senator Moran commented as follows: "Living in the breadbasket of our nation, we can often forget how prevalent hunger and lack of access to healthy food in our own communities can be. . . . However, hunger and food insecurity are very real and threaten nearly 1 in 6 Kansans."[8]

If our private, public, and not-for-profit domestic and global food system leaders can learn to work together on making the domestic and global food system more responsive to society's needs, then just maybe they can create an example for the rest of the world's economy.

I dedicate this book to the women and men who in every way and every day are doing their best to improve our global food system. This is really their book, not mine.

Case Studies by Ray A. Goldberg Related to Interviews in This Book (All Cases Published by Harvard Business Publishing)

CHAPTER 1: HEALTH AND NUTRITION

Goldberg, Ray A., and Hal Hogan. *"Restricting Foods of Minimal Nutritional Value in Texas Public Schools."* Harvard Business School Case 904-420, March 2004. (Revised August 2004.) (Susan Combs)

Goldberg, Ray A., and Noemie Myriam Delfassy. *"The Full Yield."* Harvard Business School Case 911-402, December 2010. (Revised August 2012.) (Zoe Finch Totten)

Goldberg, Ray A. *"Zipongo: Improving Health by Redesigning the Food Chain."* Harvard Business School Case 915-416, March 2015. (Jason Langheier)

Goldberg, Ray A., and Vincent N. Willis. *"Wegmans: The Work-Scholarship Connection Program."* Harvard Business School Case 593–030, September 1992. (Daniel Wegman)

Goldberg, Ray A. *"Wegmans and the Produce Revolution."* Harvard Business School Case 594-082, December 1993. (Revised February 1994.) (Daniel Wegman)

Goldberg, Ray A., and James Weber. *"The Electronic Product Code: Future Impact on the Global Food System."* Harvard Business School Case 905-409, November 2004. (Daniel Wegman)

Goldberg, Ray A., and Christine Snively. *"Wegmans and Listeria: Developing a Proactive Food Safety System for Produce."* Harvard Business School Case 915-412, January 2015. (Revised March 2015.) (Daniel Wegman)

Goldberg, Ray A., and Eliot Sherman. *"Food Security and The Church of Jesus Christ of Latter-day Saints."* Harvard Business School Case 508-002, September 2007. (Revised June 2008.) (Kevin Nield)

Goldberg, Ray A., Carin-Isabel Knoop, and Srinivas Sunder. *"Novartis: Betting on Life Sciences."* Harvard Business School Case 599-076, December 1998. (Revised September 1999.) (Daniel Vasella)

CHAPTER 2: FOOD SAFETY AND FOOD FRAUD

Goldberg, Ray A., and Matthew Preble. *"IdentiGEN."* Harvard Business School Case 914-408, November 2013. (Ronan Loftus)

CHAPTER 3: CREATING SHARED VALUE

Goldberg, Ray A., Carin-Isabel Knoop, and Cate Reavis. *"Friona Industries, L.P."* Harvard Business School Case 901-009, December 2000.(James Herring)

Goldberg, Ray A., Carin-Isabel Knoop, and Mary L. Shelman. *"Friona Industries: Delivering Better Beef."* Harvard Business School Case 906-405, October 2005. (Revised May 2007.) (James Herring)

Goldberg, Ray A., and Jose M. M. Porraz. *"Cargill (A)."* Harvard Business School Case 903-420, December 2002. (Revised April 2007.)

Goldberg, Ray A., and Jose M. M. Porraz. *"Cargill (B)."* Harvard Business School Supplement 907-415, April 2007. (Revised August 2009.) (Gregory Page)

Goldberg, Ray A., and Matthew Preble. *"CHS Inc.: Cooperative Leadership in a Global Food Economy."* Harvard Business School Case 911–409, November 2010. (Revised January 2012.) (John Johnson)

Goldberg, Ray A., and Andrew Otazo. *"Bay State Milling."* Harvard Business School Case 915-413, April 2015.

Goldberg, Ray A. *"Bay State Milling Co."* Harvard Business School Case 594-080, December 1993. (Brian Rothwell)

Goldberg, Ray A., Carin-Isabel Knoop, and Matthew Preble. *"Associated British Foods, Plc."* Harvard Business School Case 912-402, November 2011. (George Weston)

Goldberg, Ray A. "Monsanto." Harvard Business School Case 913-404, October 2012. (Hugh Grant)

Goldberg, Ray A. *"The Climate Corporation: New Options for Farmers."* Harvard Business School Case 915–415, April 2015. (Hugh Grant)

Goldberg, Ray A. *"Aracruz Celulose S.A.: Managing a Renewable Resource."* Harvard Business School Case 595-047, November 1994. (Erling Lorentzen)

Goldberg, Ray A., and Lorin A. Fries. *"Nestlé: Agricultural Material Sourcing Within the Concept of Creating Shared Value (CSV)."* Harvard Business School Case 913-406, December 2012. (Revised August 2013.) (Hans Jöhr)

Goldberg, Ray A., and Meredith Niles. *"The China Dairy Farming Institute: New Frontiers in Innovative Collaborations."* Harvard Business School Case 915-418, April 2015 (Hans Jöhr)

CHAPTER 4: TECHNOLOGY—CODING LIFE

Goldberg, Ray A., and Juan Enriquez-Cabot. *"Technology Crises and the Future of Agribusiness: BSE in Europe."* Harvard Business School Case 597–036, September 1996. (Revised January 1997.) (Juan Enriquez)

Goldberg, Ray A., and Sarah Morton. *"GTC Biotherapeutics: Developing Medicines in the Milk of Goats."* Harvard Business School Case 910–403, November 2009. (Revised December 2009.) (Juan Enriquez)

CHAPTER 5: FARM LABOR

Goldberg, Ray A., and Michael Joseph Kennedy. *"Migrant Farmworkers in the Midwest (A)."* Harvard Business School Background Note 586-073, November 1985. (Revised October 1991.)

Goldberg, Ray A. *"Migrant Farmworkers in the Midwest (B)."* Harvard Business School Supplement 592-031, September 1991. (Baldemar Velasquez)

CHAPTER 6: LARGE-SCALE FARMING

Goldberg, Ray A., and Jose M. M. Porraz. *"Fonterra: Taking on the Dairy World."* Harvard Business School Case 903-413, December 2002. (Revised May 2003.) (Andrew Ferrier)

CHAPTER 7: SMALL-SCALE FARMING AND ECONOMIC DEVELOPMENT

Goldberg, Ray, and Ian McKown Cornell. *"Amul Dairy."* Harvard Business School Case 914-405, July 2013. (Rahul Kumar)

Goldberg, Ray A., Carin-Isabel Knoop, and Srinivas Sunder. *"Amul and India's National Dairy Development Board."* Harvard Business School Case 599-060, November 1998. (Revised December 1998.) (Rahul Kumar)

Goldberg, Ray A. *"Mumias Sugar Co. Ltd.: A Success Story."* Harvard Business School Case 590-039, October 1989. (Revised November 1989.) (Jonathan Taylor)

Goldberg, Ray A. *"Social Impact of Agribusiness: A Field Study of ALCOSA in Guatemala."* Harvard Business School Case 581-140, April 1981. (Revised June 1982.) (Robert Ross)

Goldberg, Ray A., Carin-Isabel Knoop, and Matthew Preble. *"Jain Irrigation Systems Limited: Inclusive Growth for India's Farmers."* Harvard Business School Case 912-403, November 2011. (Revised February 2012.) (Bhavaril Jain)

Goldberg, Ray A., and Kerry Herman. *"Alleviating Poverty and Malnutrition."* Harvard Business School Case 907-409, March 2007. (Revised October 2007.) 9-907-409 (Nancy Barry)

Goldberg, Ray A., Laura Winig, and Kerry Herman. *"Alleviating Poverty and Malnutrition: Successful Models."* Harvard Business School Background Note 907-412, March 2007. (Revised December 2007.) (Djordjija Petkoski)

Goldberg, Ray, Carin-Isabel Knoop, and Djordjija Petkoski. *"Seeding Growth in the Democratic Republic of the Congo."* Harvard Business School Case 914–401, December 2013. (Revised April 2014.) (John Ulimwengu)

CHAPTER 8: THE IMPORTANCE OF CHINA

Goldberg, Ray A., and Kefei Yang. *"Transformation of COFCO in a Changing Environment."* Harvard Business School Case 909-403, November 2008. (Revised December 2008.) (Frank Ning)

Goldberg, Ray A. *"Shuanghui Acquisition of Smithfield Foods."* Harvard Business School Case 914-413, December 2013.

CHAPTER 9: CREATING A FAIR AND RESPONSIVE FOOD SYSTEM

Goldberg, Ray A., Robert Lawrence, and J. Katherine Milligan. *"Brazil's WTO Cotton Case: Negotiation through Litigation."* Harvard Business School Case 905-405, September 2004. (Revised January 2005.) (Pedro de Camargo)

Goldberg, Ray A., Kerry Herman, and Irina Tarsis. *"Brazil Sugar and the WTO: Agricultural Reform in the European Union."* Harvard Business School Case 906-408, November 2005. (Revised April 2006.) (Pedro de Camargo)

Goldberg, Ray A., and Jose M. M. Porraz. *"Water Policy Priorities along the U.S.-Mexico Border."* Harvard Business School Case 903-414, November 2002. (Revised March 2003.) (Joseph Glauber)

Goldberg, Ray A., and Jessica Droste Yagan. *"McDonald's Corporation: Managing a Sustainable Supply Chain."* Harvard Business School Case 907-414, March 2007. (Revised April 2007.) (Robert Langert)

CHAPTER 10: FUTURE TRENDS AND THE IMPACT ON THE GLOBAL FOOD SYSTEM

Goldberg, Ray A., and James M Beagle. *"Tobacco and the Future of Rural Kentucky."* Harvard Business School Case 902-412, November 2001 (Lorin Fries)

Goldberg, Ray A., and Juan Enriquez-Cabot. *"Chiapas: Reconciling Agriculture and Ecology."* Harvard Business School Case 587-089, December 1986. (Revised March 1987.) (Lorin Fries)

Goldberg, Ray A., Jessica M. Newman, and Jessica Grisanti. *"Nestle's Commodity* Systems *Approach in Venezuela: Laying the Foundation for Shared Value in a Time of Crisis."* Harvard Business School Case 917-409, May 2017. (Fausto Costa)

SELECT PUBLICATIONS BY PROFESSOR RAY GOLDBERG

Books

The Nonpartisan League of North Dakota: A Case Study of Political Action in America (Midwest Printing and Lithography Company, 1948; second printing 1955)

The Soybean Industry: With Special Reference to the Competitive Position of the Minnesota Producer and Processor (University of Minnesota Press, 1952)

A Concept of Agribusiness with John H. Davis (Division of Research, Graduate School of Business Administration, Harvard University, 1957)

Agribusiness Coordination: A Systems Approach to the Wheat, Soybean and Florida Orange Economies (Division of Research, Graduate School of Business Administration, Harvard University, 1968)

Agribusiness Management for Developing Countries—Latin America (Ballinger Publishing Company, 1974)

Farmers Cooperatives and Federal Income Taxes with Lee F. Schrader (Ballinger Publishing Company, 1975)

Agribusiness Management for Developing Countries—South East Asian Corn with Richard C. McGinty (Ballinger Publishing Company, 1979)

Brand Strategy in United States Food Marketing: Perspectives on Food Manufacturers' and Distributors' Brands in the United States with William Applebaum (Division of Research, Graduate School of Business Administration, Harvard University, 1967)

New Technologies and the Future of Food and Nutrition edited with Gerald E. Gaull (John Wiley & Sons Inc. New York, 1991)

The Lessons of Wage and Price Controls edited with John T. Dunlop and Kenneth J. Fedor (Division of Research, Graduate School of Business Administration, Harvard University, 1977)

Harvard Business Review *Articles*

"Profitable Partnerships: Industry and Farmer Co-ops," pp. 108–121, March–April 1972

"U.S. Agribusiness Breaks Out of Isolation," pp. 81–95, May–June 1975

"Food Supply and the Third World," pp. 68–72, May–June 1979

"Transforming Life, Transforming Business: The Life Sciences Revolution" with Juan Enriquez, pp. 94–104, March–April 2000

List of Interviewees

Barry, Nancy—President, Enterprise Solutions to Poverty

Beagle, James—CEO, Grapery

Cackler, Mark—Manager of Agricultural Global Practice, World Bank

Church, George M.—Professor of Genetics, Harvard Medical School

Combs, Susan—Past Commissioner of Agriculture, State of Texas

Costa, Fausto—President, Nestlé Venezuela

De Camargo, Pedro—Former Secretary of Trade, Ministry of Agriculture, Brazil

De Waal, Caroline Smith—Director of Food Safety, Center for Science in the Public Interest

Enriquez, Juan—President and CEO of Biotechonomy, LLC

Ferrier, Andrew—CEO, Fonterra

Fries, Lorin—Associate Director for New Vision of Agriculture, World Economic Forum

Glauber, Joseph—US Agricultural Trade Representative for the Doha Round and Chief Economist of the US Department of Agriculture

Grant, Hugh—Chairman and CEO, Monsanto Company

Herring, James—President and CEO, Friona Industries

Hunt, Jack—Past President and CEO, King Ranch

Jain, Anil—Managing Director, Jain Irrigation

Jain, Bhavaril—Founder and Chairman, Jain Irrigation

Johnson, John—President and CEO, CHS

Jöhr, Hans—Corporate Director of Agriculture, Nestlé Company

Kumar, Rahul—Managing Director and CEO, Amul Dairy

Langert, Robert—Vice President of Corporate Responsibility, McDonald's Corporation

Langheier, Jason—CEO and Founder, Zipongo

Lavin, Sheldon—CEO, OSI Group

Loftus, Ronan—Cofounder of IdentiGen and CEO of IdentiGen's American operations

Lorentzen, Erling—Chairman, African Forestry Economic Development Program

Luter III, Joseph—Chairman, Smithfield Foods

Muir, Warren—Executive Director, Division on Earth and Life Studies, National Academy of Sciences

Nestle, Marion—Paulette Goddard Professor of Nutrition, Food Studies, and Public Health, New York University

Nield, Kevin—Director, Bishop Storehouse Warehouses of the Church of Jesus Christ of Latter-Day Saints

Ning, Frank G.—Chairman, COFCO

Offutt, Ron—Chairman and CEO, RDO Company

Page, Greg—Chairman, Cargill

Penn, J. B.—Former U.S. Undersecretary of Farm and Foreign Agricultural Services

Petkoski, Djordjija—Director of Business Competitiveness, World Bank Institute

Ross, Robert—Past President, Latin American Agribusiness Development Company

Rothwell, Brian—President, Bay State Milling

Schumacher, August—Cofounder and Executive Vice President, Wholesome Wave

Singh, Rajiv—CEO, North American Branch of Rabobank

Taylor, Jonathan—President, International Basic Economy Corporation (IBEC)

Taylor, Michael—US Deputy Commissioner of Food and Veterinary Medicine

Totten, Zoe Finch—CEO, The Full Yield

Ulimwengu, John—Senior Adviser to the Prime Minister, Democratic Republic of Congo

Vasella, Daniel—President and CEO, Novartis

Velasquez, Baldemar—President, Farm Labor Organizing Committee (FLOC)

Wegman, Daniel—Chairman, Wegmans Inc.

Weston, George—CEO, Associated British Foods

Willett, Walter C.—Chairman of the Nutrition Department, Harvard T.H. Chan School of Public Health

Notes

FOREWORD

1. Mark Bittman, "Rethinking the Word 'Foodie'," *The New York Times*, June 24, 2014, p. A23.
2. Goldberg, Ray A., and Jose M. M. Porraz. *Cargill (A)*. Harvard Business School Case 903-420, December 2002. (Revised April 2007.)

CHAPTER 1

1. Goldberg, Ray A., and Hal Hogan. *Restricting Foods of Minimal Nutritional Value in Texas Public Schools*. Harvard Business School Case 904-420, March 2004. (Revised August 2004.)
2. Goldberg, Ray A., and Noemie Myriam Delfassy. *The Full Yield*. Harvard Business School Case 911-402, December 2010. (Revised August 2012.)
3. Goldberg, Ray A. *Zipongo: Improving Health by Redesigning the Food Chain*. Harvard Business School Case 915-416, March 2015.
4. Goldberg, Ray A., and Vincent N. Willis. *Wegmans: The Work-Scholarship Connection Program*. Harvard Business School Case 593-030, September 1992; Goldberg, Ray A. *Wegmans and the Produce Revolution*. Harvard Business School Case 594-082, December 1993. (Revised February 1994.); Goldberg, Ray A., and James Weber. *The Electronic Product Code: Future Impact on the Global Food System*. Harvard Business School Case 905-409, November 2004; Goldberg, Ray A., and Christine Snively. *Wegmans and Listeria: Developing a Proactive Food Safety System for Produce*. Harvard Business School Case 915-412, January 2015. (Revised March 2015.)
5. Goldberg, Ray A., and Eliot Sherman. *Food Security and The Church of Jesus Christ of Latter-day Saints*. Harvard Business School Case 508-002, September 2007. (Revised June 2008.)

6. Goldberg, Ray A., Carin-Isabel Knoop, and Srinivas Sunder. *Novartis: Betting on Life Sciences*. Harvard Business School Case 599-076, December 1998. (Revised September 1999.)

CHAPTER 2

1. Goldberg, Ray A., and Matthew Preble. *IdentiGEN*. Harvard Business School Case 914-408, November 2013.

CHAPTER 3

1. Goldberg, Ray A., Carin-Isabel Knoop, and Cate Reavis. *Friona Industries, L.P.* Harvard Business School Case 901-009, December 2000; Goldberg, Ray A., Carin-Isabel Knoop, and Mary L. Shelman. *Friona Industries: Delivering Better Beef.* Harvard Business School Case 906-405, October 2005. (Revised May 2007.)
2. Goldberg, Ray A., and Jose M. M. Porraz. *Cargill (A)*. Harvard Business School Case 903-420, December 2002. (Revised April 2007.); Goldberg, Ray A., and Jose M. M. Porraz. *Cargill (B)*. Harvard Business School Supplement 907-415, April 2007. (Revised August 2009.)
3. Goldberg, Ray A., and Matthew Preble. *CHS Inc.: Cooperative Leadership in a Global Food Economy*. Harvard Business School Case 911-409, November 2010. (Revised January 2012.)
4. Goldberg, Ray A., and Andrew Otazo. *Bay State Milling*. Harvard Business School Case 915-413, April 2015; Goldberg, Ray A. *Bay State Milling Co*. Harvard Business School Case 594-080, December 1993.
5. Goldberg, Ray A., Carin-Isabel Knoop, and Matthew Preble. *Associated British Foods, Plc*. Harvard Business School Case 912-402, November 2011.
6. Goldberg, Ray A. *Monsanto*. Harvard Business School Case 913-404, October 2012; Goldberg, Ray A. *The Climate Corporation: New Options for Farmers*. Harvard Business School Case 915-415, April 2015.
7. Goldberg, Ray A. *Aracruz Celulose S.A.: Managing a Renewable Resource*. Harvard Business School Case 595-047, November 1994.
8. Goldberg, Ray A., and Lorin A. Fries. *Nestlé: Agricultural Material Sourcing Within the Concept of Creating Shared Value (CSV)*. Harvard Business School Case 913-406, December 2012. (Revised August 2013; Goldberg, Ray A., and Meredith Niles. *The China Dairy Farming Institute: New Frontiers in Innovative Collaborations*. Harvard Business School Case 915-418, April 2015.

CHAPTER 4

1. Goldberg, Ray A., and Juan Enriquez-Cabot. *Technology Crises and the Future of Agribusiness: BSE in Europe*. Harvard Business School Case 597-036, September

1996. (Revised January 1997.); Goldberg, Ray A., and Sarah Morton. *GTC Biotherapeutics: Developing Medicines in the Milk of Goats*. Harvard Business School Case 910-403, November 2009. (Revised December 2009.)

CHAPTER 5

1. Goldberg, Ray A., and Michael Joseph Kennedy. *Migrant Farmworkers in the Midwest (A)*. Harvard Business School Background Note 586-073, November 1985. (Revised October 1991.); Goldberg, Ray A. *Migrant Farmworkers in the Midwest (B)*. Harvard Business School Supplement 592-031, September 1991.

CHAPTER 6

1. Goldberg, Ray A., and Jose M. M. Porraz. *Fonterra: Taking on the Dairy World*. Harvard Business School Case 903-413, December 2002. (Revised May 2003.)

CHAPTER 7

1. Goldberg, Ray, and Ian McKown Cornell. *Amul Dairy*. Harvard Business School Case 914-405, July 2013; *Amul and India's National Dairy Development Board*. Harvard Business School Case 599-060, November 1998. (Revised December 1998.)
2. Goldberg, Ray A. *Mumias Sugar Co. Ltd.: A Success Story*. Harvard Business School Case 590-039, October 1989. (Revised November 1989.)
3. Goldberg, Ray A. *Social Impact of Agribusiness: A Field Study of ALCOSA in Guatemala*. Harvard Business School Case 581-140, April 1981. (Revised June 1982.)
4. Goldberg, Ray A., Carin-Isabel Knoop, and Matthew Preble. *Jain Irrigation Systems Limited: Inclusive Growth for India's Farmers*. Harvard Business School Case 912-403, November 2011. (Revised February 2012.)
5. Goldberg, Ray A., and Kerry Herman. *Alleviating Poverty and Malnutrition*. Harvard Business School Case 907-409, March 2007. (Revised October 2007.)
6. Goldberg, Ray, Carin-Isabel Knoop, and Djordjija Petkoski. *Seeding Growth in the Democratic Republic of the Congo*. Harvard Business School Case 914-401, December 2013. (Revised April 2014.)

CHAPTER 8

1. Goldberg, Ray A., and Kefei Yang. *Transformation of COFCO in a Changing Environment*. Harvard Business School Case 909-403, November 2008. (Revised December 2008.); Goldberg, Ray A. *Shuanghui Acquisition of Smithfield Foods*. Harvard Business School Case 914-413, December 2013.

CHAPTER 9

1. Goldberg, Ray A., Robert Lawrence, and J. Katherine Milligan. *Brazil's WTO Cotton Case: Negotiation through Litigation*. Harvard Business School Case 905-405, September 2004. (Revised January 2005.); Goldberg, Ray A., Kerry Herman, and Irina Tarsis. *Brazil Sugar and the WTO: Agricultural Reform in the European Union*. Harvard Business School Case 906-408, November 2005. (Revised April 2006.)
2. Goldberg, Ray A., and Jose M. M. Porraz. *Water Policy Priorities along the U.S.-Mexico Border*. Harvard Business School Case 903-414, November 2002. (Revised March 2003.)
3. Goldberg, Ray A., and Jessica Droste Yagan. *McDonald's Corporation: Managing a Sustainable Supply Chain*. Harvard Business School Case 907-414, March 2007. (Revised April 2007.)

CHAPTER 10

1. Goldberg, Ray A., and James M Beagle. *Tobacco and the Future of Rural Kentucky*. Harvard Business School Case 902-412, November 2001; Goldberg, Ray A., and Juan Enriquez-Cabot. *Chiapas: Reconciling Agriculture and Ecology*. Harvard Business School Case 587-089, December 1986. (Revised March 1987.)
2. Goldberg, Ray A., Jessica M. Newman, and Jessica Grisanti. *Nestle's Commodity Systems Approach in Venezuela: Laying the Foundation for Shared Value in a Time of Crisis*. Harvard Business School Case 917-409, May 2017.

CONCLUSION

1. Ted Levitt, "Marketing Myopia," *Harvard Business Review 38*, July–August 1960, pp. 24–47.
2. Jacob Bunge, "Cargill Invests in Startup That Grows 'Clean Meat' from Cells," *Wall Street Journal*, August 23, 2017, https://www.wsj.com/articles/cargill-backs-cell-culture-meat-1503486002.
3. Katy Askew, "Food Makers Expected to Deliver on Health but Trust Lacking, Survey Finds," *Food Navigator*, August 10, 2017, http://www.foodnavigator.com/Market-Trends/Food-makers-expected-to-deliver-on-health-but-trust-lacking-survey-finds.
4. Tonya Garcia, "Campbell Soup to Withdraw from Food Group by Year-End," *Marketwatch*, July 19, 2017, http://www.marketwatch.com/story/campbell-soup-to-withdraw-from-food-industry-group-by-year-end-2017-07-19.
5. Abigail Watt, "Six Candy Companies Pledge to Stop Advertising to Children under 12," *Candy Industry*, April 13, 2016, pp. 1–2, http://www.candyindustry.com/articles/87219-six-candy-companies-pledge-to-stop-advertising-to-children-under-12.

6. Dyanne Weiss, "Mars to Label Foods Whether They Should Be Consumed Only Occasionally," *Liberty Voice*, April 15, 2016, p. 1, http://guardianlv.com/2016/04/mars-to-label-foods-whether-they-should-be-consumed-only-occasionally/.

7. "Senators Introduce Legislation to Fight against Food Deserts," *Specialty Food News*, August 10, 2017, p. 1, https://www.specialtyfood.com/news/article/senators-introduce-legislation-fight-against-food-deserts/.

8. "Senators Introduce Legislation to Fight against Food Deserts," *Specialty Food News*, August 10, 2017, p. 1, https://www.specialtyfood.com/news/article/senators-introduce-legislation-fight-against-food-deserts/.

Index

Printed in the USA/Agawam, MA
October 15, 2018

685654.008